Introduction to Computer Science and Technology

Introduction to Computer Science and Technology

Edited by

Adele Kuzmiakova

ARCLER PRESS

www.arclerpress.com

Introduction to Computer Science and Technology

Adele Kuzmiakova

Arcler Press
224 Shoreacres Road
Burlington, ON L7L 2H2
Canada
www.arclerpress.com
Email: orders@arclereducation.com

ISBN: 978-1-77407-740-5 (Hardcover)

ABOUT THE EDITOR

Adele Kuzmiakova is a computational engineer focusing on solving problems in machine learning, deep learning, and computer vision. Adele attended Cornell University in New York, United States for her undergraduate studies. She studied engineering with a focus on applied math. While at Cornell, she developed close relationships with professors, which enabled her to get involved in academic research to get hands-on experience with solving computational problems. She was also selected to be Accel Roundtable on Entrepreneurship Education (REE) Fellow at Stanford University and spent 3 months working on entrepreneurship projects to get a taste of entrepreneurship and high-growth ventures in engineering and life sciences. The program culminated in giving a presentation on the startup technology and was judged by Stanford faculty and entrepreneurship experts in Silicon Valley. After graduating from Cornell, Adele worked as a data scientist at Swiss Federal Institute of Technology in Lausanne, Switzerland where she focused on developing algorithms and graphical models to analyze chemical pathways in the atmosphere. Adele also pursued graduate studies at Stanford University in the United States where she entered as a recipient of American Association of University Women International Fellowship. The Fellowship enabled her to focus on tackling important research problems in machine learning and computer vision. Some research problems she worked on at Stanford include detecting air pollution from outdoor public webcam images. Specifically, she modified and set up a variety of pre-trained architectures, such as DehazeNet, VGG, and ResNet, on public webcam images to evaluate their ability to predict air quality based on the degree of haze on pictures. Other deep learning problems Adele worked on include investigating the promise of second-order optimizers in deep learning and using neural networks to predict sequences of data in energy consumption. Adele also places an emphasis on continual education and served as a Student Leader in PyTorch scholarship challenge organized by Udacity. Her roles as the Student Leader were helping students debug their code to train neural networks with PyTorch and providing mentorship on technical and career aspects. Her hobbies include skiing, playing tennis, cooking, and meeting new people.

TABLE OF CONTENTS

LIST OF FIGURES

LIST OF ABBREVIATIONS

AI	artificial intelligence
ARPA	Advanced Research Programs Agency
CS	computer science
CTR	calculating-tabulating-recording firm
DBMS	database management structure
DPI	deep-packet inspection
FICSS	factors influencing computer science studies
GIGO	garbage in garbage out
IC	integrated circuit
ICT	information communications technology
ISO	International Organization for Standardization
ISTAHC	Global Society for Technology Appraisal in Health Care
LAN	local-area-network
LSI	large scale integration
MOS IC	MOS assimilated circuit
MOS	metal-oxide-semiconductor
PC	personal computer
PDA	personal digital assistant
PISA	Program for International Scholar Assessment
RAM	random access memory
RAS	reliability, availability, and serviceability
RTL	resistor-transition logic
SAGE	semi-automatic ground ecosystem
SFINAE	substitution failure isn't an error
SI	system of units
SNPs	single nucleotide polymorphisms
SPI	Stateful-Packet Inspection

TA	technology assessment
TTL	dual transistor logic
UI	user-interface
WAN	wide area networks
WEEE	waste electrical and electronic gear

PREFACE

Information on computer science and technology is very variable. Different researches related to these two aspects have been carried out and presented in different books and reports. However, the information is dispersed and does not offer a comprehensive overview to the real association between computer science and technology. Therefore, this volume was written after doing a thorough scrutiny of different journals, articles, research, and a wide array of computer science and technology books. The main objective of preparing this volume is to offer the best information based on the field of computer science and technology.

Computer science and technology have revolutionized how things are done in various sectors all around the world. Every sector is looking for ways to improve on its product and technology has proved to be a good way to do that.

This volume extends previous work by examining how computer science and technology can be used to improve the livelihood globally. The importance of this volume cannot therefore be overemphasized. It is hoped that this volume will provide an understanding of the actual technologies used in day to day activities.

Students taking computer science and technological courses will benefit from this volume because it will act as a reference in their daily course work.

The volume has 10 chapters, and each chapter discusses about a specific topic under computer science and technology. Chapter 1 introduces the concepts of computer science and technology; Chapter 2 offers basic information on basic concepts of computer; Chapter 3 discusses on scientific methods of computer science; Chapter 4 discusses on modern usages of computers; Chapter 5 discusses on history of computer science; Chapter 6 focuses on principal areas of study within computer science; Chapter 7 discusses about the relationship between science and technology; Chapter 8 discusses on benefits of computer science; Chapter 9 tackles on barriers to studying computer science; and lastly, Chapter 10 offer details on leveraging current momentum in computer science and technology.

These 10 chapters were lengthily prepared for the readers to have a preview of how computer science and technology relate to each. The author paid more emphasis on the simplicity of the content in order to make the book comprehensible and understandable to all readers.

Chapter 1

INTRODUCTION TO COMPUTER SCIENCE AND TECHNOLOGY

CONTENTS

1.1. INTRODUCTION

The field of computer science has proven to be one of the fastest-growing as well as the highest paying careers. However, the supply of teachers and students is decreasing due to a lack of interest in computer science. This is all due to the lack of exposure that students have towards technology and their resources and also whether or not the students are gaining any source of encouragement to explore the field of computer science.

When you educate students in computer science, even those who are less interested in the field are benefited. Due to the rise in the digital age, it is important for there to be the development of logical thinking as well as the ability to solve problems, which is part of the curriculum in computer science. It is important for students to be able to use computers to write reports, research on specific subjects, and even create files, regardless of the field that the student is interested in. Every industry and if you stopped it has more job openings that require for one to have knowledge in computer sales. There are projections that a showing that there will be growth by twice the rate of any job when it comes to job openings.

Figure 1.1. There are many online courses that are making it easier for people to study computer science.

Source: *https://www.mastersavenue.com/disciplines/computer-science-it.*

Computer science has proven to be a way to pull students and communities out of poverty because the job perspective for computer science is developing at a high rate. It is also becoming an important way to improve innovations in the world which can lead to even more job opportunities. A study, however, has shown that the exposure to computer science has been mainly on white male students. The study showed that there is a lack of focus on females, blacks and Hispanics students. This lack of resources and educators who can teach this science has led to a gap in education between white males and colored/female students.

1.2. WHAT IS COMPUTER SCIENCE?

Computer science is the study of the procedures that interrelate with data and that can undergo representation as data in the sense of programs. Computer science is also called computation science or computing science. It enables for there to be the usage of algorithms so as to cause manipulation, storage, and communication of digital information (Dasgupta, 2016). A computer scientist deals with the study of the theory of computation and the practice of creating software systems.

Computer science has both theoretical and practical disciplines. The theoretical aspects of computer science are highly abstract, what are the practical aspects that deals with computer graphics emphasizes applications in the real world. The language used for programming has a theory that deals with the approaches to the explanation of computational processes, while computer programming itself deals with the utilization of the programming languages and complex systems. The interaction between humans and the computer considers the hardships in making computers useful, usable, and accessible.

The invention of the modern digital computer was the earliest foundation of what was going to be the computer science predate. Machines such as the abacus, that were used to calculate fixed numerical problems, have existed for a very long time. They have helped in computation such as division, multiplication, addition, and subtraction of large numbers. Algorithms that are used to perform computations have been in existence for a very long time, even before the creation of sophisticated computing equipment (Dasgupta, 2016).

Figure 1.2. Computer science involves using technology to perform different duties in the world today.

Source: *https://blogs.sas.com/content/sascp/2018/12/03/so-what-is-computer-science/.*

Degrees in computer science are structured in a way that is incremental, where they give students an overview of the principles that are basic. It involves units such as pattern recognition, computational theory, network, and systems theories or machine learning. People studying computer science are also taught on how modern computer science fits into the society, either in terms of the discipline's history or on a business or enterprise module in terms of computer science. Computer science courses also deal with teamwork so as to deliver a certain project. There are some universities that do this by using some of their partners in industries and businesses at this level, so at to allow their students to have the opportunity to design for a real-world client.

If the students want to become specialists and attract future employers, they need to acquire transferable skills. Some of the advanced skills they can acquire are patterns and signals, data structures, complexity theory, or software product engineering (Dasgupta, 2016).

1.3. WHAT IS A COMPUTER?

A computer is a machine that can follow instructions to perform sequences of operations that are logical and arithmetic in an automatic manner using computer programming. Computers in the modern time are able to do a set of operations that are generalized. These are called programs. These programs allow computers to do very many tasks. A computer system refers to a computer that is complete with an operating system, hardware, and the peripheral equipment that is needed and utilized for the full operation of the computer. This term also refers to a group of computers that work together due to connections, this is a computer network or cluster (Dasgupta, 2016).

A wide range of industrial and consumer devices use computers as control systems. They include special purpose devices that are simple, such as remote controls, ovens, microwaves, factory devices such as computer-aided designs, industrial robots, and even devices used for general purposes such as personal computers and even smartphones. Computers help to connect the world to the internet and they also help in connecting hundreds of millions of other computers and the people using them (Shelly, Freund, &Vermaat, 2010).

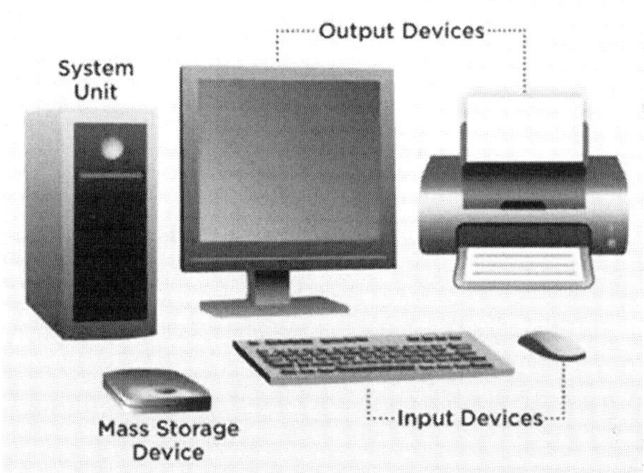

Figure 1.3. Above are the different parts of a computer.

Source: *https://www.webopedia.com/TERM/C/computer.html.*

In the past, computers were mostly used as calculating devices. Abacus helped people make calculations manually. There were some mechanical devices that were created as to make long tedious tasks easier to do, such as guiding patterns for looms. There were also much more sophisticated machines that were created to do specialized calculations that were analog in the early 20th century. During the World War II, the first digital electronic calculating machine was developed. In the late 1940s, the first semiconductor transistors were created, followed by the MOS transistor as well as the IC chip technologies in the 1950s, which was later followed by the revolution of the microprocessor and microcomputer in the 1970s (Gary B. Shelly, Steven M. Freund, & Misty E. Vermaat, 2010).

Computational speed, power, and versatility have been improving at a high rate ever since the 1970s, with the counts if the MOS transistor rising at a high rate. This was well predicted by Moore's law and caused the digital revolution between the 20th and 21st centuries.

Normally, a modern computer has at least one processing element, which is a central processing unit that is created with a metal-oxide-semiconductor microprocessor, together with a certain type of computer memory, where they mostly use MOS semiconductor memory chips.

Arithmetic and logical operations are carried out by the processing element, and the orders of operation in response to stored information can be changed by the sequencing and control unit. Some of the peripheral devices include the joystick, mice, keyboard, etc. some of the output devices include printers, monitors, etc.

Those that perform both functions (input and output) include the 2000s-era touchscreen. The peripheral devices create the possibility for information to be gotten from a source that is external and they also allow for the results of operations to undergo retrieval and saving.

1.4. KEY CHARACTERISTICS OF A COMPUTER

1. It Responds to a Specific Set of Instructions in a Well-Defined Manner

There is a set of instructions that a computer may respond to. When it comes to the computer processor, the set of instructions refers to a segment of code containing a set of steps that required to undergo execution by the processor. For a computer to be able to perform any tasks, it needs to be given a certain set of instructions.

For example, when you ask a computer to create a square, you need to have a set of instructions that tell the computer how the square should be created. The human gives the computer instructions using either a keyboard or another form of input device.

The computer uses an operating system or software to be able to interpret the instructions it is given. These systems are also programmed by humans so as to be able to translate the commands of the user into a function that the computer is able to understand.

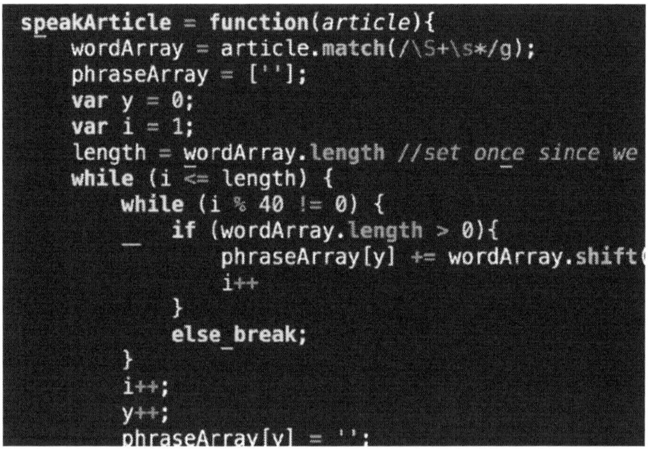

Figure 1.4. The computer used algorithms that are set by programmers to perform a certain action.

Source: *https://www.wsj.com/amp/articles/whats-hot-in-the-art-world-algorithms-1432687554.*

Instructions that are given to the computer are considered a set of steps that involve the information on how the computer software or hardware should be operated, undergo performing, or be maintained. If there is an instruction manual or instructions found online included in a program or hardware device, it is important to review these instructions before using the computer. Instructions are important in programming so as to be able to tell the computer to perform a certain function. These set of instructions are normally stored on a hard disk drive or another different form of storage device. These, however, are not executed, up to the point when they are run by the user.

2. It Can Execute a Pre-recorded List of Instructions (A Program)

Computer programs involve a collection of instructions that are able to perform a task that is specific when it undergoes execution by a computer. Most of the devices are able to use programs to make certain programs properly. Computer programs are normally written by computer programmers in a programming language (Henderson, 2009).

Figure 1.5. Computer programs help the computer in performing a list of instructions that were pre-recorded.

Source: *http://www.scienceclarified.com/Ci-Co/Computer-Software.html.*

Assemblers or compilers are able to derive machine code from programs that are in human readable forms of source code. This involves a form that has instructions that the computer can perform directly. Alternatively, and interpreter can be able to execute a computer program. A software is a collection of computer programs, related data, and libraries. When it comes to categorization, computer programs may be categorized along functional lines. This includes system software as well as application software. The main method that is normally used in calculating and manipulating problems is referred to as an algorithm.

Computer programming involves being able to give the computer instructions on what the computer should do. These instructions are normally referred to as code. They are normally written by computer programmers so as to deal with tasks and problems. Normally, the end goal is to create something, such as a webpage, or a specific software, or even just a nice photo. This is why computer programming is normally described as both an art and a science. It is normally both technical and analytical at the same time very creative (Henderson, 2009).

3. It Can Quickly Store and Retrieve Large Amounts of Data

Computer data storage is a hard subject to explain but it can be divided into three main processes. First, data normally undergoes conversion into simpler numbers that make it easier for the computer to store. Second, these numbers are then recorded by the computer hardware into the computer. Third, the numbers undergo organization and then are transferred to a storage that is temporary and manipulated using either programs or software.

Figure 1.6. Above is a hard disk drive that can act as a secondary storage when connected to the computer.

Source: *https://simple.wikipedia.org/wiki/Computer_data_storage.*

The hard disk drive is normally the main data storage region for most computers. It is a disk that has magnetic coatings and heads, which are able to interpret or create magnetic information, in a way that also the cassette tapes work. Actually, the earlier computers in the past used cassette tapes to store data. Binary numbers are normally written as a series of small areas on the disc which are magnets either north or south. All of the memory storage devices for a computer use magnetism to write binary numbers. These include floppy disk and tapes. The data recorded on these devices can be destroyed if they come too close to a magnet (Henderson, 2009).

Some of the new computers especially laptops utilize solid-state drives to store primary data. These have chips to store memory that is similar to those used in USB keys, SD cards, cell phones, etc. Binary numbers are written through charging or not charging a couple of tiny capacitors in the chip. Storing data using electricity is much more rugged than when magnetism is used.

1.5. COMPUTER INTERFACE LAYERS

1.5.1. Hardware

A computer hardware involves the parts of the computer that are physical and tangible such as the central processing unit, monitor, cabinet, keyboard, graphics card, speakers, motherboard, and sound card. It is referred to as "hard" when it comes to changes or modifications. They are normally directed by the software to perform any instructions or commands. When you combine the software and hardware, this creates a computing system that is usable, although other systems, can exist with a hardware.

The hardware in a computer can undergo categorization as having external or internal components. The internal ones include the motherboard, central processing unit, hard drive, Random Access Memory, heat sink, power supply, chips, transistors, graphics processing unit, network interface card and the Universal serial bus ports. These internal components work together to process and store instructions that are given to them by the operating system or the program (Henderson, 2009).

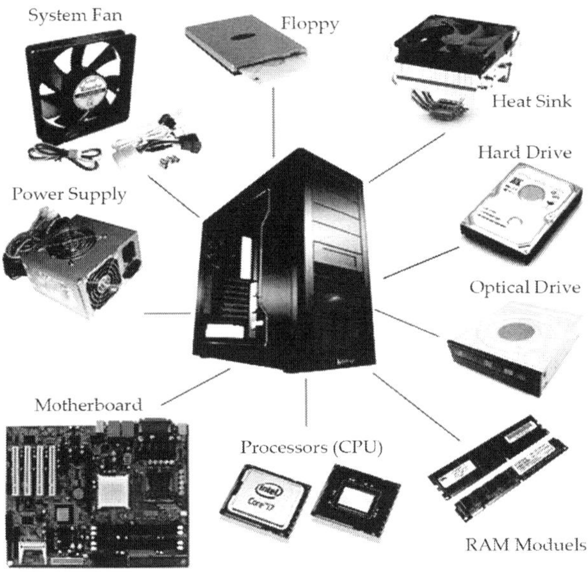

Figure 1.7. Above are the components of the computer hardware.

Source: *https://www.kenresearch.com/blog/2019/08/global-computer-hardware-market-outlook-ken-research/.*

The external components are also called peripheral components and they are normally connected to the computer, which can control its input or output. Some of the input components include the keyboard, camera, mouse, microphone, joystick, stylish, memory card or USB flash drive. Those components that are for output include the monitors, headphones, printers, etc. All these devices are created so that they can give instructions to the software so as to come up with an execution.

It is normally common for businesses or individuals to buy computer hardware and then after a while replace or upgrade it. Individuals and companies can also lease virtual or physical hardware's from providers of the service. These providers are then left responsible for ensuring that the hardware is kept up to date, both in terms of the components and the software that is running on it.

The abstraction of physical computing resources from the software that uses the resources is called hardware virtualization. This is normally possible due to the use of a virtual machine manager that is called a hypervisor. In real terms, the hypervisor is able to create versions of internal hardware that are virtual, so that resources are efficiently shared and used more. In cloud computing, hardware virtualization is normally involved with infrastructure as a service.

The equipment that is used for input, output and data storage is called an auxiliary computer hardware. It includes an adapter that allows for one type of device to communicate with a different type of device and a complementary metal-oxide-semiconductor, an onboard, a semiconductor chip that is powered using a battery inside a computer that is able to store data, including the settings of the system hardware and the time and date of the system (Page & Gamboa, 2019).

1.5.2. Operating System

The operating system is a program that has the ability to act on the interface between the software and the computer hardware. It involves the integration of a set of programs that are specialized, and are used to manage the operations of the computer as well as all the other resources. It controls and monitors the execution of other programs that are inside the computer, including other system software and application programs.

The operating system has specific functions:

- It works to ensure that the computer system is convenient to use in a manner that is efficient.
- It is also able to ensure that their hardware resources are not recognized by other users.
- It gives the user of the computer an interface that is convenient to operate the system.
- The operating system also acts as the link between the person using the computer and the hardware, which makes it easy for the

user to access and use other resources.

- It helps in managing computer system resources.
- It also keeps track of the person using the specific computer resources, it also is able to grant requests as well as mediate any requests that may be conflicting from different users and programs.
- It also provides the sharing of resources in a manner that is efficient and fair among the users in the programs.

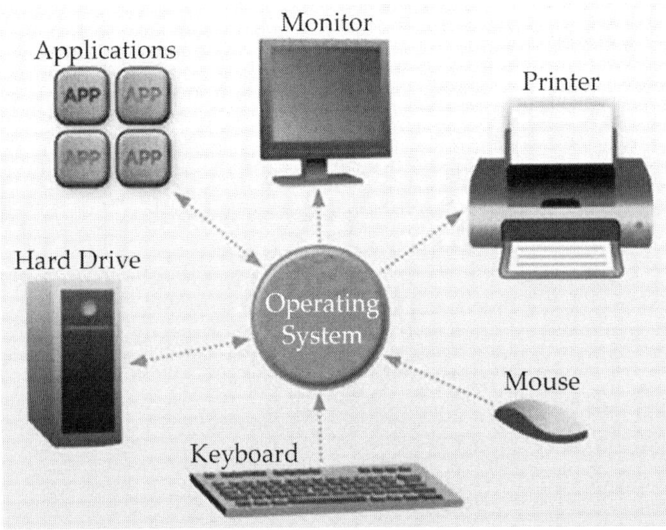

Figure 1.8. The operating system also monitors the health of the computer hardware. It allows us to see how well the hardware is performing.

Source: *https://medium.com/computing-technology-with-it-fundamentals/operating-system-its-functions-and-characteristics-c0946e4215c6.*

Single-tasking and multi-tasking operating system are one of the types of operating system. The single tasking system is able to run only one program at a time and the multitasking system makes it possible for there to be more than one program running at a time.

This is achieved in a manner where they processor time that is available undergoes division between multiple processes. This is called timesharing. These different processes are each interrupted a couple of times using a subsystem that schedule tasks in the operating system. The multitasking system is divided into two types: the preemptive and co-operative type. In preemptive multitasking, the operating system is able to slow the time for the CPU and also is able to dedicate a slot to each program that is being used. In co-operative multitasking, the system is able to do this as it relies on each process to give its own time to the other process in a manner that is defined (Page & Gamboa, 2019).

Another type operating system in the single-user and multi-user system. The single-user operating system is able to allow for more than one program to run at the same time, however, it cannot distinguish the users.

A multi-user operating system can also allow for more than one program to run at the same time, and it is also able to identify the processes and resources that may belong to the different users of the system, and also allows for many users to use the system at the same time. Operating systems that can share time are able to schedule tasks that allow the system to be used efficiently and is also able to do accounting software for the allocation of costs in the processor time, mass storage, and other resources that may be available to a couple of users.

1.5.3. Application

An application software is a program or a group of programs that are designed to meet the needs of the user. Some of the examples of the common applications that are used daily include: spreadsheets, an accounting application, a web browser, a spreadsheet, and aeronautical flight simulator, or a photo editor, among others.

Application software stands for all the applications that are in a computer. It is possible for an application to be published separately or put together with the computer in the system software. It can also be coded as an open source, or university project. Applications that are created for mobile platforms are called mobile applications (ITL Education Solutions Limited, 2011).

Application software has grown considerably since the cross-platform software became much more popular.

It is important for some of the programs that are used by specific people or businesses to be taken wherever they want to be used at any time possible. Applications have been able to enable the end-user to work in an efficient manner no matter where they go.

Figure 1.9. Applications are end user programs that allow the user to perform many different tasks.

Source: https://www.informationq.com/application-and-types-of-computer-applications/.

They are designed to make work easier on a CPU compared to the traditional software, which requires for there to be more resources and normally uses a simple user interface. Application software has been able to allow us to move away from the traditional system that required one to install the software equipped with the applications. Applications have now allowed for there to be web-based applications which reduce the stress on the systems resources, letting the Internet and the cloud take all the stress.

Application software differs from other software that may come together with the computers operating system, such as a utility. For example, disk tool is a software that is located inside the operating system and can be used to search for problems in the hard drive, delete files that are not necessary and defragmented drives. These can be used by the user, but they depend on the computers core to operate effectively. Applications may not be able to run independently but they do not rely on information from the computers core (ITL Education Solutions Limited, 2011).

One of the types of application software is the desktop application. These are normally installed into the computer, are quite high powered and are able to use the memory in the computer directly to perform a task.

They also allow people to manipulate graphics, or numbers to be able to produce an output. Examples of this application include word processes, video players, etc.

Another type is the Web-based application. This involves the applications that only exist in the web format compared to those that are normally installed directly to a machine.

These applications are able to provide space on the user's hard drive or network because they are found on the web and can be accessed from anywhere in the world at any time.

The data that they have is stored on the cloud. This also means that this application is always up to date and it updates automatically, giving the user a reduced risk in using an application that is insecure (ITL Education Solutions Limited, 2011).

1.6. CLASSIFICATION OF COMPUTERS BASED ON SIZE AND POWER

1.6.1. Personal Computer

A personal computer refers to a computer that has multiple purposes, whose size, capabilities, and cost for production is feasible for the use of one person.

Personal computers are meant to undergo operation directly by the end-user, instead of by an expert in computers or technician.

In comparison to minicomputers and mainframes, it is not possible to have many people use personal computers at the same time.

To efficiently use a personal computer in the 1960s, institutional or corporate computer owners had to generate their own programs. Despite the fact that personal computer users had to develop their own applications, normally they had commercial software, free-of-charge software, or free and open source software which they used to run their systems.

The hardware or operating system manufacturers were the ones who typically developed and distributed software's for personal computers in an independent manner (ITL Education Solutions Limited, 2011).

Figure 1.10. *Personal computers refer to all those that can only be used by one person at a time.*

Source: https://pagedesignshop.com/how-and-why-you-should-back-up-your-personal-computer/.

As of now users of the personal computer do not need to generate their own programs so as to use the personal computer, however, it is still possible to use end-user programming. This is different from mobile systems, where the software is often only available to the end-user through a channel that is supported by the manufacturer, and the development of programs by the end-user may be discouraged if it is not supported by the manufacturer. Much of the personal computer market has been dominated by Microsoft operating systems and Intel hardware since the early 1990s. Initially, with MS-DOS and then later with Microsoft Windows.

Any different operating systems from Microsoft windows occupy a small share of the industry. These include Apple's macOS and unix-like operating systems that were free and open. The development of personal computers together with the digital revolution has greatly affected the lives of people globally (Henderson, 2009).

Some of the personal computers include:

Tower model: The tower model computer refers to that which the motherboard, the supply of power, and the devices for mass storage are stacked one on top of the other in the cabinet. This is different in comparison to the desktop model, in which these components are stored in a box that is much more compact. The main advantage of these computers is that they do not have issues with creating more space, which makes installing other storage devices is easier.

Figure 1.11. Desktop computers are mainly found at the workplace.

Source: *http://www.esuppliersindia.com/the-compu-care/high-performance-desktop-computer-pr4927678-sFP-swf.html.*

Desktop model: This involves a computer that has been designed to comfortably fit on top of a desk, normally with the monitor sitting above the computer. These computers are low and wide in comparison to tower model computers that are thin and tall. Because of this shape, desktop model computers are only able to have three devices internally for mass storage. Those that are designed to be smaller than the normal ones are normally referred to a slim line model.

Notebook computer: this refers to a computer that is powered by either a battery or an AC and is generally smaller than a briefcase and can be carried from one place to another in a convenient manner. It can be used in spaces that temporary, such as an airplane, library, meetings, etc. This computer is sometimes called a laptop computer and weighs less than 4 pounds and is 2.5 inches or less in thickness. Some of the best laptop computers were made by Toshiba, Apple, Dell, and IBM. These computers and normally a bit more expensive than desktop computers yet they have the same capabilities. This expense is due to the difficulty they have in designing and manufacturing the notebook computers. A docking station can be used to effectively turn a notebook computer into a desktop computer. This is a hardware frame that works to supply connections for the devices for input and output such as a printer. Laptop computers normally come with displays that use the thin-screen technology. This screen technology works better than the dual-scan screen when it comes to the brightness and also the viewing of the output in different angles. Laptop computers also use a couple of different approaches to integrate a mouse into the keyboard. This includes using a track ball, touchpad, or a pointing stick. There is also a port that can allow for a mouse to be attached. In order to add a modem or the network interface into the laptop computer, there is a PC card that is insert able as a hardware. It is also possible to attach or build in CD-ROMs and digital versatile disc drives.

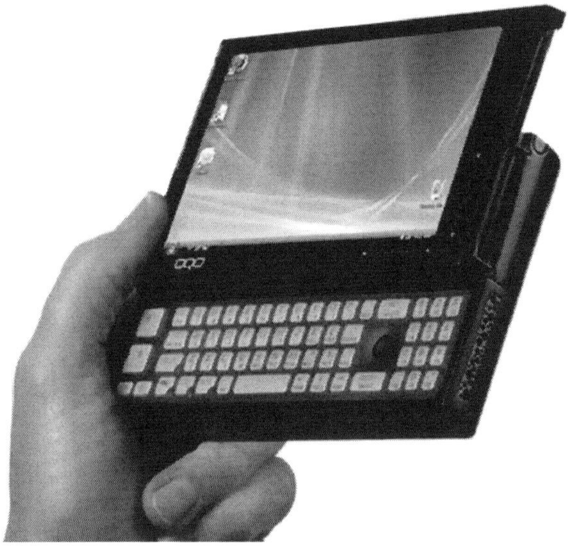

Figure 1.12. As seen above, handheld computers are small enough to fit in the user's hand.

Source: *https://www.computerworld.com/article/2474281/pocket-marvels--40-years-of-handheld-computers.html.*

Hand-held computer: this includes computers that are of a small size and can even be stored inside a pocket and used while you're holding it without having to place it on the surface. These are also called personal digital assistant (PDA) and can be divided into those that are able to input handwriting as well as those that have a small keyboard. Apple's Newton was among the first handheld computers that were able to accept handwritings. This, however, was later removed from the market.

The Palm Pilot is the popular handheld computer that accepts for one to input their handwriting. Other companies such as Casio and Philips make handhelds with keyboards. Handheld computers mostly use Windows CE and EPOC as the main operating systems. Handheld computers and mainly used as personal information managers. They have applications that help in maintaining schedules, saving names and phone numbers on the phone, performing simple calculations, writing and receiving emails as well as being able to search for information on the Internet. The keyboards have small keys that may take a while for one to get used to. Those that use handwriting instead of keyboards also need some time to get used to. Despite this small issue, handheld computers are popular in the market and appreciated by many end-users.

Palmtop: this is an electronic device that is able to fit in the palm of the users' hand. The Palm Pilot was the earliest palmtop computer and is a good example of this. Due to the size of the palmtop computer in the past, they did not have a keyboard or a mouse and often had to use a pen that used graffiti or something of the sort. The name Palmtop computer was given to these computers due to the comparison with the bigger and problematic ones. At this time small cell phones and even smartphones had not yet been created. Due to the creation of the Smartphone, this term is hardly ever used to describe a com that can fit in your hand.

Laptop computer: laptop computers are designed due to how portable they are. The components of the computer together with the keyboard are all on one panel with the second panel that has hinged containing a flat display screen. When the laptop is closed shut, the screen and the keyboard are protected in times of transportation. Laptops have batteries that are rechargeable which makes the portability even much more enhanced. The laptop uses the RAM system which helps to reduce graphic performances when compared to the desktop machine. This helps to save power, weight, and space, because the laptop and graphic codes can be integrated into the Central Processing Unit.

Due to this desktop computers anomaly preferred in comparison to laptop for gaming purposes. When compared to desktop computers, laptop computers can only have upgrades on memory and hard disk drive therefore accounting for the limited space and power available.

Both laptops and desktops have the same input and output ports that allow them to connect to displays externally, the mouse, storage devices and keyboards. Laptops, however, are a bit more expensive in comparison to desktops, because of the components that are normally used to make the laptop, which are expensive.

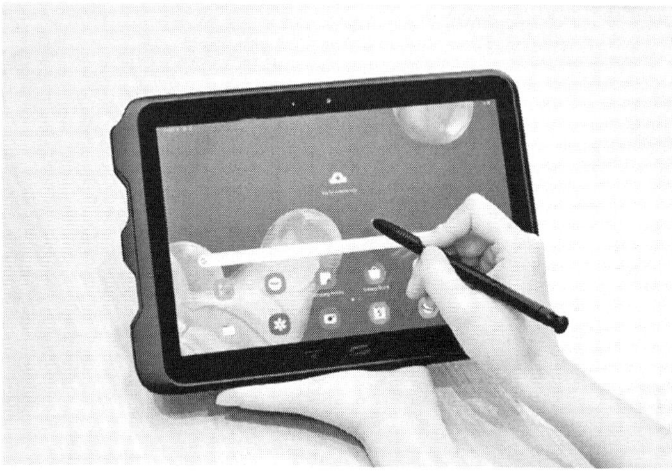

Figure 1.13. *Tablets are very convenient and have been found to be the second bought computers after smartphones.*

Source:-https://www.theverge.com/platform/amp/2019/10/30/20938223/samsung-rugged-tablet-galaxy-tab-active-pro-released-us-lte.

Tablet: tablets use a display that is touch screen and can be controlled either using the users finger or a stylus pen. Some tablets are able to have a convertible design which may offer a keyboard which can either be attached and removed, or a screen that can either be fully rotated or folded to access or hide the keyboard. There are some tablets that are able to use the desktop personal computer operating system such as Windows or Linux and others may use the operating system that was initially designed for the tablet by the manufactures. Most tablet computers have USB ports which can be used to connect mice and keyboards.

1.6.2. Sub-Notebook Computer

This is a class of laptop computers that are smaller in size and also lighter than the normal notebook. They are also called ultra-portable, super portable or mini notebook. They are sometimes confused with the ultra-mobile PC which refers to small form factor Tablet PCs. The ultra-mobile PC category has smaller laptops than in sub-notebooks category, however, they both use the usual full desktop operating systems such as Windows or Linux, instead of other software that is specialized such as Internet tablet OS (ITL Education Solutions Limited, 2011).

Sub-notebooks are also hard to differentiate from netbooks which are a completely different category of laptops that were created from the design of the mini notebooks in general. Netbooks are normally much cheaper than sub-notebooks, because they're normally used as portable Internet capable devices and they do not have enough processing power for a workstation. They sacrifice performance for power efficiency in comparison to sub-notebooks that use 18w TDP.

Figure 1.14. *They have a similar design to the laptop but were created way earlier in the early 90s.*

Source: https://boingboing.net/2019/02/02/functional-rigor.html/amp.

Sub-notebooks are much smaller than the normal full-size laptops but they are larger than handheld computers. Most of the times they have screens that are smaller, less than 15 inches, and they also have a weight that is lower than typical laptops which is usually less than two kilograms. So as to achieve the size and weight, they lack optical disk drives and ports due to their omission. They, however, can be paired with docking stations to compensate for lacking these options.

The ASUS Eee PC was created in 2007 and was the first new class of low-cost sub-notebook that is what is commonly called the netbook. This device was created to mainly use with the Internet. Netbooks normally use Atom processors while other sub-notebooks normally use other processors that are much more powerful such as the ULV types.

Apple introduced the Mac Book Air in 2008, which they claim to be the world's thinnest notebook. The Mac Book Air has a 13.3-inch widescreen and an LED-backlit display that lights up instantly. It also has a built-in camera, a backlit keyboard and a trackpad that allows for multi-touch gestures. It, however, does not have an optical drive that is built-in. It weighs around 1.35 kgs. Ultrabooks were first announced by the Computer 2011 Intel. This name was given to then to represent a laptop that is highly portable and is also light and has a long battery life.

Tablet computers were becoming increasingly popular by 2011. This led to the decline in the cells of the sub-notebook due to the tablet computers having improved computing capabilities as well as lower production costs. When the Mac Book Air went into the market, it led to increased production costs due to the revolutionized traditional keyboard as well as the display. Due to the great feedback the Mac Book Air was getting, Intel was able to promote the Ultrabook as a new high-mobility standard. The Ultrabook has gotten praises from analysts in places that the netbook did not succeed in. The netbooks of 2011 only had the low price as the strong point. They lost praises due to their design, as well as portability and the ease of use (ITL Education Solutions Limited, 2011).

Figure 1.15. *Subnotebooks were considered portable and light. They were always less than 2 kgs.*

Source: https://collection.cooperhewitt.org/objects/18649967/.

Many of the companies that were producing netbooks ceased to produce them around the end of 2012. Many products from the notebook were replaced in the market by chrome-books. Chrome-books are a type of network computer concept in the form of a netbook. The Stream 11 in 2014 was invented by HP as they re-entered the non-Chromebook netbook market. There are also other computers that are specialized that have been released to the market, and are quite similar to netbooks such as the GPD win 1 and 2.

Netbooks have become a growing trend in schools for many reasons. Children are yet to be prepared for the lifestyle that they will expect in the 21st-century, combined with many new educational tools that can be found on the Internet. There is also the growing emphasis onthe student-centered learning. These reasons have led to the rise in the use of sub-netbooks in the education sector. The first rugged netbook for the education sector was mass-produced by Dell. They have a touchscreen and a network activity light that was able to indicate to the teacher when the laptop is online (ITL Education Solutions Limited, 2011).

1.6.3. Workstation Computer

A workstation computer is a computer that is specially designed for applications that are technical or scientific. They are normally created to be used by one person at a time and are normally connected to a network in a local area. They use operating systems that are multi-user.

The phrase workstation has been over used to refer to more than just the workstation computer including the mainframe computer terminal and even a PC that is connected to the network. The main phrase normally refers to a group of hardware offered by several companies that opened the door for 3-D graphics animation revolution in the late 90s (Page & Gamboa, 2019).

Figure 1.16. *Workstation computers have proven to have much better graphics than the personal computers. Their performance has proven to be much better.*

Source: https://discountcomputerdepot.com/desktops-by-price/desktops-under-300/dell-precision-t3400-windows-10-pro-workstation-computer-core-2-duo-8g-500gb-22-lcd/.

Workstation computers have been able to offer performance that is higher than mainstream personal computers especially when it comes to the central processing unit and graphics, the capacity of memory it has, and also its capability to multitask. Workstation computers were created to optimize the visualization and manipulation of different types of data that may be complex such as 3-D mechanical designs, animations, etc.

Workstation computers are normally created in a form that is like that of a desktop computer. They have high resolution display, a mouse, a keyboard and also may have a couple of displays, graphics tablets, etc. Workstation computers were the first category of computers in the market to provide users with advanced accessories and collaboration tools (Page & Gamboa, 2019).

Workstation computers have five main features:

- Error correcting code RAM – this helps to make the computer system much more reliable. It helps to fix any errors in the memory before they can cause problems to the computer system, preventing the computer from crashing and saving one downtime.
- Multiple Processor Cores – when a computer has more processor cores, it has a higher processing ability. This, however, doesn't mean that it boosts the performance of the computer. The software that the user is using has to be programmed to take advantage of the multiple process of cores. Having them, however, is advantageous.
- Redundant Array of Independent Disks – these use a number of internal hard drives for the storage and the processing of data. There are a couple of different redundant array of independent disc systems. Depending on the system that is being used, the user can attain multiple drives to process their data, or get drives that are mirrored, which means that if one drive does not function the others will still be able to work.
- Solid-state Drives – these work differently in comparison to the conventional hard disk drives. They do not have any moving parts so they have lower chances of getting any physical failure. They are also faster than the conventional hard disk drives. The only disadvantage is that they are much more expensive and have a lower storing capacity than their normal drives.
- Optimized Graphics Processing Unit – all computers normally need a screen to provide output. Having a higher end graphics processing unit leads to ensuring your central processing unit does

less work processing the screen output. In most cases, the graphics processing unit can actually take over some of the stress from the central processing unit and makes the output processing faster. High end graphics processing units are, however, expensive.

- Most of the computers in the segment of the desktop market and expected to perform as workstation computers. However, they use PC operating systems and components. Industries that manufacture components often market components that are premium and function similar to models that are cheaper but they also feature higher level of performance.

Figure 1.17. *Above is a HP workstation computer CPU.*

Source: https://www.amazon.com/HP-Z420-Workstation-Computer-8-Cache-64GB/dp/B01GUEGGFM.

In the past, workstation computers were quite expensive, they costed several times the cost of the standard PC and sometimes they were as expensive as a new car. They were quite expensive because they used companies that were much costlier and ran faster than those that were found at the local computer store. They also use high-speed networking and graphics that were sophisticated. These features were normally not found in PCs of the time. They also allow for data to flow without being interrupted between the many different subsystems within a computer due to the balanced approach to system design. Workstation computers have higher profit margins than the PCs that were commodity-driven because they were much more specialized nature (Page & Gamboa, 2019).

1.6.4. Minicomputer

This is a class of smaller computers that were created in the mid-1960's and were much more affordable in comparison to mainframe and midsize computers from IBM and other direct competitors. In 1970, that was a consensus definition of a mini-computer as a machine that was much cheaper than US$25,000. This was equivalent to US$162,000 in 2018.

These computers had an input and output device and also a high level of storage memory of a minimum of 4000 words. It was also able to run programs in a higher-level language, such as BASIC. Minicomputers had their own software architectures and operating system. They were mainly created for the control, instrumentation, interaction with humans, and communication switching that was easy to differentiate from calculation and record keeping. The woman of them that wrestled for the final and your supplication to original equipment manufacturer. During the time the minicomputer existed, which was between 1965 and 1985, of that 100 companies that were formed only a half dozen remained (ITL Education Solutions Limited, 2011).

Figure 1.18. *Above is an example of a minicomputer which were invented in the 1960s.*

Source:https://www.wikiwand.com/en/History_of_computing_hardware_(1960s%E2%80%93present).

In around 1971, the term minicomputer came to mean a machine that is placed in the middle range of the spectrum when it comes to computing. This means it was found between the smallest mainframe computers and the microcomputer. This change in definition was due to the appearance of the single-chip CPU microprocessors that were introduced by Intel 4004. These days, the term minicomputer is rarely used. The new term is a midrange computer such as Power ISA which are high-end.

Sales of the minicomputer declined due to the reduced cost of microprocessor-based hardware, the development of local area network systems that were not expensive and also easily deployable, the development of the 68020, 80283, and the 80386 micro-processes, as well as the desire of the people using these computers to not have to rely on inflexible minicomputer manufacturers. Network workstations, file servers and PCs were able to replace minicomputers and computer templates in the beginning of the 1980s (ITL Education Solutions Limited, 2011).

There were several versions of Unix systems that used the Intel x87 microprocessor architecture that were developed, which helped to cement the change from minicomputers to PCs that were not as expensive. This was during the 1990s. This included Linux, Net BSD, Solaris, etc. The series of operating system from Microsoft windows had versions of the servers that were better able to support pre-emptive multitasking and other features that were advantageous to the user.

CPUs that have been built up from multiple components are becoming much more obsolete because microprocessors are becoming more powerful. This can be seen due to the distinguishing features that can differentiate mainframes and the midrange systems from microcomputers.

The leading computer manufacturer was once Digital Equipment Corporation which was the second-largest company that produced computers after IBM, but after the minicomputer started to decline in the market due to the production of the UNIX servers which were generic as well as the Intel-based PCs, the Digital Equipment Corporation, as well as almost all the other minicomputer companies including prime, collapsed. Some of the companies also had to merge. There are only a few architectures for minicomputers that have been able to survive up to date. The operating system from IBM which introduced many advanced concepts has been able to survive together with IBM's AS/400 (ITL Education Solutions Limited, 2011).

Figure 1.19. *This is a digital equipment corporation.*

Source: https://en.wikipedia.org/wiki/Minicomputer.

There are many companies that were able to build systems around minicomputers with specialized software. They were also able to address specialized problems through custom peripherals such as designs that were computer-aided, as well as manufacturing, process control, etc. most of the minicomputer was sold through original equipment manufacturer and value-added resellers. Most of the companies that pioneered minicomputers such as DEC, Data general and HP do not produce minicomputers any more. The

CPUs and operating systems of the PCs of today have developed a great deal by the integration of features from the minicomputers, despite the fact that they are physically microcomputers.

1.6.5. Mainframe

Mainframe computers, which are also known as big iron, are those that are used mainly by large companies and organizations for applications that are considered critical such as census, processing of bulk data, statistics of the consumers, resource planning for the enterprise, and processing of transactions, that are much bigger and have much more processing power than other computer categories such as a mini-computer, servers and personal computers.

The term mainframe originally comes from large cabinets that were called "mainframes" that were able to host their central processing unit and main memory for computers in the earlier times.

Thereafter, the phrase was used to distinguish machines that were commercially high-end from those with less powerful units. Most architecture for large scale computer systems were developed in the 1960s but they have also continued to undergo evolution.

Mainframe computers are normally used as servers.

Characteristics of modern mainframe designs include:

1. Internal engineering that is redundant and therefore results in high security and reliability.
2. Input and output facilities that are extensive and also have the ability to offload to engines that are separate.
3. Compatibility that is strict with older software.
4. Computational utilization rates that are high due to the utilization of virtualization to support massive throughput.
5. Being able to swap hardware such as memory and processors.
6. They have a high stability and reliability that allows them to run without being interrupted for a long period of time, with meantime between failures measured in decades.

Figure 1.20. *These are normally used in large companies that have a lot of critical data that needs to be processed.*

Source: https://gcn.com/articles/2018/10/02/mainframe-use-decline.aspx.

One of the main reasons that mainframes have longevity is because of their high availability. This is because they are mainly used in applications where it would be costly and catastrophic for any downtime to occur. Mainframe computers are defined by the term reliability, availability, and serviceability (RAS). So as to realize these features, it is important for there to be proper planning and implementation. Mainframes have also been noted to be much more secure than other types of computers. To update the software of a mainframe what is required to set up the operating system or push lens of the operating system, which is not disruptive only when using virtualizing facilities such as IBM Z, which supports the sharing of workload so that one system can take over the application of another system when it is being refreshed (Dasgupta, 2016).

In the past, around the late 1950s, mainframes only had the console, which is a rudimentary interactive interface, and used sets of cards that were punched, paper tape, or magnetic tape to ensure the transferring of data and programs. These were operated using a batch mode to support functions of the back office such as customer billing and payroll. They helped by using the repeated tape-based sorting and operations that one meant for merging, followed by line printing to pre-printed continuous stationery. When do use the time in those that were interactive were introduced, they were mostly used for applications instead of the development of programs. In 1970, devices such as the typewriter were still common control consoles for system operators. This is despite the fact that the keyboard and display devices had already been developed.

Interactive user terminals became a main factor for each mainframe to acquire by the early 1970s. This allowed the mainframe to operate as timesharing computers which were able to support hundreds of people at the same time along with batch processing. The end-users were able to gain access through keyboards or typewriter terminals and text terminal CRT displays which were specialized with keyboards. Later, personal computers were able to acquire terminal emulation software.

Mainframes were able to support graphic display terminals as well as terminal emulation by the 1980s. However, they were not able to support the graphical user interface.

This method of computing for the user became obsolete in the 1990s due to the development of personal computers that had Graphical User interfaces. After 2000, the classic green screens and color display terminals for end-users were phased out by Web-style user interfaces (Dasgupta, 2016).

Figure 1.21. *There not many young people that can run mainframe computers. Those who have been running them are retiring slowly but surely.*

Source: https://medium.com/@rogerkay/educational-initiatives-aim-to-head-off-potential-skills-crisis-developing-in-the-mainframe-world-607a0c970511.

Just as any other computing platform, the return on investment for the mainframe computer depends on its ability to scale. The mainframe computer can support heavy workloads, reduce the cost of labor, and deliver services that are not interrupted for business applications that are critical.

Mainframes were made in a way that allows them to handle a high-volume input and output as well as use and emphasize throughput computing. The mainframe design has always included channels or peripheral processors which help in managing the input and output volume, leaving the central processing unit free to deal only with memories at high-speed. Mainframe shops normally deal with databases and files that are massive. A mainframe with recorded files that are a gigabyte to a Tetra Byte is not unusual. In comparison to the typical PC, mainframes have hundreds of thousands of times as much data storage, and are able to access this data quite fast (Dasgupta, 2016).

1.6.6. Supercomputer

This is a computer with high-level of performance compared to other general purpose computers. We use the floating-point operations per second to measure the performance of a supercomputer instead of the million instructions per second that is used for the other general purpose computers.

Figure 1.22. *These computers provide computations that are of high performance.*

Source: https://en.wikipedia.org/wiki/Supercomputer.

Since 2017 there exist supercomputers that are able to perform over 100 quadrillion floating-point operations per second. These are referred to as petaFLOPS. Since November of the same year, the fastest supercomputers globally were using a Linux-based operating system. There are countries that are conducting additional research, such as the United States, China, Japan, and Taiwan to create supercomputers that are much faster, more powerful and technically superior.

When it comes to the field of computational science, supercomputers play an important role.

They are used in a number of computational intensive tasks in many different fields, including quantum mechanics, research on the climate, weather forecasting, molecular modeling and physical simulations, such as airplane and spacecraft is the dynamics, among others. Ever since supercomputers were invented, they have been used in the field of cryptanalysis (Anderson, Ferro, Hilton, 2010).

In the 1960s, the first supercomputer was introduced. For a long period, the fastest supercomputers were created by Seymour Cray at Control Data Corporation and other companies that has his name or monogram.

These initial supercomputers were highly tuned conventional designs that were able to run faster than the personal computers that were used for general purposes. Through the 1960s, the creators started to add on the amount of parallelism with 1 to 4 processes being the norm. In the 1970s, vector processors that were operating on large amounts of data were the main processors that were used in supercomputers. In 1976, the main supercomputer was the highly successful Cray-1. Vector computers were able to dominate all the way up to the 1990s. Between then and now, the norm became huge parallel supercomputers which had many off the shelf processors.

The United States has been the largest producer of supercomputers, first through Cray's dominance in the field which was highly uninterrupted, and later through a number of companies that deal with technology.

Japan made huge discoveries in the 1980s and 1990s, but then China overtook them and is now quite active in the field. From the year 2018, the highest-ranked supercomputer in terms of speed on the TOP500 supercomputer list is the Summit in the US. It has a score of 143.6 Penta FLOPS. The United States was able to secure five slots in the top 10 supercomputers, and china was able to secure two (Anderson, Ferro, Hilton, 2010).

Figure 1.23. *These computers may cost millions of dollars due to their size and high performing components.*

Source: https://computer.howstuffworks.com/10-types-of-computers9.htm.

For the longest period of time, being able to manage the heat density was the main issue for most centralized supercomputers. Supercomputers generate a large amount of heat which may lead to many other negative effects including, reduction in the lifetime of other components in the system. Its management has seen very many different approaches since the development of a supercomputer. One of the methods used was pumping Fluor inert through the system. Another method was through the using of air cooling with normal air conditioning temperatures. The supercomputer also takes up a lot of amount of electrical power which is all mostly turned into heat and requires to be cooled.

Copper wires are able to facilitate the transference of energy into the supercomputer with much higher power densities in comparison to forced air or refrigerant that is circulating can eliminate waste heat, this makes getting rid of waste heat a huge factor that is limited. Since the year 2015, there have been many supercomputers that exist that have much more capacity when it comes to infrastructure than the actual capability of the machine. This is achieved by the designers, when they conservatively designed the power and cooling infrastructure to be able to deal with more than the electrical power that is consumed theoretically be a supercomputer. The future supercomputers have designs that are power limited. This means that the amount that the power and cooling infrastructure can handle as well, as the thermal design power of the supercomputer, is more than what is expected when considering the normal consumption of power, but less than the power consumption of the electronic hardware in theoretical term (Anderson, Ferro, Hilton, 2010).

Despite the fact that most modern supercomputers use an operating system that is Linux-based, each manufacturer has their own specific Linux-derivative and there are no standards in the industry that exist, mainly because of the differences in hardware architecture that are needed so as to optimize the operating system to each design of the hardware.

Chapter 2

Basic Concepts of Computer

CONTENTS

2.1. INTRODUCTION

A computer is a machine that can be programmed in a manner to allow for the performance of arithmetic and logical operations, in an automatic and sequential way, on the input that is provided by the end-user. It also gives the output that is expected after processing.

The components of a computer are categorized into two major parts: the hardware and the software. The hardware refers to the machine itself which is tangible and is connected to devices that provide input and output such as the monitor, the mouse, and the keyboard. It is what you see when you look at a computer system.

The software refers to a set of programs that utilize the hardware so as to perform specific instructions and tasks.

It is not possible for a computer system to do anything on its own. This therefore means that it has to receive instructions to perform specific tasks to be able to solve problems that the end-user requires to be solved. This means that the end-user has to specify the sequence of instructions that they expect the computer to interpret and perform. This sequence of instructions is what is referred to as a program and it is written in a manner and language that the computer can understand.

Below, we will be talking about the characteristics of a computer, the organization of a computer, the computer software, computer language, and the computer security.

2.2. CHARACTERISTICS OF COMPUTERS

2.2.1. Speed

The speed and power of a computer come from the different parts within the computer system. There are critical parts of the computer that help to make the computer speedy.

- Firstly, the central processing unit is one of the main parts of a computer. The general speed of any computer is normally determined by how quick it can process its data. Computers are multitasking machines and they are used daily. The more capable a computer is when it comes to processing data, as well as the execution of certain instructions per second, will help in determining your computer speed. The first-ever computer processor to be invented had a processing speed of 740 kHz. It was able to perform processing of around 93,000 instructions per second. This seems like very many instructions per second, however, the processors that have been invented as of today are multi-core GHz processors. These are able to process over 100 billion instructions per second. The primary contribution to the speed of your computer depends on how powerful the processor is. For a person who uses the computer daily, a dual-core or a quad-core is enough for the needs (Henderson, 2009).

- Secondly, another critical aspect that affects the speed of a computer is the Cache. Despite the fact that computers of today can execute over 100 billion instructions past second, the processor is still normally awaiting instructions from the Random Access Memory and the Hard Drive. Because the random access memory and the Hard Drive are slower forms of memory, the machine uses Cache to achieve data transfer between the central processing unit, memory, and all other components that are within the computer system. The Cache is considered the fastest form of memory within a computer system. The level two and level three Cache will help in the storage and also sending of much more instructions within the computer. The more Cache a computer has, the more efficiently the computer is able to run.
- Thirdly, the Random Access Memory also helps in making a computer run faster. The Random Access Memory is where a computer stores its short-term data. This helps in storage of information when the computer is actively being used. It allows for the computer to access information in a faster manner. That Random Access Memory is what is used when there are multiple programs open at the same time.
- Fourthly, another important part of making a computer faster is the bus speed. A bus refers to a circuit that helps in the connection of different parts of the motherboard. The more data that the bus is able to handle at a time, will help in the faster travel of information. The bus speed is normally measured in megahertz. The front side bus is what the bus speed refers to. The front side bus is what helps in the connection of the central processing unit to a chipset that helps in communicating with the computer processor and also helps to control interaction with memory. This chipset is called the Northbridge (Henderson, 2009).

- Lastly, another main part that contributes to the speed of the computer is the hard drive. The Hard Disk Drive has parts that move, which may lead to read and write times that are slower. This normally depends on the specs of the hard disk drive. A 5400 RPM hard drive will perform slower than a 7200 RPM hard drive. There is another form of drive called a solid-state drive which does not have any moving parts and uses flash memory instead. This normally reads and writes time faster than the traditional hard disk drive.

2.2.2. Accuracy

Accuracy in a computer is used to describe results that are of true value or of the recognized standard. This generally refers to how close the result is to the correct value, no matter how precise the expression is. Accuracy in a computer means that:

- The results provided to have the most minimal errors.
- Every single calculation that is executed has to be true.
- The machine must perform all the commands it is provided with, without performing any error.

Computer accuracy is normally always high and the level of accuracy in each computer is dependent on the instructions that the computer receives, as well as the type of processor it uses. But for each computer, every single calculation is normally performed. In an example, the computer is able to give an accurate answer to the division of any two numbers up to 10 decimal places.

The level of accuracy of an answer that is gotten from a computer is greatly dependent on the programming method that is used, as well as how the results are interpreted. Computers can only perform what they are instructed to do, and if they are given instructions that are faulty for the processing of data, they automatically also release results that are faulty (Henderson, 2009).

A computer normally uses the principle of garbage in garbage out (GIGO). This means that if there is input of wrong data, then there will also be production of the wrong output. High levels of accuracy in a computer implies that there will be minimal error, but there is a contrast between accuracy and precision. For example, if a computer provides three places of decimals that have been computed properly, it is still much more accurate than four places of decimals that have an error.

Computer operations are highly reproducible in a properly coded program due to how binary they are in nature. This is almost equal to superhuman accuracy when it comes to operating calculations and comparison. An example of an operation that takes the full advantage of the speed and accuracy of the computer positions is searching.

Computers can have accuracy issues due to corrupted data. The memory of a computer can undergo corruption due to cosmic rays. This might be rare but also possible. The computer, however, is equipped with error correction systems help in handling corrupted memory. This is why people are advised to back up their computers (Henderson, 2009).

2.2.3. Diligence

This refers to the capacity that a computer has to perform repetitive tasks without getting tired. Computers are not able to get tired, lack of concentration, or even fatigued, etc. and can therefore be able to work for many hours without performing any errors. Even if there were over a million calculations that were performed in a computer, the computer is still able to perform these calculations with the same accuracy no matter how long it is used.

In comparison to human beings, computer can maintain a high level of consistency. They do not suffer the human traits of being tired or bored or lacking concentration. This allows them to perform voluminous and repetitive jobs in a consistent manner.

2.2.4. Versatility

Computers are versatile in nature. I love features that perform multiprocessing, which makes these computers very versatile. Computers can control a wide range of jobs in different various fields. They can also perform any job that has been provided as long as they have the set of programs together with the related data.

For example, the computer could be preparing results from a specific examination while evaluating electricity bills in the company, and at the same time assisting the secretary in the office to look for some important letters or documents in a matter of seconds. As a computer is preparing certain documents, it can also be used to write letters, or other documents at the same time and even playing a game at the same time (Dasgupta, 2016).

Computers have also been used in many different professions. They have been amazing creative tools for musicians and have also been used in the motion picture industry to create special effects. In universities, colleges, and other schools, computers have helped to impart education in an easier and better way. In the industry, robots that are computer-assisted are able to perform many different types of tedious jobs, especially those industries that are involved in the assembly of hippie machines, automobiles.

Some of the characteristics that help in contributing to the versatility of a computer include:

- The speed of the computer.
- The ability of the computer to store, retrieve and manipulate large amounts of data in a convenient manner.
- The flexibility the computer has in order to interface.

Versatility is one of the greatest natures of a computer. They are able to perform different categories of jobs in an efficient manner. So as to change the talent of a computer, all one needs to do is introduce a program with the instructions that the end-user wants the computer to perform. They are able to perform any tasks and can do so through the introduction of a series of logical steps. Computers can be found in many places across the world, including schools, hotels, airports, restaurants, etc.

2.2.5. Storage Capacity

The computer storage is a technology that consists of computer components, and media that you used for recording, which are all utilized to ensure that digital data is retained. It is a main function and component of the computer. The central processing unit is what helps in the manipulation of data by performing competitions. All computers have a hierarchy when it comes to storage which helps to place the storage options that are fast, expensive and small closer to the central processing unit and the storage options that are slower, larger and cheaper much further. Normally the technologies that are fast and volatile (they lose data when the connection to power is interrupted) are referred to as memory, while those that are persistent and slow are referred to as storage (Dasgupta, 2016).In easier terms, the storage is where data is stored for safekeeping or for future use. Storage devices are connected to the computer through an input and output process. This allows the computer to retain data, either for a short while or for long-term purposes. Data can be saved in a computer in either the optical form or the electromagnetic form.

There are two types of data backup options. There is the local storage option and the remote storage option. Another local storage options, the examples are:

- *External Hard Drive*: this is equal to a hard drive that has been installed into a computer, however, the difference between this and that is that this hard drive can be plugged and also be removed from the computer.
- *Solid-state Drive*: in terms of the looks, this looks like a hard drive but then it has no moving parts within it.
- *Network Attached Storage*: this involves having one or more regular integrated drive electronics or serial AT attachment hard drive connected to a network hub.
- *USB Thumb Drive or Flash Drive*: this is similar to a solid-state drive but it is a smaller in terms of its size and capacity.
- *Optical Drive*: this refers to a CD or a DVD which is ideal for storing media as well as software with purpose is to distribute.

When it comes to the remote storage option, there is only one form of storage and this is called the cloud storage. This refers to a storage space which one can access from any computer as long as we have connection to the Internet.

Today's computers are able to store a large amount of data. Computations that were once recorded or stored in a computer cannot be forgotten by the computer and it can also be retrieved almost immediately.

Computer users should be able to plan for two categories of storage. These will help to accommodate any data that needs to be stored internally on the computer, as well as any data that requires to be backed up, transferred and archived. When choosing an external data storage device, one needs to ask themselves how much data they are required to store and whether this archive for external data will be subject to incremental change or random access (Dasgupta, 2016).Due to the development of technology, there are many computer users who do not have to back up their data to a media that can be removed or an external hard drive because the files that need to be stored can be stored and backed up on the network servers of the company. People have you been able to do this at home. Also, those who are using cloud computing are now able to store at least some of the data on the Internet, therefore saving storage space in hard drives as well as in the computers. In addition, those who are not using online applications and processing power are still able to back up a moderate amount of data on the Internet, and most of the time it is free.Files that are stored or backed up online can be stored on a hard disk. The hard disk is remote to your computer, yet it can still be accessed from anywhere and backed up by the provider of this service. This can make storing and backing up data online very attractive. Actually, when Google added 1 GB of free online storage in their Google doc's office Suite, they wanted to eliminate the need for people to carry and use USBs.

2.3. COMPUTER ORGANIZATION

2.3.1. Functional Units of a Computer

Input unit: In computer science, an input device refers to a component of the computer hardware that is used to provide control signals as well as data to a system that processes information, such as the computer or information appliance. Some of these include a mouse, a joystick, a keyboard, a microphone, a digital camera, etc.

Input devices can be categorized in terms of;

- The form of input, e.g., Mechanical motion or audio and visual.
- If the input being provided is discreet or continuous.
- The level of freedom involves in the input.

Input devices help in entering data and commands into a computer system. This data can either be in the form of words, actions, numbers, etc. Input devices have the main function of directing commands and data into computers. After this data is directed to the computer, the computers then utilize the central processing unit to process this data and produce an output.

Figure 2.1. *Above are some of the input devices that are or were used together with computers.*

Source: https://www.examplesof.net/2017/08/10-examples-of-input-devices-of-computer.html.

Some examples of input devices include:

- *Keyboard* – this is one of the main input devices that is used to direct data and commands to the computer. The keyboard has arrow keys, control keys, a keypad, function keys, and letters and numbers. They can be connected to the computer with the help of a USB cable or Bluetooth.
- *Mouse* – this input device controls the coordinates and the cursor. It could be connected to the computer using a USB cable or it could be wireless. It allows the user to select, scroll, drag and drop, open and execute a program, Hover, etc.
- *Digital Camera* – this helps to take pictures in a digital manner. It allows for images to be stored as data on memory cards. The digital camera has an LSD screen that gives an opportunity to the end-user to view the images. They are popular because they store thousands of photos in their memory card and also they allow users to choose and pick the photos they will save or develop. They also do not take up much space and can be carried in an easy.
- *Scanner* – this device helps in reading images and converting them into a digital file. It can be connected to a computer using a USB cable. There are different types of scanners: Flatbed scanner – this scans documents on a flat surface; Sheetfed scanner – this works when a paper is fed into the scanner where it works like a laser printer; Handheld scanner – it works by dragging it over the pager one wants to scan; Card scanner – this is used to scan business cards.
- *Storage unit:* Storage devices are part of the computer hardware to store and remember data. There are many types of storage device:
- *Hard disk drive* – these are magnetic storage devices that are not volatile and are capable of storing a large amount of data. They have an electromagnet in the read and write head that charges the surface of the disk with either a positive or negative charge. This is how the binary numbers one or zero are represented. The head is then able to detect the magnetic charges that are left on the surface of the disc and this is how the data on the disk is interpreted. The surface of the disc is divided into two parts: concentric circles and sixes. This division helps to provide specific locations which

can help in remembering where the data was saved. Coordination of the rotating disk and swinging actuator arm are carefully done by the circuit board which gives the opportunity to the read and write head to find access to the specific locations in a fast manner. Hard disk drive capacities on measured in Terabytes. They can be installed into the computer or bought in format that is portable. One of the disadvantages of hard disk drives is that they can break and wear out easily due to the moving parts.

- *Solid-state drive* – these devices are not volatile and are also able to hold a large amount of data. They use millions of transistors that have been wired in a series on its circuit board. This is called NAND flash memory. This means that they do not have any mechanical moving pads and that can be instantaneous access to the data. Solid-state drives are able to perform much quicker than the normal hard disk drives but they are also quite expensive. The capacities of solid-state drives are measured in gigabytes. Due to their expense, one can compromise by using two disc drives inside one computer. This involves having a solid-state drive as the main drive for storing important programs and the operating system and the normal traditional hard disk drive to store pictures, music, etc. solid-state drives are as for portable devices because they do not have moving parts making them reliable.

Figure 2.2. *Storage devices help in facilitating the safekeeping of data for use at a different time.*

Source: https://meropaper.com/difference-between-primary-and-secondary-memory/.

- *Random Access Memory* – this is the computer's primary memory. It is a solid-state storage medium that is very fast and can be accessed directly by the central processing unit. When the computer is being used, the Random Access Memory where open programs or files are stored temporarily. The Random Access Memory is volatile and any data that is stored will be lost immediately the power is eliminated. This means that this form of storage is not suitable for long-term storage of data. If the data is needed, it is copied from the secondary storage into the Random Access Memory. This is because when you use the secondary storage such as the Hard Disk Drive, it will make the computer perform slower. The Random Access Memory is quite expensive and its capacity is measured in gigabytes. Computers would benefit from better performance and multitasking if the computer is operating with the capacity of Random Access Memory above the recommended minimum.

- *Output Unit:* Computer output device refer to those that are able to receive information from the computer and transfer the data that has undergone processing in the computer, to the person using it. These devices provide data in many different forms including audio, visual, etc. They are normally used for the display, projecting, or physical reproduction of data. The most commonly known output devices used with the computer and monitors and printers.

Figure 2.3. *These help in relaying information that has been processed by the central processing unit.*

Source: https://www.examplesof.net/2018/09/examples-of-output-devices.html.

All output devices are connected to computers using cables or by wireless networking and they are peripheral hardware. Computers are able to function without output devices, however, one will not be able to know what the computer is doing. There will be no way to know if the computer is performing errors or if one needs to add another input. For example, if a computer does not have a monitor, the computer will still be able to work, but it would not be as helpful.

Some of the output devices include:

- Monitor – this is the most widely used computer output device. It works by creating a visual display which is used by the user to visualize data that has been processed. They come in different sizes and resolutions. Some of the examples are:
- Flat Panel Screen – this monitor uses liquid crystals or plasma to give an output. It works when light passes through liquid crystals so as to create pixels.
- Cathode Ray Tube – This monitor generates pixels through phosphorescent dots to display images.
- Printers – this device helps in generating a tangible copy of the data that has been processed, such as photographs or documents. The computer is able to send this image data to the printer, which then is able to re-create that image physically and this is normally on paper. There are different types of printers:
- Inkjet – This printer is able to stream mini small dots of him onto the surface to create an image.
- Laser – this printer uses magnetized pigment to roll it on toner drums that transfer the pigment onto a surface.
- Dot Matrix – these devices are able to set images on a surface using an ink ribbon using a print head.
- *Processing Unit:* The processing unit is considered the brain of the computer. It performs all the types of operations to process data. It also stores data, results that are intermediate and programs. It helps in controlling the operations of the whole computer system. The central processing unit has three components:
- Memory or Storage Unit – this unit is able to pop on the storage of data, instructions, and intermediate results. It supplies information to other components of the computer when required. It is also known as the main memory. The size of your task will affect the capability, speed, and power of the computer. Its main role is to start all the data and instructions needed to process data. It also

stores the data that has been processed before the final result is shown or received by an output device. The main memory is where all the inputs and outputs are transmitted.

- Control unit – this unit helps in controlling all the parts of all the components in the computer system. However, it does not process any actual data. It works to control the transference of data and instructions to other parts of the computer. It also ensures the managing and coordination of all computer units. It is able to receive instructions from the memory unit, and interpret them so as to direct the operations of the computer. In addition, it helps with communication of the computer with the input and output devices, so as to ensure the transference of data or results from the storage.

Figure 2.4. *Just like a brain controls the body, so does a central processing unit control the computer.*

Source: https://simple.wikipedia.org/wiki/Central_processing_unit.

- Arithmetic Logic Unit – this unit has two subsections. It has the arithmetic section which works to ensure that there is performance of arithmetic operations such as subtraction, addition, multiplication and division. It performs all the complex operations by ensuring repetition of the above operations. The second subsection is the logic section which performs operations such as selecting, comparing, merging, and matching of data.

Arithmetic Logic Unit: The arithmetic logic unit is a part of the CPU that takes in the data from the memory registers. It is able to perform mathematical operations such as addition, multiplication, division, subtraction, logical shifts and logical operations the digits and values that are found in the register of the processor or the accumulator.

The word-size of a processor is determined by the size of the word that the Arithmetic Logic Unit can handle. This means that a processor with 32-bit is one with a 32-bit ALU. After the instructions are processed, the result they get is stored in the Accumulator. Control signals are generated by the Control Unit, which direct the Arithmetic Logic Unit to perform specific tasks. Data is stored by the accumulator as a default register.

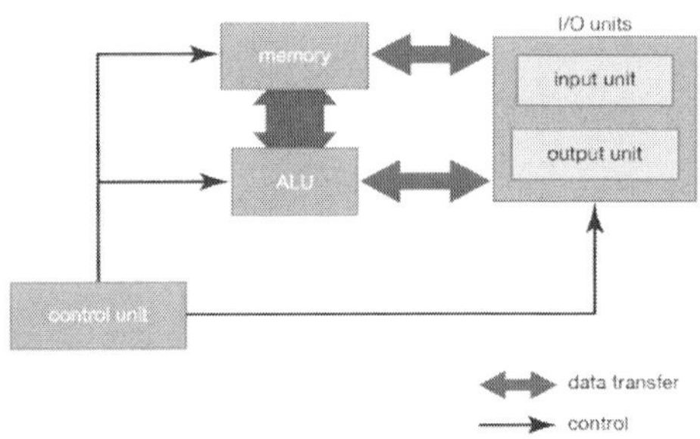

Figure 2.5. *Above shows how data is transferred to and from the Arithmetic logic unit and the memory and Input/output unit.*

Source: https://www.britannica.com/technology/arithmetic-logic-unit.

The simplest Arithmetic Logic Unit only performs addition, complement operation, and is able to perform the shifting of a words by a step to the right or left, all the other operations that are arithmetic that are synthesized from sequences of these operations that are primitive. Modern processors, however, are having an increased tendency in implementing extra arithmetic functions in the hardware. This involves dedicated multiplier or divider units.

The Arithmetic Logic Unit was once known to be the main core of the computer, considering the fact that it was the only section performing all the calculations. This, however, is not true, due to the modern architecture of the processors, because there are now more than one ALUs in each unit. ALUs are now expected to perform more than just the calculations that are required by the program of the user. They now also perform many other internal calculations that are necessitated by the processor, such as deriving addresses for certain instructions that utilize addressing modes that are different. This job can, however, be distributed into separate storage units in the modern architecture (Page & Gamboa, 2019).

Control Unit: This is a part of the central processing unit that helps in directing the processor's operations. It directs the memory of the computer, the arithmetic logic unit, as well as the output and input on how they are meant to deal with any instructions that have been delivered to the processor.

It helps in directing these operations by giving them signals for timing and control. Most of the resources for the computer undergo management by the control unit. It promotes the direction of data between the central processing unit and other devices.

The control unit is found in the processor and it helps to co-ordinate the data movement sequence in, out of and also between the sub-units of the processor. These routed data movements through the different sub-units provide a result that produces data that is manipulated and expected by the software instructions (Anderson, Ferro, & Hilton, 2010).

It also aids in the conduction of data flow within the processor and also helps to provide several control signals that are external to the rest of the computer so as to ensure that the data and instructions are further directed to and from the processor external destinations.

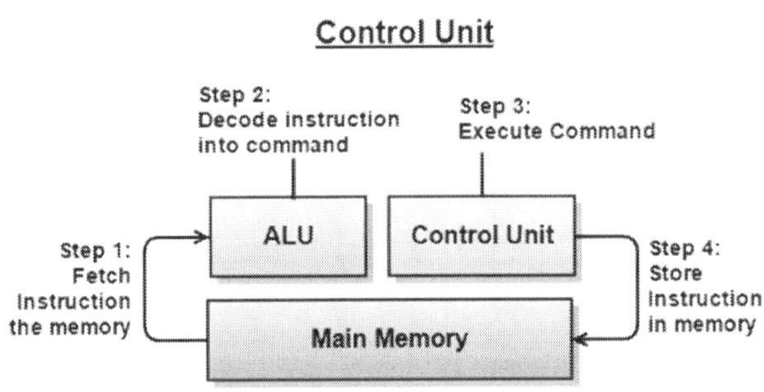

Figure 2.6. *The control unit sends commands that is has executed to the main memory for storage.*

Source: https://www.assignmenthelp.net/assignment_help/what-is-control-unit.

The devices that need a control unit are the central processing unit and the graphics processing units. The control unit is able to receive instructions that are external as well as commands, which it can then convert into a sequence of control signals that the control unit is able to apply to the path of data so as to implement a sequence of operations that are on the register-transfer level.

2.3.2. Memory

2.3.2.1. Primary Memory

Random Access Memory: This is a form of computer memory that is able to be read and changed without any specific order, especially when storing working data and machine code. A random-access memory device helps in allowing the data items to undergo reading or writing in about the same amount of time regardless of where the data inside the memory is located. This is different when you come to other direct access data storage media such as DVD-Rws, CD-RWs and older magnetic tapes and drum memory, because the time that they require to read and write data items is different in a significant manner depending on where they are located physically on the recording media, due to limitations that a mechanical such as the speeds of media rotation and movement of the arm.

Random-access memory has multiplexing and DE multiplexing circuitry that helps it in connecting the data lines to the address storage, so as to read and write the entry. Random-access memory devices mostly have multiple data lines. They are known to be 8-bit or 16-bit, etc.

Figure 2.7. Two types of random access memory: static RAM and dynamic RAM.

Source: https://en.wikipedia.org/wiki/Random-access_memory.

Random Access Memories is created in the form of metal oxide semiconductor memory cells with integrated circuit chips. Random-access memory is volatile and any stored information is lost when the power is eliminated. However, there has been development of Random Access Memory that is not volatile. There are other Random Access Memories that may allow for the random access for reading operations, and are not volatile, however, they may not allow for writing operations and they may also have other limitations (Anderson, Ferro, & Hilton, 2010).

Read-only memory: It is a type of memory that is not volatile and is used in computers as well as other electronic devices. Any data that is stored in the read-only memory cannot be modified electronically after the memory device is manufactured. This type of memory is used to store software that is hardly changed during the life of the system. This software is known as firmware. The software applications that are used for devices that are programmable can undergo distribution as plug-in cartridges containing read-only memory.

Read-only memory refers to a type of memory that is hardwired, and cannot be changed electronically after it has been manufactured. This is such as the diode matrix or a mask read-only memory integrated circuit. Despite the fact that discrete circuits can undergo alteration in principle, integrated circuits cannot. New devices need to be manufactured so as to replace the installed device, in case of correction of errors or updates to the software (Henderson, 2009).

Figure 2.8. *Read-only memory does not lose data when the power is switched off.*

Source: https://www.thoughtco.com/definition-of-rom-958317.

The electrically erasable programmable read-only memory together with an erasable programmable read-only memory, are the ROM devices that can be reprogrammed, however, it can only be done at a relatively slow speed, and one may need special equipment for this to be done. It can also only be done a few times.

The term read-only memory can sometimes be used to refer to an ROM device that has a specific software, or a file that has a software that needs to be installed into electrically erasable programmable read-only memory or flash memory.

2.3.2.2. Secondary Memory

Hard disk: This is an electro-mechanical data storage device that utilizes the magnetic storage to ensure the storage and retrieval of information that is digital by using one or more platters, which are rigid rapidly rotating disks, that have a magnetic coating. These platters are normally arranged on an actuator arm that is moving and are paired with magnetic heads so as to ensure reading and writing of data onto the platter surfaces. The data is then accessed in a random-access manner. This means that the specific individual blocks of data can undergo storage or retrieval in any random order instead of it sick sequential. Hard disk drives are a form of storage that is not volatile, which means it can maintain the storage of data even after power is eliminated.

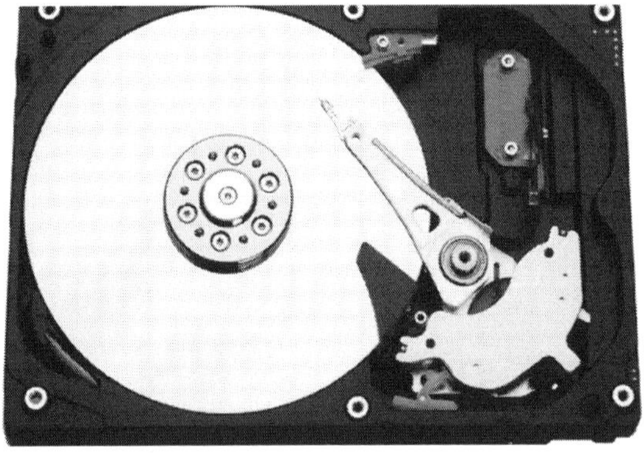

Figure 2.9. *Hard disk capacity limits are becoming too low and there is a need to create storage devices with higher capacities.*

Source: https://www.itprotoday.com/storage/storage-shift-time-may-be-right-new-form-factor.

How did describes were introduced by ABM in the year 1956. They were the dominant devices for secondary storage for computers that were used for general purpose in the early 1960s, Hard disk drives were able to maintain this position into the era of servers and personal computers in the modern era, despite the fact that devices for personal computing, such as tablets and cell phones, that were produced in large volumes, relied on flash products.

There are very many companies that have been able to produce hard disk drives according to history. The main manufacturers of hard disk drive, however, were Seagate and Toshiba. The largest volume of storage produce for servers is dominated by hard disk drives. The production, however, is growing slowly and the sale revenues together with the unit shipments have come to a decline due to the fact that solid-state drives have been seem to have rates for data transfer that are higher, storage density that is higher, much more reliability, and much lower times for latency and access (Henderson, 2009).

Compact disk: The compact disc which is normally known as a CD is a digital optical disk data storage format that was initially developed by both Phillips and Sony in the year 1982. It was initially created to store and play only recordings of sound but was later developed to store data as well. There are other formats that while data developed including, rewritable media, write once audio and data storage, photo CD, video compact disc, etc. The first audio CD player that was commercially available was released in 1982 in Japan. It was the Sony CDP-101.

The normal standard compact discs have a diameter of 120 mm and can hold up to 80 minutes of audio that is uncompressed or around 700MiB of data. The mini compact discs have a couple of different diameters that range from 60 to 80 mm. They are able to store around 24 minutes of audio. They can also deliver device drivers.

When the compact disc was invented in 1982, it could store more data than any hard drive for any personal computer, which could hold on 10 MB. Later on, in 2010, hard disk drives were able to store as much space as 1000 CDs, while their prices had lowered to commodity level. The sales of audio CDs, CD-ROMs and CD-Rs had reached about 30 billion days in just 2004 globally. By 2007, there were sales of 200 billion CDs globally.

Figure 2.10. *CDs have been used globally to distribute softwares.*

Source: https://www.britannica.com/technology/compact-disc.

Compact discs were being replaced by other forms of digital storage in the early 2000s. By 2010, the number of audio compact discs that were sold in the United States had reduced by about 50%, however, they are still the main method of distribution for the music industry.*Digital Video Disk:* The abbreviation for this is the DVD which is a digital optical storage format that was created in 1995. This form of storage is able to store any type of data that is digital, and us greatly utilized for storing software and other files from the computer, as well as video programs that are viewed using DVD players. They provide a storage capacity that is higher than that of compact this but they have the same size.

DVDs that have been pre-recorded are produced in large numbers using molding machines that physically insert the data by stamping it onto the DVD. Such disks are a type of DVD-ROM, because the data that is in this can only be read and it cannot be changed or erased. DVD discs that are blank and recordable can be used to record once using a DVD recorder and then after that, they act as a DVD ROM. DVDs that are rewritable can be used to record and erase many times (Henderson, 2009).

DVDs can be used into formats: the DVD video consumer digital video format and the DVD audio consumer digital audio format. They can also be used to hold high definition material when the written in special AVCHD format. When a DVD contains a different type of information can be referred to as a DVD data disk.

Figure 2.11. *This looks very similar to the CDs, however, they cannot be used interchangeably.*

Source: https://archive.org/details/CanonDVC200W.

There were a couple of different formats of video recording on optical discs before the DVD was invented. In 1963, the technology of optical recording was created by David Paul Greg and James Russell. It was then patented in 1968. There was a consumer optical disk data format that used much larger disks than the format of this day, and where brought into the market in 1978. They were called Laser Disc. These, however, were not adopted by the consumers due to the high cost of the players and the disks (Henderson, 2009).

DVDs are read by DVD drive which can be found on a computer. There are also DVD players which do not need a computer to function that can also read both DVD-video and DVD-audio disks.

2.3.3. Input Devices

Keyboard: This is a typewriter style device which uses a sequence of buttons and keys that have arranged to act as levers that are mechanical or switches that are electronic. After punch cards and paper tapes declined, this became the main method of input for computers.

There are characters that are engraved or printed on the buttons on the keyboard. Each key when pressed corresponds to the single Luton symbol for underneath. There are some symbols that may require for one to press and hold more than one key at the same time or in a sequence so as to produce them. Despite the fact that pressing a keyboard key will produce a letter, number or sign, there are other buttons or simultaneous sequences to press the keys that can help in producing actions or performing computer commons.

When used normally, the keyboard is utilized to enter texts so as to type a text or a number into the word processor or any other program that may support this function. In modern computers, the software is left to interpret the key presses. The keyboard of the computer is able to distinguish each physical key from the other as well as reports all presses of the keys to the software that is controlling it. Regular keyboards or specific keyboards with special gaming features can be used for computer gaming. The specific keyboards for gaming and able to expedite keystroke combinations that are frequently used (Page & Gamboa, 2019).

Figure 2.12. *Keyboards and electric typewriters both have buttons that have letters, numbers and characters.*

Source: https://www.computerhope.com/jargon/k/keyboard.htm.

There are keystroke combinations such as control-alt-delete that are used to give commands to the operating system of the computer. This combination was initially used to force a reboot, however, now it brings up system security options on the monitor. There is a user interface that is fully navigated by the keyboard, it is called the command-line interface.

Mouse: This is a pointing device that is handheld and is able to detect two-dimensional motion in relation to a surface. This motion is normally translated into a pointer that is moving in a synchronized manner on the display, which helps in the smooth controlling of the graphical user interface. The mouse was first publicly demonstrated to control a computer system in 1968. In the modern times, mice are cordless in comparison to initially when they had to be wired to a computer. Being wireless forces them to rely on short-range video communication with their connected system.

Originally, mice had a rolling ball on their lower surface to help in detecting motion, but now in the modern times, they have been able to detect motion using optical sensors without any moving parts. Computer mice cannot only move the cursor, but also allow operations such as selection of menu items on a display, due to them having more than one button on them. Additional control and dimensional input can be enhanced on mice when they have other elements such as touch surfaces and wheels (Page & Gamboa, 2019).

Figure 2.13. *This is an example of a desktop computer mouse that has two buttons and a wheel.*

Source: https://www.computerhope.com/jargon/m/mouse.htm.

In general, the mouse controls the pointers movements in two dimensions in a graphical user interface. The mouse turns the movement of the hand into electronic signals that are equivalent to the hand movements, which in turn moves the pointer on the screen. Whatever direction the hand moves, is the direction the pointer moves on the screen. In other words, the movement of the hand is replicated by the pointer. When one stops the movement while the cursor is within a certain area, you can select a file, program or action from small images that are called icons or even a list of names.

Trackball: This is a pointing device that has a ball that is held by a socket which has sensors that are able to detect when the ball rotates about axes. It actually looks like a mouse that is upside down with the ball protruding. The person using the device uses the thumb, fingers, or the palm of the hand to position the pointer on the screen. One can use fingertips to press the buttons on the trackball.

When comparing a trackball and a mouse, with a trackball, the person using it has to lift their finger, thumb or hand to re-position the ball so as to continue rolling, while when using a mouse, you would have to lift the mouse so as to re-position it. Some trackballs have low levels of friction, and since they are made of glass, they can be spun so as to make them coast. The buttons on the trackball may be found like on a mouse or in a style that is unique to suit the user (Reilly, 2003).

Figure 2.14. *It helps in entering motion data into computers and other electronics.*

Source: https://www.adesso.com/product/imouse-t40-adesso-2-4-ghz-wireless-4-button-desktop-trackball/.

CAD workstations have been seen to use large trackballs to increase the level of precision. Before the touchpads were invented, small trackballs were commonly found on portable computers. This was common because there was hardly any desk space to run a mouse. There are some thumbballs that were created to attach to the side of the keyboard and have the main buttons with similar functions as those on a mouse.*Touchpad:* This is a device that is used as a pointer. It has a tactile sensor, a surface that is specialist to ensure the translation of motion and position of the user's fingers to a position that is in relation to that on the operating system, which is then turned to an output on the screen. These are mainly found one laptop computers in comparison to using the mouse on my desktop, and also are substitute for when there is not enough disk space to use a mouse. Because they come in many different sizes, it is possible to also find them on personal digital assistants as well as some portable media players. There are also touch-pads that are wireless and can be found as detached accessories.

In 2010 the most common technology was able to send the change of capacitance where a finger touches the pad. These touch-pads are not able to sense the tip of a pencil or other implements that are ungrounded or non-conducting. Fingers that are covered using a glove may also be a problem to use (Reilly, 2003).

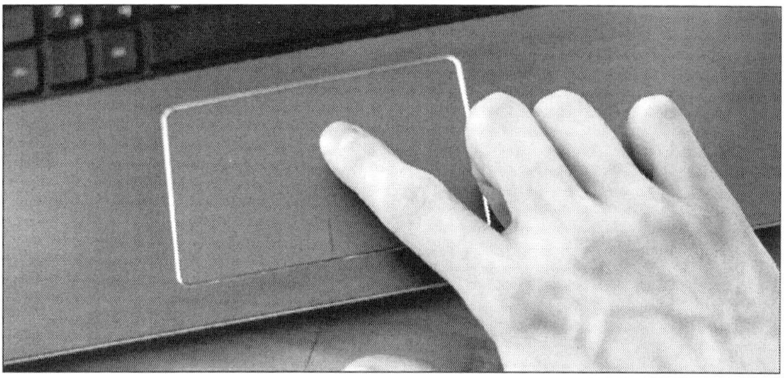

Figure 2.15. There are laptops that allow for one to tap wither once or twice on the touchpad to click.

Source: https://www.howtogeek.com/441083/how-to-disable-or-enable-tap-to-click-on-a-pcs-touchpad/amp/.

Despite the fact that touch-pads are able to sense the specific position, their size can be a huge factor in limiting the resolution. As it is commonly used for pointing, the motions of dragging the finger is translated into a finer motion that is relative of the cursor on the output to the display on the operating system, which is similar to how a mouse is handled when it is lifted and put back on the surface. They also have hardware buttons that are similar to the left and right buttons that are found on the mouse but are positioned at the bottom of the touchpad.

Touch screen: This is both an input and output device and is normally found on top of an electronic visual display, in a well-layered manner, of a system that processes information. A user is able to use simple or multi-touch gestures by touching this screen with either their fingers or a special stylus, so as to input or control the system for processing information.

Some of the touch screens require either ordinary or special cotton gloves to function, well others can function using a special stylus pen. It is possible for the user to react to what is displayed using the touch screen, and sometimes the system can allow the user to control how the output is displayed, for example zooming in. Touch screens allow the user to interact in a direct manner with the output that is being displayed, instead of having to use a mouse, or other devices. A stylus is optional for most touch screens in the modern time (Reilly, 2003).

Figure 2.16. *These work both as output and input devices.*

Source: https://theeventco.uk/product/dell-27-led-touchscreen-monitor/.

Devices such as personal computers, electronic a voting machines, etc. have touch screens on them. It is also possible to attach a touch screen to a computer, as a terminal, to a network. They have a huge role in the design of some digital appliances, such as personal digital assistants. They are also used to a great deal in educational settings such as campuses and classrooms.

Light pen: This is a computer input device that is created in the shape of a wand. It is light sensitive and is used together with the cathode-ray tube of the computer's display. It gives the opportunity to the user to point to objects that have been displayed on the screen or even draw on the screen in a way that is similar to using a touch screen but with much greater accuracy when it comes to positioning.

The light pen is able to work with any cathode ray tube-based display, however, the ability it has to work with Liquid Crystal Display is not quite clear. The light pen has the ability to detect any brightness changes of screen pixels that are close by when is scanned by the cathode ray tube electron beam, and it thereafter sends details on the time at which this event occurred to the computer (Reilly, 2003).

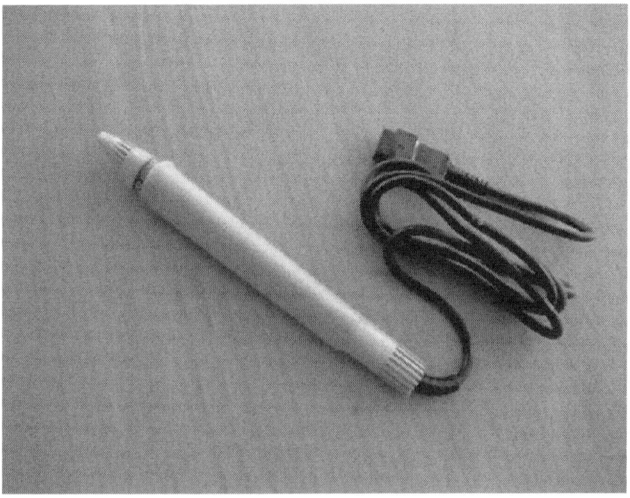

Figure 2.17. *This has fallen out of use as a general purpose input device.*

Source: https://atariwiki.org/wiki/Wiki.jsp?page=Atari%20CX70%20Light%20Pen/Light_Pen_CX70-5.jpg.

Because the cathode ray tube is able to scan the whole screen one pixel at a time, it is possible for the computer to ensure that it is keeping track on the expected time of scanning various locations on the screen using the beam and be able to know the position of the pen from the last time it was stamped.

The first time the light pen was created was in 1995 as part of a project in MIT called the whirlwind project. Graphic terminals such as the IBM 2250 commonly used the light pens in the 1960s. They were also available for the IBM 3270 text-only terminal.

Magnetic ink character recognition: This known as the MICR code in short. It is a technology that was created to recognize characters and was mainly used to streamline the processing and clearance of cheques and other documents in the banking industry. The magnetic ink character recognition encoding, which is called the magnetic ink character cognition line, is normally found at the bottom of cheques as well as other vouchers and it includes the bank account number, cheque number, bank code, the document type indicator, the cheque amount, and a control indicator. The format for the account number of the bank as well as the code is specific for different countries.

Figure 2.18. *These help in providing a secure, high-speed method of scanning and processing information.*

Source: http://www.themeskanon.com/explanation-of-magnetic-ink-character-reader/.

Technology has allowed the magnetic ink character recognition reader to scan and interpret the information found on the cheque into a device that collects data, in a direct manner. In comparison to barcodes and other technologies that are similar, magnetic ink character recognition characters are easily read and interpreted by humans. Magnetic ink character recognition encoded documents undergo easy processing and this is done in a fast and accurate manner, in comparison to the conventional OCR encoded documents (Reilly, 2003).

Optical mark recognition: This is also called the optical mark recognition and it is the method of interpreting data that has been marked by humans from documents such as exams and surveys. They are used to determine the results of questionnaires and multiple-choice examination papers that have been marked using lines or shading.

Most of the traditional optical mark recognition devices function with a scanner device that is dedicated to shine a beam of light onto the paper so as to detect where the marked area is. The difference in reflection at the positions that were determined previously on a page, is then used to note where the marked areas are, because they do not reflect more light than the area of the paper that is blank.

Some optical mark recognition devices use the method of forma that have been printed previously on trans-optic papers so as to determine the amount of light that we will be able to pass through the paper. This means that when the paper is marked on either side, the amount of light passing through the paper will be reduced.

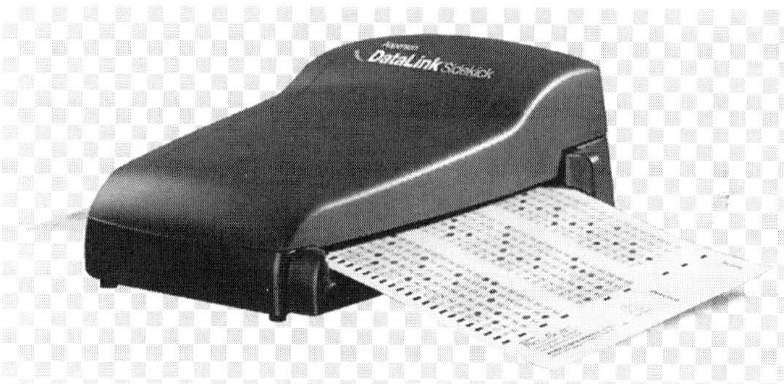

Figure 2.19. *The IBM 805 test scoring machine was the first mark sense scanner.*

Source: https://www.uihere.com/free-cliparts/optical-mark-recognition-image-scanner-optical-character-recognition-computer-software-input-devices-scanner-1827310.

In comparison to the dedicated optical mark recognition device, the desktop optical mark recognition software can allow a user to create forms on their own in a word processor then use a laser printer to print them. The optical mark recognition software then functions together with a common desktop image scanner which has a feeder for documents, so as to process the forms once they have been marked. The optical mark recognition is normally differentiated from the optical character recognition due to the fact that it does not require a pattern recognition engine that is complicated (Reilly, 2003).

Barcode reader: This is a scanner that is optical and allows for the reading of printed barcodes, recording of that data that is found on the barcode and sending that data to a computer. It is similar to a flatbed scanner because it has a light source, a lens, and a light sensor that can translate the optical impulses into signals that are electrical.

In addition, almost all barcode readers have circuitry for decoding that can help one in analysing the barcode data on the image that has been provided by the sensor, and this allows it to send the content of the barcode to the output port of the scanner.

The resolution of the scanner is determined using the dot size of the light that is released by the barcode reader. The reader can produce an output that is wrong if the dot of light is wider than the barcode it is reading or the space in the barcode, because it will lead to the overlapping of two elements: two spaces or two bars (Reilly, 2003).

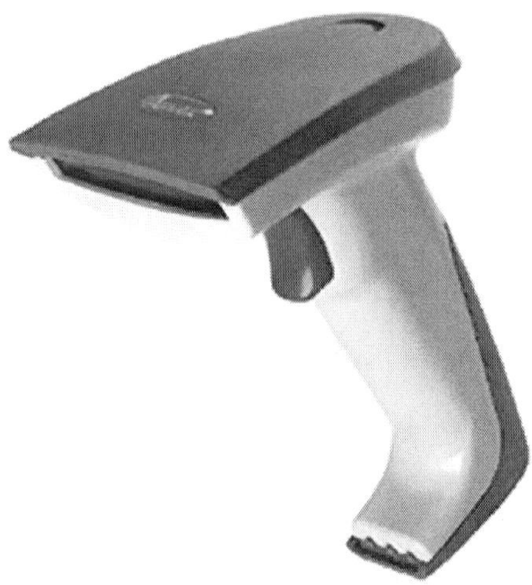

Figure 2.20. *The scanners used the supermarkets are called horizontal scanners.*

Source: https://en.wikipedia.org/wiki/Barcode_reader.

Cell phone cameras have been able to act as scanners as well in these modern times. They are able to read the common barcode formats as well as QR codes. They can do so in a fast manner when the autofocus is used.

Scanner: This is an image scanner that scans images, texts that are printed, handwritings or an object, using optical technology, and turns this into a digital image. The flatbed scanner is the variety that is often used in offices. It has a glass window where the document being scanned is placed.

There are also handheld scanners that work by moving the scanner by hand over the document being scanned. This is an evolution from wands that were used to scan texts. These days there are 3D scanners that are used in industries for designs, tests and measurements, orthotics, and many other applications. There are also scanners that are driven mechanically to replace flatbed scanners which would be impractical for large-format documents (Shelly, Freund, &Vermaat, 2010).

The scanners used these days normally use a charge-couple's device or a contact image sensor to sense the image. Drum scanners were developed much earlier but they are still commonly used to provide images of the highest quality. These use a photomultiplier tube as the sensor for the images.

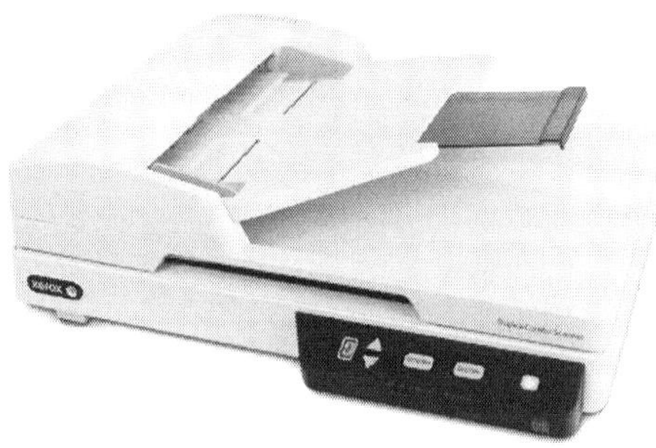

Figure 2.21. *They are used to capture images for display of computers.*

Source: https://www.xeroxscanners.com/xdcs.

Those that are used for document scanning at a high speed are rotary scanners. These use charge-couple's device array instead of using the photomultiplier. Those that photograph delicate books and documents are non-contact planetary scanners. All the scanners that have been mentioned above are able to produce images that are in two dimensions of subjects that are normally flat, and sometimes they could be solid. 3D scanners are the only scanners that can produce outputs that are in the three-dimensional structures of the solid objects.

2.3.4. Output Devices

Monitor: This is an output device that helps in displaying information in a form that is pictorial. The components of a monitor are the circuitry, display device, the power supply and the casing. In the modern devices, the monitors use a thin film transistor liquid crystal display which is equipped with LED backlighting which was used to replace the cold-cathode fluorescent lamp backlighting. The monitors from earlier utilized the cathode ray tube.

Monitors are normally connected to a computer using a digital visual interface, Display Port, HDMI, low voltage differential signaling, VGA and other connectors and signals. Initially, computer monitors were only used to process data, while television sets were utilized to provide entertainment. Since the 1980s, computer monitors have been used in processing data as well as entertainment, while televisions have been able to implement some computer functionality as well.

Figure 2.22. *Monitors are found on all computer devices. Without them, one will not be able to know what the computer is doing.*

Source: https://deprimesolutions.co.ke/product/ex-uk-dell-st2220lc-22-lcd-widescreen-computer-monitor-vga-dvi-hdmi/.

It is now easier to interchange modern computer monitors with conventional television sets. This, however, may be limited by the fact that computer monitors are not able to integrate speakers, and therefore it may not be able to work without external components.

Printer: This is a peripheral device that makes representations that are persistent of graphics or texts on paper. Despite the fact that most output is readable by a human, barcode printers are an example of printers that have an expanded use.

Personal printers a mainly created to be used by individual users, and they can be connected to only one computer. These printers are created in a way that only allows low volume, and jobs that have a short turn-around for printing, that only require a short set up time to give the hard copy of the document that is required. These printers are, however, slow and print 6-25 pages per minute. They do this and yet the cost per page is high. This, however, is not affected as it has an on-demand convenience.

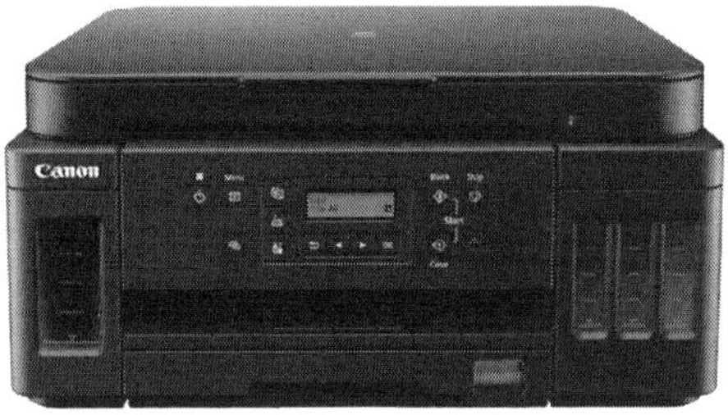

Figure 2.23. *Printers are used all over the world to re-create the output that has been processed by the computer.*

Source: https://www.pcmag.com/review/369454/canon-pixma-g6020-mega-tank-all-in-one-printer.

Shared printers are made in a way that allows them to print high volume and at high speeds. They are normally connected to many different computers from different users on a network and can print at speeds of around 45 to 100 pages per minute.

A virtual printer is referred to as a piece of computer software that resembles a printer driver in terms of the interface and the Application program interface, however, it is not connected with a computer printer that is physical. This printer is an able to create files that are images of the data which is meant to be printed, for purposes to join the archive or as a form of input for a different program, for example creating a PDF.*Plotter:* This is able to produce drawings that are vector graphics. They produce lines on paper by using a pen. In the olden days, plotters were utilized in computer-aided designs and other applications, because they were able to draw lines in a faster manner and also of a higher quality than the other printers which were conventional, and the plotters that were small and used for the desktops were normally used for business graphics. Despite the fact that plotters were able to retain the dominant position of producing drawings that were quite large for a long period of time, they are now almost fully replaced by wide format conventional printers.Plotters were able to offer a way that is fast and efficient to produce a drawing that was very large and also vector-based artwork that had a high-color resolution, when the computer memory was quite expensive and the power for processing was very limited. This was also the case because the other printers had output capabilities that were limited in terms of the graphics.

Figure 2.24. *These are mainly used by graphic industries to recreate works of art.*

Source: https://www.amazon.com/Cutter-Plotter-Cutting-Signmaster-Software/dp/B00WTUHSGI.

PIN protesters have as of now become obsolete, and they have undergone replacement by large format inkjet printers as well as LED toner-based printers. These devices are able to understand some of the vector languages that were initially used by the plotter, because many a times, they are much more efficient to raster data.*Facsimile:* This is normally known as the fax machine and it can also be called a Telescoping machine. It helps transmit scanned printed material in a telephonic manner, this could be both texts and images, normally to a telephone number that has undergone connection to a printer or another device that can provide output.

Figure 2.25. *Fax machines are rarely used these days, but some countries use them almost every day.*

Source: https://www.technected.com/fax-machine-reliance-in-healthcare-whats-the-alternative.

The document that is original is normally scanned with a fax machine, which then allows for processing of the contents as a graphic image that has been fixed in a single manner, then converted into a bitmap, and then transmitted through the telephone system using tones that are of audio frequency.

The fax machine that is receiving this data is able to interpret those audio frequency tones and then re-construct the image by printing a copy on paper. The systems that were used earlier, used continuous or analog ways, in the direct conversion of image darkness to tones that were in the audio form. Most fax machines use digital representations of the page to modulate the transmitted audio frequencies. This digital representation is compressed so as to allow for quick transmission of areas either all-white or all-black.

Most businesses are able to maintain some kind of fax capability, however, this technology has gotten a lot of competition from alternatives that are Internet-based. In some countries, fax machines continue to enjoy support in the business because electronics signatures and contracts are still not accepted by the law, while contracts that have been faxed with copies of the signature are.

In countries such as Japan, fax machines are still used widely for graphemic and cultural purposes and are also utilized in sending documents to recipients who may be available domestically or internationally from over 82% of all convenience stores in the nation. These convenience stores are only able to print the content of the sent fax, in an A4 paper size, in a manner that is slightly re-sized in the electronic confirmation slip (Shelly, Freund, &Vermaat, 2010).

Sound-cards and speakers: A Sound card is also referred to as an audio card and it is an internal expansion card that is able to provide both input and output of signals that are in the audio form to and from a computer that is being controlled by computer programs. This term (sound-card) is also normally used to refer to external audio interfaces that are used in applications for professional audios.

It is possible for the sound functionality to undergo integration into the motherboard, by utilizing the components that are the same as those found on plug-in cards. This system that is integrated is normally also referred to as a sound-card. Modern video cards with HDMI to output sound also have sound processing hardware and can also attain video using a connector. They previously connected to the sound-card or the motherboard using a S/PDIF connection.

Speakers are normally sold to be used with computers although they can also be used with other audio sources such as MP3 players. Most of them have an internal amplifier and also require to have access to a power source to work, which may be a mains power supply that is normally connected to the speaker using an AC adapter, batteries, or a USB port (Shelly, Freund, &Vermaat, 2010).

Figure 2.26. *Speakers work as an audio output device. One is able to listen to music or videos through them.*

Source: https://rondamo.co.ke/product/z130-logitech-speakers/.

Normally, the connector that provides the signal input is normally a jack plug that is 3.5mm, and is mainly color-coded lime green. It is also possible to use an RCA connector or a USB port which may also supply both the signal and the power. There are also wireless Bluetooth speakers that are powered using a battery. These do not require any connections. Most computers use built-in speakers that are low power and quality. When one chooses to connect an external speaker to the computer, these built-in speakers are normally disabled (Shelly, Freund, &Vermaat, 2010).

2.4. COMPUTER SOFTWARE

2.4.1. System Software

This is a software that has been designed to ensure a provision of a platform for other software. Some of the examples of systems that are commonly used include operating systems such as Ubuntu, Microsoft Windows, MacOS, game engines, industrial automation, computational science and software's that are used as applications for service.

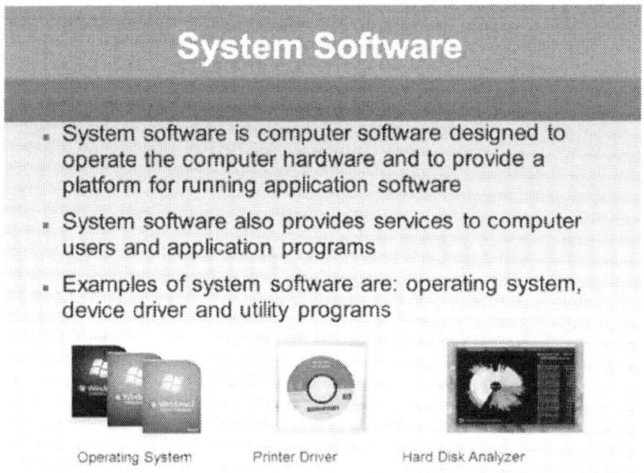

Figure 2.27. *Above is a different perspective on what a system software is.*

Source: https://slideplayer.com/amp/6671912/.

The system software is different from application software, which allow users to perform user-oriented tasks such as listening to music and playing games. Application software were mostly designed by the computer users so as to cater for their specific hardware and their specific needs. The system software, however, was normally provided by the manufacturer of the computer hardware end it was designed in a manner that allowed it to be used by most or all of the users of the specific system (Henderson, 2009).

A software cannot be considered a system software if it can be uninstalled from the computer without causing problems to the functioning of other software. The only exceptions for this rule can be web browsers such as Internet Explorer, where it was argued out by Microsoft that it should be a system software that one can choose to uninstall if they wanted to.

Current examples are Firefox OS and Chrome OS where the functions of the browser are the only way to run programs because they are the only user interface, and other web browsers are not able to be installed to replace them. This can build a conversation on whether they are part of the operating system and thus the system software (Henderson, 2009).

Another contradictory example is a cloud-based software. This software allows for the software client, which is normally a JavaScript application running in the web browser or a web browser itself, instead of the user in a direct manner, and is therefore referred to as a system software. System programming methodologies, as well as system programming languages, are normally used to develop the cloud-based software. However, when it comes to the perspective of functionality, there is not a big difference that is seen when you compare the word processing application and the word processing web application

2.4.2. Application Software

This is referred to as an app in its short form and it is a program or a group of programs that are created to suit the needs of the end-user. Some examples include a file viewer, a media player, a photo editor, an accounting application, etc. It is possible for applications to be created in a bundle with the computer together with the system software or to be developed separately.

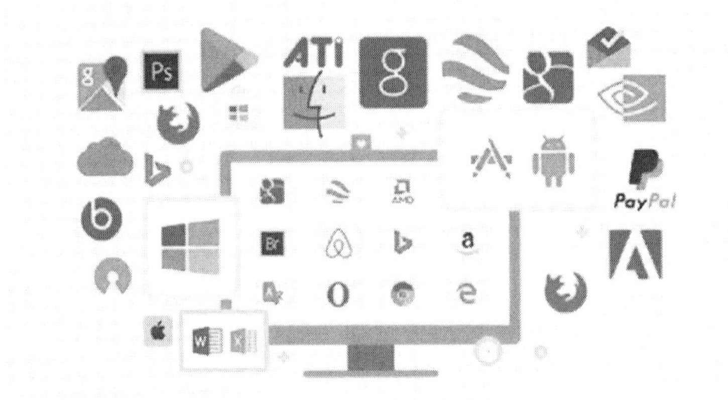

Figure 2.28. *Application softwares account for all the applications that are found on the computer so suit the user's needs.*

Source: https://www.quora.com/What-are-the-types-of-application-software.

They are created so as to ensure that the work is made easier on a central processing unit in comparison to the traditional software, which requires for there to be more resources and normally uses a simple user interface. Application software's have been able to allow us to move away from the traditional system that required one to install the software equipped with the applications.

Applications have now allowed for there to be web-based applications which reduce the stress on the systems resources, letting the Internet and the cloud take all the stress.

Application software is different from other software's that may come together with the computers operating system, such as a utility. For example, disk tool is a software that is normally inside the operating system and can be used to search for problems in the hard drive, delete files that are not necessary and defragmented drives.

These can be used by the user, but they depend on the computers core so as to operate effectively. Applications may not be able to run independently but they do not rely on information from the computers core (Henderson, 2009).

Types of application software

- Word processing software: The word processing software is known as a word processor and is a computer program that helps in providing for input, formatting, editing and output of specific data, and most of the times, it has some features that have been added. In the past, word processors used to have the specific function of processing texts, as they were stand-alone devices, however, the word processors in this modern world are web processor programs that are being run on almost all general purpose computers. Word processors are designed to function as simple text editors and also as desktop publishing programs that are fully functioning. However, after 2010, these distinctions have changed and they are now quite unclear. Word processors were not developed from computer technology. Actually, they were able to evolve from machines that were mechanical, and only later they were able to merge with the computer field. Processing has helped to automate the physical aspect of writing and editing and technology has had to refine it so as to make sure it is available to corporations and individuals. In the 1970s the term word processing was introduced to American offices. Initially, it was meant to streamline the work to typist, but this, later on, shifted towards automating the editing of texts. Ever since word processing was invented, there have been three different types: electronic, mechanical, and software.

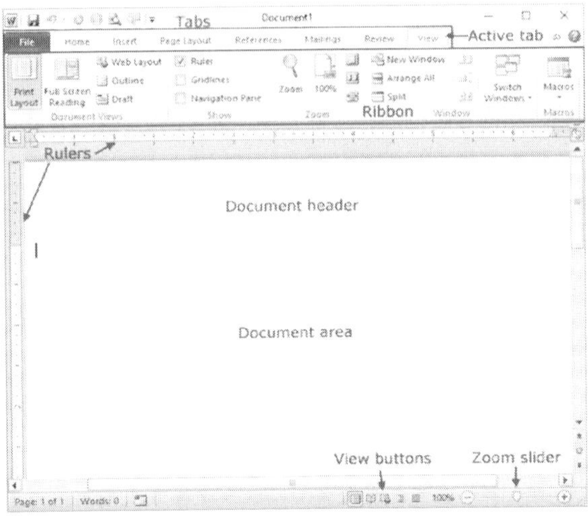

Figure 2.29. *The word processor helps users write documents on the computer that could be letters, essays, reports, etc.*

Source: https://www.computerhope.com/jargon/w/word-processor.htm.

- Database software: The database software is created in a manner that allows it to produce databases and ensure the storage, management, changing, searching, and extraction of information that is found inside them. A database software program that is comprehensive is normally called a database management system.

A database was created to ensure the protection of information in the database and also to ensure that this information is both accurate and consistent. The function of a database software is: storage of data; the backup and recovery of data; presentation and reporting of data; provide access control to multiple users; management of the data security; and communication with the database. These days, there are online database software's that make it possible for users to create web-based applications that are customized without any experience in coding. It normally involves a functionality that includes editing and collaboration. This allows members from one team to share files and also discuss projects. Depending on the platform that is being used, it is possible for the user to also create forms that can be stored in a website and can also deliver data directly to a database. Most of these database software's that are online have capabilities to perform advanced reporting. An example of a database software is an analytical database software which provides the opportunity for the user to withdraw data from a couple of databases and perform examinations on them so as to assess their performance quantitatively.

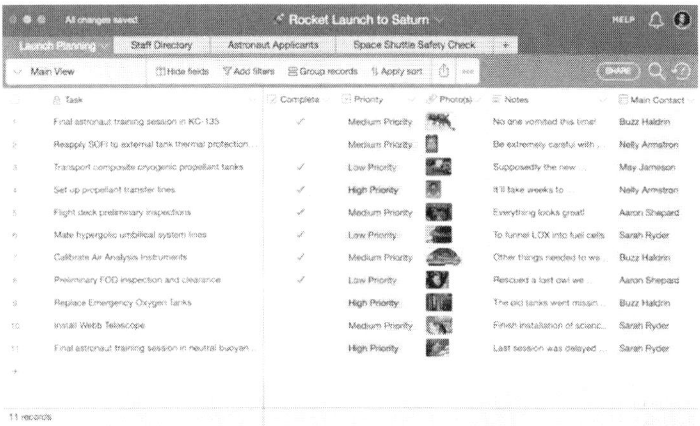

Figure 2.30. *Database help in backing up and recovering data.*

Source: https://blog.capterra.com/free-database-software/.

- Spreadsheet software: This software is a computer application that is interactive and allows one to organize, analyze and store data in a tabular form. Spreadsheets were developed to represent the analogs of worksheets that were used for accounting. The software works on the data that is inputted in sales on a table. Each cell may have either a number or a word in it or results from certain formulas that are calculated and valued based on the content of other cells automatically. It is also possible for a spreadsheet to also refer to such an electronic document. Users of spreadsheets are able to address values that have been stored and also observe the effects on the values that have been calculated. Spreadsheets are useful for analysis of "what-if" cases because it is easy to investigate them without manual recalculation. It is possible for the spreadsheets that are used these days to have multiple sheets that are interactive, and they can be able to display data in either numerical and texts, or graphical forms. In addition to performing basic mathematical and arithmetic functions, the spreadsheets of today have functions that have been built in to help in the operation of financial and statistical tasks. Calculations such as standard deviation and net present value are easily applied to tabular data with a function that has been preprogrammed in a formula. Spreadsheet programs are also able to provide expressions that are conditional, functions that are able to help in conversion between texting numbers, and functions that operate on the strings of texts. Peppa Pig systems have been replaced by spreadsheets all around the world. Despite the fact that they were initially created for accounting and bookkeeping tasks, they are now utilized in many different ways extensively.

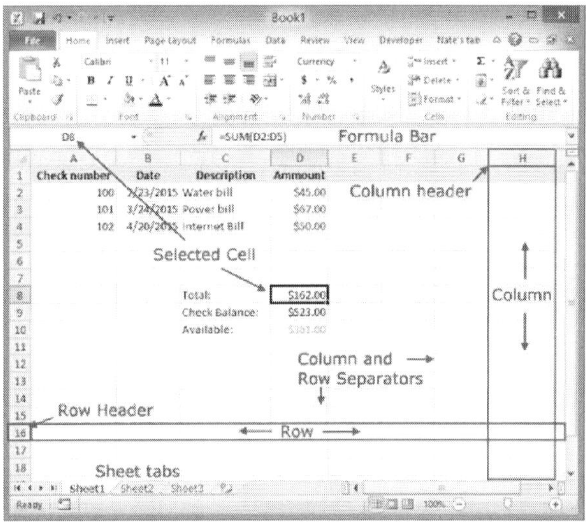

Figure 2.31. *Spreadsheets have been used to perform mathematical and arithmetic problems by many office workers.*

Source: https://www.computerhope.com/jargon/s/spreadsheet.htm.

- Presentation software: This is a software package that helps in the displaying of information using slides in a slide show. It has three main functions: it helps for the insertion and formatting of texts; it provides a proper method for the insertion and manipulation of graphic images; and it has a system that allows the displaying of the content in a slideshow. In comparison to traditional presentation media, presentation software in the modern times can be seen as helping to enable categories that are functionally specific, of electronic media with their own cultures and practices that are distinct. This mode of delivery for presentations has proven to be pervasive in all aspects of communications when it comes to businesses, especially in planning of businesses as well as in conferences that are academic or even professional settings. They can also be used in the knowledge economy generally, where ideas is normally an output from work. Presentations can also work perfectly in political settings, especially where persuading the opposite side is what determines the outcome of the group in workplace politics. Most of the rooms that are used to hold meetings and conferences have presentation electronics configured inside them. These include overhead projectors that can be used to display the slides to make a presentation, and they are often driven by the laptop of the person presenting, which is normally controlled directly by the presentation program that was used to develop this specific presentation. These presentations, in terms of slideshows, are normally used as a visual aid to track the lectures coverage and also for the audience, especially when the audience prefers audiovisual presentations.

Figure 2.32. *Presentations are a perfect audiovisual way of explaining something.*

Source: https://business.tutsplus.com/articles/best-presentation-software-alternatives-to-powerpoint--cms-28697.

- Multimedia Software: This is a type of software which helps to combine texts, audio, videos and image files. This software helps to enhance any form of text document by adding photos that are interesting, chats, animations and also graphics. The software normally provides tutorials that help the user to learn on how to properly make this happen. This allows the user to use this software without having to have computer skills. This software can help in providing entertainment in addition to being useful. It provides the opportunity for one to listen to different songs, play music, add speech recordings and even make interesting sound effects. With the multimedia software it is possible to listen to legit pronunciations of phrases, listen to sounds from animals or songs from musical, see artwork from all over the world and even hear music from famous composers as well as watching movies. Multimedia software is able to provide a wide selection of options that the user can enjoy, and this is one of its greatest advantages. It can even be quite advantageous in different fields such as science and technology, history, geography, sports, arts, health, medicine, etc. This software normally requires a large storage and can be obtained in the format of a CD.

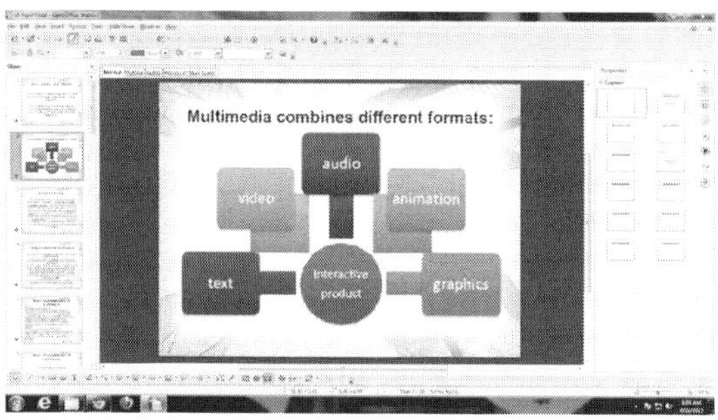

Figure 2.33. *Multimedia software combines the formats of videos, audios, texts, graphics, and animations to create a product that is interactive.*

Source: https://manilynricafort21.wordpress.com/application-software-multimedia-software/.

2.5. COMPUTER LANGUAGE

2.5.1. Machine Language

This is also called the machine code, which is a computer program that is developed in the language of machines to provide instructions that can be directly executed by the central processing unit of a computer. Each instruction commands the central processing unit to perform a task that is very specific such as loading, storing, jumping, or an arithmetic logic unit operation on either one or more than one units of data in the memory of the central processing unit (ITL Education Solutions Limited, 2011).

This language is strictly numerical and it is expected to run as fast as possible, and it may also be considered as the level of representation that is the lowest, of an assembled computer program or as a programming language that is primitive and dependent on hardware. Despite the fact that it is possible to directly write computer programs in machine code, it is a job that is tiring and it is prone to errors when it comes to managing individual bits and calculating addresses and constants that are numerical manually. Therefore, it is very rare to find programs being written directly in machine code, especially in the modern time, however, it can be used for lower level debugging, program patching and assembly language disassembly.

Most of the practical programs as of now are developed in languages that are of a higher level or assembly languages. The source code then undergoes translation to machine codes that can be executed by utilities such as assemblers, linkers and compilers, having the great exception of interpreted programs, which have not undergone translation into machine code. The interpreter itself, however, typically consists of machine codes that can be executed directly. It may be seen as a processor or an executor which is performing the source code instructions (ITL Education Solutions Limited, 2011).

Machine codes have been defined as the lowest level of programming detail that can be utilized by a programmer, however, there are many processes that use microcode and there are others that optimize and transform instructions from the machine code into sequences of micro-ops, internally. This, however, is not considered to be a machine code.

Every processor or processor family is equipped with its own set of instructions. These instructions are referred to as bit patterns that are physically designed to correspond to different commands to the computer. This means that the instructions are developed in a specific manner so as to be specific to a class of processors using the same architecture.

2.5.2. Assembly Language

This is a low-level programming language which has a great correspondence when it comes to the instructions in its language and the machine code instructions of the architecture. Every assembler has its own assembly language because assembly normally depends on the instructions of the machine code. Each assembly language is normally designed for when specific computer architecture. Symbolic machine code is another name for assembly language.

Utility programs that are referred to as assemblers will help convert the assembly code into machine codes that can be executed. This process of conversion is normally referred to as assembly. It files to the assembly of the source code. The assembly language normally has one-to-one ratio when it comes to having one statement per machine instruction. However, statements and comments that are directives of the assembler, macros, and levels that are symbolic of the program as well as memory locations can be supported (ITL Education Solutions Limited, 2011).

Each assembly language is strict when it comes to being specific to a specific computer architecture and even sometimes to an operating system. However, some assembly languages have no provisions for this specific syntax or operating system calls, and most assembly languages can be used with any operating system universally, because the language that has been provided normally helps in giving access to the full capabilities of the processor, whereby, all call mechanisms of the systems are able to rest.

Most high-level programming languages are normally portable across different architectures, but they also required to be interpreted and compiled, which is much more complicated than assembling.

Developers may choose to use assembly language to:

- Write codes for systems that have processors that are old and that have high-level language options that have been limited.
- Create a code that can use direct interaction with the hardware, for example in interrupt handlers.
- Account for high repetitions of interruptions in embedded processors, which need the shortest number of cycles per interrupt.
- Develop programs that require to use instructions that are specific to the processor and not set by the compiler.
- Develop executables of compact size that can stand alone are required and they are meant to execute without recourse to the complement run time or libraries that have associations with high-level language.
- Develop real-time programs such as simulations, navigation systems for flights and even medical equipment. For example, it is important for the telemetry for the fly by wire system to undergo interpretation and be acted upon within a time constraint that is strict. Such systems have to have the elimination of any source of delays that may be unpredictable, which may be created

by languages that have been interpreted, garbage collection that is automatic, paging operations, or multitasking that might be preemptive. There are some languages that are of a higher level that are able to incorporate run time components in system interfaces that operate in a perfect manner and still introduce such delays. When wenches are lower level languages for such a system, it gives greater visibility and control over the details that are being processed, to the programmer.

Assembly language is still normally taught in programs that deal with computer science and electronic engineering. Despite the fact that there are only a few programmers who use assembly language as a tool regularly, the underlying concepts of assembly language is still very important. Topics such as the location of memory, stock processing, binary arithmetic, compiler design and interrupt processing are had to study in detail without understanding how the computer works at the hardware level and understanding the lower level languages.

2.5.3. High Level Language

High level language refers to a programming language that has an abstraction that is strong from the details of the computer. When compared to low-level programming languages, high-level programming languages are easier to use, use natural language elements, and they can also automate videos of computing systems that are significant, such as their memory management, making it simpler and more understandable when trying to develop a program in comparison to when one is using a lower level language. The quantity of obstruction that is provided helps in defining how high-level a programming languages (Dasgupta, 2016).

Auto-codes were high-level programming languages that utilized compilers to function.

These were invented in the 1960s. An example of an auto-code is Fortran. Plankalkül was the first ever high-level programming language that was designed for computers. It was created by Konrad Zuse. This high-level programming language was, however, not implemented in his time, and the contributions that he had originally made were highly isolated from other developments due to the world war that was occurring.

Fortran was the first high-level language to significantly spread globally. It was a high-level language that was independent of machines and was developed by IMBs auto-codes that had been invented earlier.

Algol was introduced in 1958 and 1969 by computer scientists from Europe and America. It was the first language that had a clear distinction between the name parameters and value together with their corresponding semantics. Algol was also able to introduce programming concepts that were well structured whose syntax was the first to be described in formal notation (Dasgupta, 2016).

The abstraction level of high-level language is higher than that of the machine language. Instead of dealing with registers and call stacks, it deals with, addresses, complicated arithmetic, subroutines and functions, locks among other computer science concepts that focus on the usability by the user instead of the efficiency of the program.

High level languages hardly have any language elements that translate directly into the native opcodes of the machine. It is also possible for the language to have features such as input and output, object-oriented language features, and other features such as routines that handle strings. This language is common in causing detachment and separation of the computer from the programmer.

This is different when compared to low-level languages, such as assembly languages. It is possible for a high-level programming to amplify the instructions of the programmer and cause a lot of movement of the data in the background without the knowledge of the programmer. This is because all the executing instructions as well as the power of responsibility has been handed over to the computer by the programmer (Dasgupta, 2016).

2.5.4. Compiler and Interpreter

A compiler refers to a translator which is able to transform high-level language into machine language.

An interpreter is a program which is able to closely imitate the execution of programs that have been created in a source language. Compilers are you able to convert one whole program in one try where the interpreters convert the program by doing so to a single line at a time.

Humans are able to understand anything they would like to understand using languages that are natural, but computers cannot. The computers require for the languages in the human readable form to be translated by the translator, and to be re-written in a form that his computer readable. Both of the interpreter and the compiler are forms of language translators (Henderson, 2009).

A language translator refers to a software that is able to translate programs from a language source that is in a form that can be read by humans into an equivalent program in machine language. This source language is normally and mostly a high-level programming language, and it is normally translated to the machine language of the actual computer.

A compiler is a program that allows for there to be reading of a program that has been written in a high-level language and the compiler is able to convert it into either a low-level language or a machine language and it is also able to report any problems and errors that may be in the program. It is able to convert the whole source code in one try and it is also able to do so by taking multiple tries, however, in the end, the user is able to get the code that has been compiled and is ready to execute (ITL Education Solutions Limited, 2011).

And interpreter on the other hand is a program that works as an alternate option for making sure that programming language is implemented and it does the same work as a compiler. It helps in performing tasks such as parsing and type checking in a similar way as a compiler. However, the interpreter accesses expressions by directly processing the syntax tree and it also executes statements instead of generating codes from the syntax tree.

The interpreter may require to process the syntax tree more than once and that is why interpretation is normally slower in comparison to executing a program that has been compiled.

A compiler and an interpreter can be combined so as to ensure implementation of a programming language. In this situation, the compiler is meant to generate intermediate level code then the code undergoes interpretation instead of being compiled to machine code. When your employ and interpreter, it is very beneficial when it comes to the development of programs, where the most important function is to ensure that you can be able to test the modification of a program faster rather than be able to run the program efficiently (ITL Education Solutions Limited, 2011).

2.5.5. Open Source Software

This is a type of computer software in which there is release of a source code under a license whereby the holder of the copyright is able to grant the user the ability to study, change, and distribute the software to any other person and for many other different purposes. This software can be developed in a public manner that is collaborative.

The development of open source software can lead to perspectives that are diverse, instead of those of one company. In 2008, there was a report that was done that showed that software's that have an open source model have been able to result in savings of more than 60 billion per year for the customer.

In open source software, the users are meant to be treated as co-developers. This means that they should also be able to access the source code of the software. In addition, the users are normally encouraged to ensure submission of any changes that they may make to the software including additions, code fixes, bug report, documentation, etc. (Anderson, Ferro, & Hilton, 2010).

Having more co-developers has helped to increase the rate of evolution of a software. This is because when the source code is viewed by many users, they are able to find all the bugs and be able to give suggestions on how to fix them. In addition, there are some users who have programming skills that are advanced, and the machine of each user helps in providing a testing environment that is additional to the one that was previously used. This testing environment that is new helps in offering the ability to find and fix new bugs.

Software's that are open source are normally easier to get in comparison to proprietary software's, that often leads to an increased use. In addition, there can be an increase in the adoption of that standard is the availability of an open source implements the standard. Open source systems have also helped in building the loyalty of developers, because the developers gain empowerment and a sense of ownership of the end product (Anderson, Ferro, & Hilton, 2010).

2.6. COMPUTER SECURITY

2.6.1. Virus

A virus it is a computer program that, when it undergoes execution, it is able to replicate itself by causing modification of other computer programs and this leads to insertion of its own code. When there is success in replication, the areas that have been affected are said to be infected with a computer virus.

Figure 2.34. *Viruses can infect parts of the computer hardware and cause the computer system to crash.*

Source: https://www.ictworks.org/10-signs-your-computer-infected-viruses-malware-or-trojans/amp/.

The people who write viruses use deceptions in social engineering so as to exploit knowledge that is detailed on the vulnerabilities of the security system, so as to initially cause infection of systems and spread the virus. Most viruses normally target systems that run Microsoft windows, where there are variety of mechanisms that are employed to cause infection of the new host, and most of the time this is done by using anti-detection strategies that are complex to evade the antivirus software (Tedre, 2014).

The people who create viruses do so, so as to seek profit, send messages that are political, personal amusement, to show the system that there's a vulnerability that exist, sabotaging the service, or just because they want to explore the issues that are involved with cyber security, artificial intelligence and evolutionary algorithms.

Computer viruses can lead to damage each year that may be worth billions of dollars. This is because they cause the failure of the system, wastage of the computer resources, corruption of data, increased maintenance costs, etc. There has been development of open source antivirus tools so as to deal with this issue. Industries have created antivirus software's that are being sold or being distributed for free so as to protect various operating systems from viruses.

By 2005, there were no antivirus software that were existing and were able to uncover most of the computer bases, especially the new ones. As of now, there are researchers who deal with computer security. They are actively looking for new ways to ensure that anti-viruses arc a better solution to detect emerging viruses effectively, before they have been distributed widely (Tedre, 2014).

2.6.2. Protecting Computer System Using Antivirus Software

When the hardware starts to behave in an unusual manner, the default reaction is normally to think that a virus has infected your computer. Despite the fact that a virus is normally a possibility, there is always a possibility that the problems could have arisen due to an infection that is known as a malware.

Viruses and malware can be prevented using:

- Using antivirus and malware software that is trusted.
- Ensuring that you update the operating system.
- Make sure that you only use networks that have been encrypted.
- Ensuring that you maintain a tight grip on your personal information.
- Keeping track with the latest attacks.

There are normally more than 2 million malware threats that occur each and every day. Viruses and malware are very prevalent in at the same time can be quite frustrating, time-consuming, and annoying, regardless of whether it was created so as to give you a hard time or to hijack an operating system.

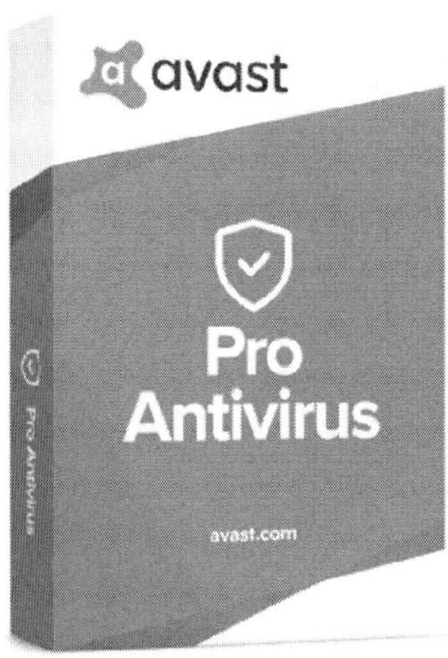

Figure 2.35. *Above is an example of an antivirus that is commonly used by most personal computer users.*

Source: https://www.bhphotovideo.com/c/product/1369454-REG/avg_avs_pav18t24enk_01_avast_pro_antivirus_2018.html.

There are normally antivirus software downloads that are free on the Internet, but these are not advisable because it is not good to trust your computer with just any form of software. In addition, antivirus programs that are completely free and also potentially unwanted programs.

This is because most of them have a kind of spyware that has been installed.

It is always advisable to invest in a high-quality antivirus software. In comparison to hijacking and crypto-jacking that could bring many problems to your personal computer, it is a small price to pay.

It is also important to download software updates immediately they are available. An antivirus software that is good will help in preventing viruses and malware for a long period of time, because they can detect and eliminate the viruses as long as all the other programs and software is updated (Page & Gamboa, 2019).

All major providers of software equip laptops with their own operating systems, and each of them also have their own line of defense against an antivirus. They still, however, have to ensure updates on a regular basis so as to deal with for vulnerabilities that may be newly discovered.

Despite the fact that users may feel that restarting and upgrading your system to a version that is newer is unnecessary, it is important for one to know that these updates are designed in a way that helps to decrease the exposure to possible viruses (Page & Gamboa, 2019).

2.6.3. Precautions to be taken Against Viruses

There are ways in which one can prevent the computers from being infected by viruses.

- Firstly, every computer should have an antivirus software. This is a must-have protection and it is always the first step in ensuring that your computer does not get infected with a virus.
- Secondly, it is important to ensure that your antivirus software is always kept up to date. Having a free antivirus software may not be the best option, however, it is still better than nothing. Microsoft normally provides a security package that is for free and this is much more decent considering that one pays for their windows license.

Figure 2.36. *Above are some of the ways one can protect their computer from computer viruses.*

Source: https://www.slideshare.net/wafahani/computer-virus-and-antivirus-50766843.

- Thirdly, running scans that regularly scheduled with your antivirus software is an important way to avoid infection. This can be done by setting up the software to run scans at regular intervals. This is normally advised to be at least once a week but not longer than a week between scans. It is normally had to work on your computer when it is running scans for viruses. To avoid this, it is advised for one to set this scan to run at night when the user is not using the computer. This, however, cannot happen if you turn off your computer at night. This means that it is important to set the antivirus software to run on one specific night, and on this night the computer should be left running.
- Fourthly, it is important to ensure that your network is secure. Many computers use the Wi-Fi connection to connect to files, printers or even the Internet. It is important to use WPA or WPA2 encryption and avoid broadcasting and open Wi-Fi connection. If possible when should also avoid broadcasting the name of the Wi-Fi network. It is still possible to access the Wi-Fi on your computer, however, when will have to type in the name of the Wi-Fi network and the password. If the user has many guests that use the WiFi, it is important to just provide your guests with a guest SSID that has a different password. This can help with preventing hackers accessing your files.

- Lastly, it is important to avoid websites that have materials that are pirated. This also includes opening email attachments from unknown people or unknown companies. Users need to avoid clicking on links that are found in unsolicited emails.

Chapter 3 Scientific Methods of Computer Science

CONTENTS

3.1. INTRODUCTION

There are a number of disciplines that computer science gets its foundations from. Many different concepts from many different fields are utilized in studying computer science. Computer science uses theory and practical, as well as general and specific aspects. There is a great number of different sciences that are able to help in much more communication, not only because the methods of communication are developing to be quite convenient and efficient, but also because there is an increased need for getting views in this world that are holistic.

Computer science does not only depend on the use of computers, technology or programs and data. It is considered a science that deals with mathematical aspects that are abstract and also includes an aspect of engineering. The aspect of engineering deals with having the skills to design, while the aspect of mathematics deals with finding answers to problems, or showing proof that the problems do not exist.

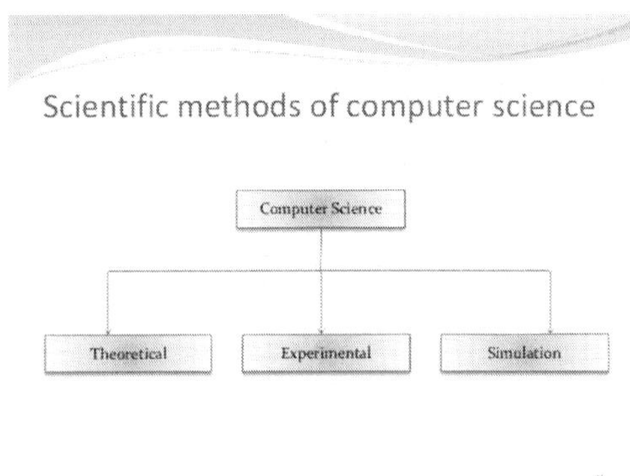

Figure 3.1. *Above are the main methods of computer science.*

Source: https://www.slideshare.net/parindarajapaksha/scientific-methods-in-computer-science.

Normally, there are characteristic features that are found in computer science that are derived from classical scientific methods. Computer science is built on different components in different areas of science. Computer science has the specific factor based on the fact that its objects of investigation are related to the computer itself. These objects develop together with the growth of the theories that describe them and also with the practical experience as they are being used.

This can be seen in the fact that computers that were used in the past are definitely not the same as those that are used right now. The definition of a computer in the 1950s is also different from that which we use right now. The scientific methods of computer science can be divided into modeling, theoretical, simulation computer science, and experimental computer science.

3.2. MODELING

Modeling is always included in sciences. It is utilized in a way that shows that the issue of interest needs to be made into a manner that is much simpler, so as to be studied. Models are meant to ensure that the main features of a certain issue are considered. This is considered to be the first step of abstraction. In other words, it refers to knowing the features that are important in a certain concept. This is made possible by the fact that there will always be a ground that is theoretical and which we begin from when doing science.

When you have a model that has been simplified, of a certain concept, this means that it has been described in a certain way using a language that is symbolic and which can help us in the prediction of consequences that may either be observable or measurable of certain changes in a system. Theoretical Computer science, Experimental Computer Science and Simulation Computer Science are all about models of phenomena (Barry, 2015).

During the modeling process, there are a few questions that one must ask themselves:

- In creation of the model – What are the factors that one needs to pay attention to? What should one avoid when creating the model? What formalism needs to be utilized in creating the model?
- Suitability of the model – Is it able to perform the tasks it is set out to perform? Is the level of resolution and abstraction appropriate?
- Does the model vary from what the expectation is in terms of its features and behaviors?
- Are there any other models that exist, or results that are experimental, when it comes to varying from the reality?
- Is the model validated to perform its expected purpose?
- There are normally some constraints that are specially applied on certain models, such as conservative models. These arc normally used in systems that are in relation to safety. This means that this

is done under an assumption that the parameters that are either not modeled or those that are not included in the system of modeling have a credibility value that is not quite favorable.

One needs to make an analysis of the pros and cons of new models against old models by making an analysis in the differences between the old and the new models. This is referred to as benchmarking. This necessary in making new models and also in ensuring that the model created works well.

Figure 3.2. *Computer modeling is a basis for all other scientific methods of computer science. It can be used to create models for 3D objects.*

Source: https://www.udemy.com/course/learn-computer-modeling-for-3d-printing/.

Modeling involves using the real world as it is to create a modeled phenomenon. This means it needs to start from the world as it is. One should then use this modeled phenomenon to create a model that is simplified which is in correspondence to predictions and hypothesis, then make a comparison between the two on whether the simplified model is easy and suitable to work with. This is in correspondence to making observations that are new and doing tests. Selection then has to be done amongst theories that are competing to choose a fully acceptable theory.

In the field of computer science, there is a conceptual model. It is referred to as a domain model so as to help in distinguishing it from the other types of models. This model is mainly chosen because it does not depend on designs or even for concerns to be implemented. This includes data storage. This model aims at expressing what the terms and the concepts that are utilized by the experts of domain, mean. This is done so at to ensure the discussion of problems, and also in finding the appropriate relationships when different concepts are compared.

This model tries to fully explain what different ambiguous terms mean, and also make sure that there are no issues that can occur when it comes to the different interpretations of the concepts used as well as the terms. Stakeholders could be easily confused by the different meanings and interpretations, especially those that involve implementation and design of a solution, where there is a major factor of understanding and having clarity about the business that is provided by the conceptual model. After there has been modeling of the domain concepts, this model then is a basis that is stable for the later developing of applications in the domain (Tedre, 2014).

There are different notations that are used to describe conceptual models. First, The Unifying Modeling Language Notation, which describes the conceptual model with a diagram divided into classes, where the classes are used to describe concepts. The relationships between the concepts are represented by associations. The modeled concept in the different situations are represented by the types of roles in an associated.

Secondly, Entity Relationship modeling describes conceptual modeling using an entity relationship model diagram, where the concepts are represented the entities and the relationship between the concepts are represented by the number of elements in the set and the different options that are available. No matter which notation is utilized, the meaning of the business that is shown in the conceptual model should not be compromised in clarity and richness. This means that one needs to ensure that it is expressed in a direct manner in a way that the concerns of implementation influence it.

All in all, computer modeling refers to the use of abstract representations that are based on mathematics, of an event, behavior, system or phenomenon that is natural, found in the real world. Computer models are developed in a manner that allows them to behave just like the system in real-life. The more accurate a computer model is, the closer it is to matching real-life (Tedre, 2014).

3.3. THEORETICAL COMPUTER SCIENCE

This is a section of general mathematics and computer science that deals more with topics to do with computational mathematics and it also deals with the computational theory. Being able to restrict theoretical areas within limits in a precise manner is hard.

Theoretical Computer science deals with many different topics such as the structure of data, complexity of computing, algorithms, computations that may be problematic, the theory of information, biology of computation, the geometry of computation, algebra, etc. This field mostly deals with techniques based on mathematics (Page & Gamboa, 2019).

In 1931, it was proven that it is possible to have fundamentals that have limitations on the statements that can be accepted and those that cannot be accepted. This shows that mathematical proof had previously existed. Logic and computability can now be studied efficiently due to the development of theoretical computer science. In 1948, the theory of information was included into this field by Claude Shannon. A mathematical model was also included in this same decade. This model included learning the brain. There was a lot of biological data that was used to back this information, thus helping for the development of neural networks and processing that was distributed in a parallel manner. There were computer scientists, in 1971, who proved that there are relevant problems that are practical and are landmarks results in competition and complexity theory.

After quantum mechanics was developed in the early 20th century, there was a concept on the fact that it was possible to perform operations that were mathematical on a wave function of a particle. This means that one was able to compute certain functions on different states at the same time. This led to the development of quantitative computer later on in the same century. This concept showed that it was possible to use these methods to factor huge numbers in a time that was polynomial, and if these methods were used, they would lead to making the cryptography systems that are modern (Page & Gamboa, 2019).

Some of the topics included in Theoretical Computer science include:

Algorithms: An algorithm is a procedure for calculations that is designed in a step by step manner. They are used to calculate, process data, and automate reasoning. It is a method that is efficient and is expressed as a fine list of instructions that have been defined in a proper manner so as to make calculations on a certain function. They normally start from an empty state, where the instructions are used to explain the computing method, that when utilized, goes through successive states that have been defined in a proper manner, which then leads to the developed into an output and then ending in a state that is finale. It is not compulsory for one state to transit to another in a manner that has been determined. It is possible for some algorithms to have an input that is random.

Automata theory: This is the study of machines and moving mechanical devices that are abstract, together with the problems that are used in solving them. This theory is found in a subunit of mathematics and computer science. This theory involves studying virtual machines that can operate on their own, so as to help understanding the process of inputting and outputting in a logical manner. This is done with or without stages of computing that are intermediate.

Coding theory: This theory involves studying the different properties of codes as well as checking on how fit they are for a specific use. Codes are normally utilized for compression of data, correcting of errors, cryptography, and these days they are used for network coding. There are many different scientific disciplines that study codes. Some of these include engineering, mathematics, etc. They study these codes so as to design methods to transmit data that are reliable and efficient. They help to remove any redundant codes and also detect and correct any errors in data that is being transmitted.

Computational biology edit: This involves developing and applying theoretical methods, techniques for computational simulation, data analysis methods, social and biological and behavioral systems. This field deals with applied mathematics, statistics, Computer science, animation, biochemistry, anatomy, and even neuroscience. Computational biology and biological computation are two different things. Biological computation is a section of computer science and engineering that uses biology and bioengineering to develop computers, but it is almost the same as bioinformatics, which uses computers for storing and processing data that is based on biology.

Computational complexity theory: This is a subunit of the computational theory that deals with the classification of problems to do with computation in a matter that deals with their complexities, and looking for relations between these classes. Problems to do with computing are believed to be a task that should be solved by the computer, which is similar to stating that these problems can be fixed using mathematical steps, for example, an algorithm. A problem can be described to be difficult if the solution that is used needs major resources, regardless of whatever algorithm is used. This theory introduces models that are mathematical, so as to ensure studying of these problems and being able to quantify the number of resources that are required to deal with them, such as the time and storage. There are other measures that are also used and these are complex, such as the level of communication, the number of gates that are used in a circuit, and the number of processors. This theory is mainly used for the determination of the main limits of what computers are able to do, and what they are not able to do

Computational geometry: This is a subsection of computer science that deals with the study if algorithms that are able to be defined in geometrical terms. Some problems that are mainly based on geometry are brought up due to the study of geometric algorithms that are computational. These problems at the same time are said to be a section of computational theory. Despite the fact that computational geometry is a development that has recently arisen, it has a history that makes it one of the oldest fields in the computing sector. The main impulsion for computational geometry to be developed as a discipline was aided by computer-aided design. However, there majority of the issues that arise in this theory are classical in nature, and may arise due to the visualization of mathematics. Computational geometry is also normally used in robotics, integrated circuit design, computer vision, geographic information systems, computer-aided engineering, etc.

3.4. EXPERIMENTAL COMPUTER SCIENCE

Experimental computer science refers to the development of, or experimenting with or on software and hardware systems that are nontrivial. This may not be a sufficient definition as an improved definition would include the need to understand artifacts that help in understanding the field in a much for efficient manner. There is also a need to understand the difference between the experimenting that is done in experimental computer science and in biology or physics (Barry, 2015).

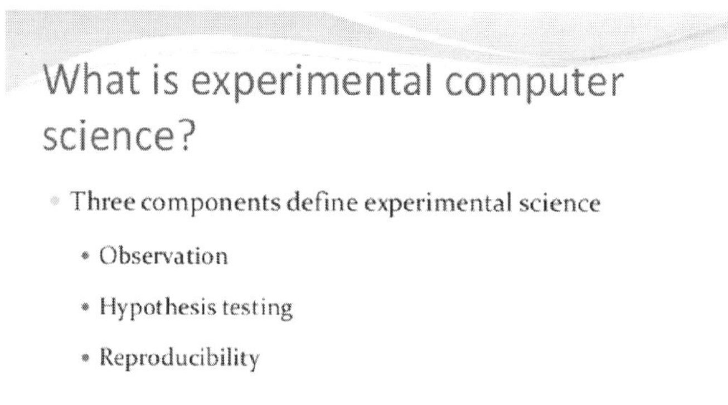

Figure 3.3. *Above are three components that help in defining experimental computer science.*

Source: https://www.slideshare.net/goharkhan6/experimental-economics-and-experimental-computer-science.

So as to cover all these issues, a better definition is described using six main characteristics. These will help in better understanding of the diverse phenomena. The main factor is that experimental Computer Science deals with artifacts such are software and hardware systems. These artifacts need to be explained for there to be an understanding on how complex artifacts are, how they depend on technology, how the phenomena are approved universally, and how they do not rely on the theory.

Experimental computer science is a discipline that is highly synthetic. This means that it was human made and not already available by nature. At the extremes of the field is where the level of synthetics is at the same level with the physical aspect e.g., In the technology for chips for the semiconductors that are metal-oxide in nature.

Practitioners are able to be creative due to the few physical constraints. It is very exciting to create your own ideas in a computer that is working. This, however, can be difficult because of the synthetic property, because there may be issues that have not been brought up to researchers who are in other fields (Barry, 2015).

There may be problems in bringing up the qualities that cannot be touched in creating research, having difficulties assessing the artifacts contribution and how the experimental systems are interrelated.

Artifacts in experimental computer science refers to implementing one or more than one computational aspects. The artifact is able to embody different manipulations and transformations because the aspects that are being studied are algorithms, processes, mechanisms and those that help in the manipulation and transformation of information.

Some of the artifacts are software systems and hardware systems. These include applications and computers respectively. The artifact can be used as the main topic of study, the main aspect that is used to conduct the study or both. It often deals with a huge portion of the knowledgeable contribution of research that is experimental, and the aspect that has been created represents great intellectual effort (Tedre, 2014).

The name artifact is normally used together with electronic hardware or software systems; however, it is used in a much broader manner. Experimentalists normally like to use graphic images and animations, data that is hard to construct, such as tests and benchmark suits. This is all in addition to computers and chips which are hardware systems and editors, computer-aided design and expert systems which are software systems. There are also many other things that are built and studied by experimentalists which may be defined as artifacts, however, not all of them are accepted by practitioners. Some example includes: protocols, languages in programming, methodologies, architectures, etc.

The issue when it comes to definitions comes from the fact that some of the cases are derived from the fact that there are certain artifacts that are implemented from abstractions, which can end up being considered as a concept that is abstract. The concept and the instance may depend on the abstract thinking of a specific individual. Different individuals map through different artifacts and ideas. This is, however, unnecessary, because the issues that arise during the creation of artifacts as well as their study are applied to both the wide and narrow interpretations.

Artifacts are the main aspect of experimental Computer Science, due to the fact that the study is done on the algorithms, processes, mechanisms, and the ability to transform information, which helps in describing certain behaviors when responding to different inputs, and they are also generally complicated, in terms of the general number of component parts (Tedre, 2014). These characteristics may lead to the overwhelming of the ability to compromise them using direct analysis because they are very complicated. All in all, how the parts interact is normally more important. This refers to the dynamics of their behavior. It is hard to predict how a computational idea will perform, on the basis of an analysis, either theoretical or logical, because the temporal characteristics of the interactions, the large amount of program, or the state of the hardware can make the problem worse. Regardless, the algorithms, mechanisms, and processes need to undergo implementation, to ensure that how the system behaves and also how the components interact, is able to be observed while in action.There are many theories of computer science that are being tested and also there are some that are still being tested. For example, there are methods such as object-oriented programming, functional programming, and methods that are formal, which are all supposed to lead to the improvement of the productivity of programmers, the quality of the program, or both. These, however, have not undergone testing in a systematic manner, despite the fact that they are more than 20 years old, and there has been a lot of effort that has been put into the development of languages used for programming, and techniques that are formal (Tedre, 2014).Human-computer interaction is one field of computing, together with some sections of software engineering that have to consider also humans in their forms of the phenomena that is being investigated. This is, therefore, an approach that is empirical and is much for used for humanities and social science.

3.5. COMPUTER SIMULATION

The third research methodology that is used within computational science in the recent years of computation involves modeling and simulation, doing this while complementing theory and experimentation. In both investigation and experimentation that is theoretical, computational science has shown up at the level where computer science, science disciplines and applied mathematics intersect.

Being able to master the tools of computational science such as modeling with visualization in 3D and computer simulation, being able to efficiently handle a large amount of data sets, being able to access a large number of resources that are well distributed, and ensuring collaboration with other specialists that are found on the internet, etc. are now things that university graduates are expected to be specialized in, not only those that have majored in computer science (Dasgupta, 2016).

These skills have become a part of the culture; the scientific culture. We have been able to deal with problems of today that may be quite difficult due to the environment and methods of computing that are making it possible. It is more obvious these days to have computational sciences that are much more flexible and dynamic, due to the many huge changes that are occurring in computing.

This is where computer simulation comes it. It allows us to use it in the investigation of regimes that's are far off the current capabilities of experimenting, and also in the studying of phenomena that is hard to replicate in the lab, such as experiments on how the universe will evolve. In the scientific aspect, one can use theory as well as experimentation to guide computer simulations, whereby the results after computation are able to help in the suggestion of new experiments and models that are theoretical.

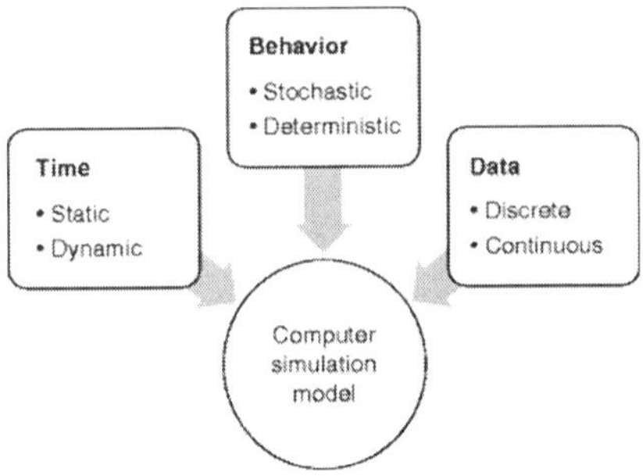

Figure 3.4. *A computer simulation model refers to a program or algorithm on a computer that helps in the simulation of changes of a system that has been modeled in response to input signals. Above is a representation of the model.*

Source: https://link.springer.com/10.1007%2F978-1-4419-1428-6_500.

One can explore very many different design options in engineering through computer models, in comparison to building those that are physical, and all this is done at a small fraction of the cost and less time. It is possible to use very powerful computers to conduct galaxy formation studies. Science only develops more when there is a lot of research activity being done. Despite the fact that the name 'simulation' has been used for many years, it shows us how science will be dealt with in the years to come (Dasgupta, 2016).

Scientists will be able to do experiments in the computer, as well as being able to test hypotheses that are scientific by using real physical objects that can be used to investigate. Computer simulations are also seen as a representation pf a major discipline on its own, despite of the main application. It involves being able to use computers, mainly supercomputers, to visualize and simulate complex and large-scale phenomena. Computational science using computer simulation has helped in the studying of weather predictions, molecular dynamics, finite analysis of elements, pre-surgeries, etc.

If one can base computer science on computability theory, then it is also possible to base computer simulation on computational science. Below are some of the past systems that we can use to describe potential or existing roles that computer simulation can play:

- Chaos and complex systems – the aspect that one is able to succeed in observing complexity in a deterministic model that is structurally simple, is a major thing. The features of linear systems have a qualitative topological phase space, are able to undergo determination in a statistical manner, however, one has to use simulations for those that are not linear.

- Virtual Reality – this refers to being able to involve the person analyzing into the world that is being simulated. Despite the fact that most times, people see it as being similar to the interfaces that are man-machine hardware, it is important for the technology to ensure incorporation methods so as to build virtual worlds, which normally a problem of computer simulation.
- Artificial Life – this is normally an outcome of computational science that helps in challenging the main definition of the word 'experiment.' An experiment that is conducted using life that is artificial is one where there is writing of a computer program to help in the simulation of life forms that are artificial. This is normally referred to as mutation or genetic reproduction.
- Physically-based Modeling and Computer Animation – this process has moved forward greatly within computer graphics, and this has been a pace that can be well noticed.

These days, present-day machines have a high computing power that allows us to produce simulations of a wide variety of processes and phenomena; especially those that are not linear. This method is made very user-friendly and attractive due to modern graphic capabilities.

Despite the fact that there are many characteristics that lead to the differences between the younger filed of computer science from that which has been on the earth for a thousand years of sciences such as logic, natural sciences and mathematics, it is possible to state that computer science can be describes as a science due to the large amount of scientific features it has. Generally, it is important to talk about how all the sciences that are modern are greatly connected to technology. This is seen in chemistry, biology, physics, and mostly even for computer science. This is naturally so, because most of the research that is done and leads to modern computers developing is mostly done in the industry. The parts of computer science that deal with engineering have a connection to the physical aspects of the computer. Theoretical Computer science is in the same way as other parts of science. It is based on mathematical and logical grounds. The computer in these terms is not the main focus of the investigation. It is, however, a tool that is normally able to change so as to accommodate theoretical concepts that are much more powerful (Dasgupta, 2016).

Chapter 4

Modern Usages of Computers

CONTENTS

4.1. INTRODUCTION

Computers have been able to change the lives of many different people all over the world. It is hard for anyone of us to imagine a life without a computer. We use them every day is almost everything we do. They have helped in making our lives easier and have also brought comfort into our lives.

Computers have helped us in terms of communication, allowing us to stay in touch with very many people from all around the world. People are even able to drive cars that are computerized. Even the airplanes we use to travel are computerized. Employees have been able to have employers who work for them without even having to meet them.

Computers are also referred to as the electronic brain. Human being greatly depends on them to run their daily tasks. Computers are important for people in the business industry and also for the people who require them to do work, study and entertain. These days, schools are also trying to integrate computers into the education system for young boys and girls.

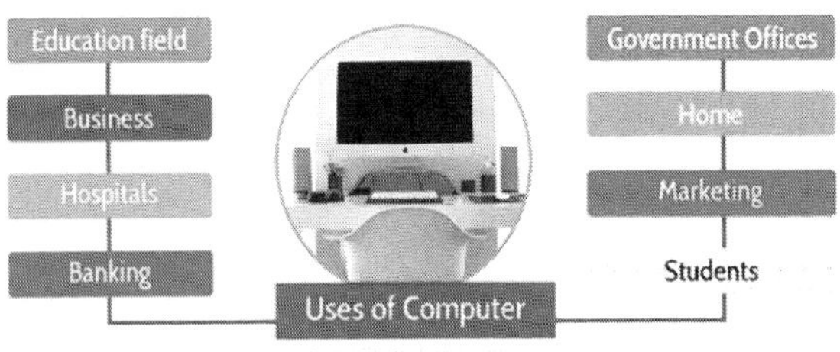

Figure 4.1. *Computers are being used for many different purposes in this modern time. Above are some of the common uses.*

Source: https://www.quora.com/What-are-the-uses-of-computers.

A while ago computers were only owned by the rich. As of today, they are something that we cannot avoid, so as to achieve success and development. They are no longer acquired only through stealing and by those who are extremely rich, they are, however, now and in the future, going to be used by many people all over the world to achieve success and global development. India is an example of a country that will benefit greatly from the accurate knowledge and utilization of computers. It will eliminate illiteracy and also promote efficiency, productivity, optimism, high quality work and productivity (LaMarco, 2019).

4.2. FOR BANKING PURPOSES

Computers that are normally utilized in the banking industry have helped to improve customer service provided by the employees and even their productivity when it comes to the managing of accounts, which does this at the same time as it helps in the streamlining of the activities in the back-office. Small banking institutions are able to use an equal level of technology when compared to larger banking institutions. This allows the smaller banks to effectively compete with the larger banks for business. Competition is one of the biggest impacts in this area. Computers are used in different ways:

Figure 4.2. *Computers have made it easier to manage accounts of the many people that use banks these days. It is much easier than the previous ways of bookkeeping.*

Source: https://www.moneyunder30.com/best-budgeting-tools.

4.2.1. Account Management

Automating of customer accounts is where the activities start in banking. This allows for the creation, updating and maintenance of customer records by the personnel. Accuracy of accounts that the personnel in the banking sector process, has been enhanced and made effective by the software and hardware that is used in banking. Customer transactions are normally carried out using a data record system that is centralized. All banking information systems are set up using account management, which is paramount and the first step.

4.2.2. Hardware Technology

Banking hardware in the 1960s involves a mainframe and a machine for punching cards. The punch cards were equipped with all the information of the customers' accounts. The punch card machine is what was used to read the information on the punch cards into the main system. Entire banks can be run by configuration of midrange and server hardware. In addition, they can also help in the receiving of transactions from bank branches that are affiliated. These hardware technologies that are new, are able to process many more transactions than hardware systems for legacy banking. These technologies have promoted the use of wireless banking as well as banking using telecommunications.

4.2.3. Electronic Transactions

Electronic transactions are an everyday thing for banking systems. An example of a transaction that is electronic is a direct deposit. Computers are the ones that normally process these transactions that are electronic, and these computers need to have the capability of encrypting hardware and software, so as to ensure that the data is not compromised as it is being transmitted. After the performance of the electronic transmissions, the computer is able to transfer the information it has transmitted to the main computer system so that is can process and update the information. Landlines and cell phones, the internet and ATMs, have helped to extend the capabilities of transacting in an electronic manner.

4.2.4. Web-Based Banking

These systems utilize a server that is dedicated through a network system in the bank. There is a specific section in the system of the bank that is set aside for applications on the internet. According to the law, it is compulsory for banking systems that are based on the web to include certificates that are authenticated and servers that are secure in regards to the transactions that are from the Federal Reserve Board and the Federal Deposit Insurance Company. The customers who prefer to bank online are able to find their accounts thanks to an interface that is found on the web. This web interface helps in ensuring integration with the main computer. The customer details, including the password and ID, end up passing through a couple of checkpoints before joining the main system of the computer so as to perform a transaction that is based on the web.

Figure 4.3. *Computers have made it easier to bank. There are many banks that have provided their users with online banking, making banking much more convenient.*

Source: https://www.dreamstime.com/royalty-free-stock-photography-computer-banking-image1328807.

There are many different types of computers that are used to carry out the different operations that are used daily. These computers promote efficiency and effectiveness, allowing the personnel to work and carry out transactions, ensure the needs of the customer are processed, foresee any new trends, ensure preparation of reports that may be both external and internal, communicating with the main customers, and even to promote the generation of profits. The different computers used are as below:

- *Mainframe computers* – These computers are utilized in banks to able to store information on the records of the client, operations that are either domestic or international and other information for processing that may be important. When it comes to a large bank, they could have their mainframe computer in the HQ of the bank and then link the terminals that are found in each branch with it. The ability to perform time-sharing is this computer's main advantage in the banking industry. This advantage helps in allowing more than one user to have access, in a simultaneous manner, to the same computer as well as the resources it has to provide. These computers are able to process data at a very high speed and they also have fault tolerance mechanisms that have been built within them. They also help to reduce the costs of labor and can also support a great workload which can be processed without any interruptions. An example of a mainframe computer that banks normally use include the BS2000 machine.

- *Minicomputers* – These are machines that perform computational processes and can range is size either between the mainframe computers which are large and the personal computers which are small. These computers play a role as servers of the internet and also the network in operations carried out in the bank. They have helped the banks shift from a method of processing that is centralized to one that is distributed. They are used as systems for storing files, running email systems and performing operations on the internet. This computer is able to support more than 65 terminals. An example of this is the VS series from Data General.

4.3. IN HOSPITALS, SUCH AS ICU

The medical field these days highly relies on computers, and this has occurred in a short period of time, just a few decades. Computers have been used in the medical field to provide diagnostic and treatments that are advanced, to patients. Computer technology is being used in: clinical labs, operations within the hospital, storage of medical records and systems for imaging. They are also used in the business offices of these providers of health care. Using computers in the health sector has proven to be very advantageous to doctors as well as researchers in medical science that is advanced. They are also being used to promote the improvement of patient health care levels (LaMarco, 2019).

4.3.1. Medical Imaging

This involves the computers that are used to process images of the human body, so as to be used in the studying and creation of diagnoses of patients. Some of the technologies involved in medical imagine include Ultrasound, X-Rays, MRIs and CT scans. All these forms of technology are normally controlled by computers. Since the early 20th century, there has been use of X-ray imaging. These days, computers are used together with X-ray machines so as to ensure proper transfer and adjustments.

4.3.2. Patient Monitoring

Monitoring of patients that is done using computers allows for the automatic monitoring and collection of vital signs such as respiratory rate, blood pressure, heart rate, etc. in a digital form. These computers help in reducing the time that is taken by the health personnel on making routine tests on the patients. Hospitals that are equipped with this technology are able to update the charts of their patients in an automatic manner, as well as inform the staff in the hospital of any changes that may occur to the vitals of the patient.

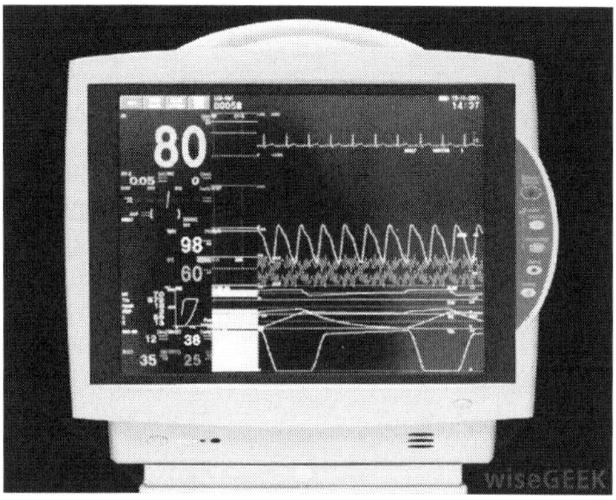

Figure 4.4. *Above is a machine that is used to monitor patient heart rate, blood pressure, etc. It is a cardiac monitor.*

Source: https://www.wisegeek.com/what-are-the-different-types-of-icu-equipment.htm.

4.3.3. Surgery That Is Assisted by Computers

Computers are used to plan, teach and perform a variety of procedures that are surgical. Robotically-assisted surgery is one of the latest innovations when it comes to computer technology in the health sector. This robotic device helps the surgeon's complete procedures that are minimally invasive. In this situation, the surgeon is still the one in control and normally shows the robot what to do.

4.3.4. Networks and Digital Communication

The means of communication has increased between medical practitioners thanks to the internet and computer networks. Some of the modes of communication include emails, webinars, and video chats. Health care practitioners are able to keep up with the newest medical developments as they occur, due to digital connections. They are also able to have consultations with their co-workers in real-time and also be able to get a different opinion for differential diagnoses as well as different options for treatment.

4.3.5. Telemedicine

Telemedicine has become a concept that has promoted house visits. Medical professionals are able to use video chats to meet with the patients in a remote manner thanks to computers and smartphones. Besides the fact that this is advantageous to patients who live in areas that have limited options when it comes to healthcare, telemedicine has also really helped even when it comes to natural disasters and also in areas with war.

4.3.6. Electronic Health Records

This is perhaps one of the newly developed methods in health care. An electronic health record refers to the provision of a paper chart in version that is digital, of the patient that is instantly available to health providers that are authorized. Healthcare providers in the United States are advised by the government to use electronic health records through their incentive programs.

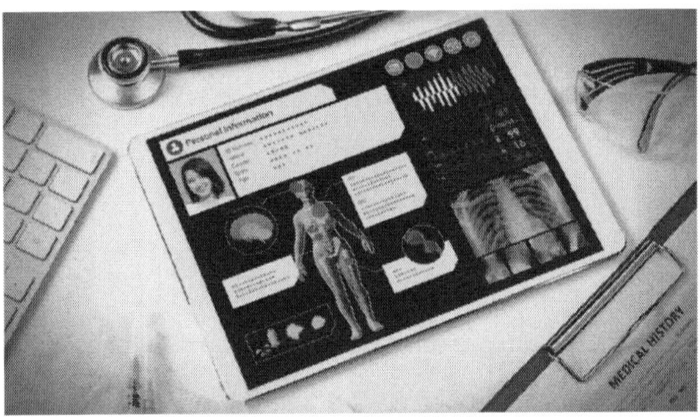

Figure 4.5. *Electronic health records have proven to be a major key in health care. They have automated patient data.*

Source: https://givingcompass.org/article/universal-electronic-health-records-might-be-key-to-healthcare-trust/.

4.3.7. Medical Databases

There are many useful solutions of software in the medical field that have been brought by the development of computers. There are organizations that have huge databases of information in relation to health statistics and diseases, for example, the world health organization. There are also databases that are public which are equipped with data on substances that are toxic, drug coverage and results of clinical research.

4.3.8. Medical Research

There are complex computer simulations that are created, in the research being done currently, on diseases that cannot be cured such as cancer and HIV. Hence, So us to be able to handle large amounts of research data as well as be able to ensure the analysis of millions of outcomes that may be possible, healthcare facilities are equipped with supercomputers and distributed computer systems. For example, computers are developing more and more in the sector of medical research such as in the mapping of the human genome.

4.3.9. Computers and Hospital Administration

So as to ensure the proper handling of patient records, scheduling of personnel, and many other details that are important in ensuring the care for a patient, most hospitals rely heavily on computers, and also software's that are specialized, to perform these actions. Almost every department in the hospital uses computers. The larger hospitals are probably equipped with their own computer servers that are private and specialists who are able to maintain them.

4.4. IN CODING AND PROGRAMMING

Not only coders are affected every day by coding. People come across coding and programming immediately they step out of their houses even without knowing. The effects of programming and coding are almost everywhere in the world of today. In the streets, at the workplace, and even at the grocery store and almost everywhere you go. Individuals interact with scanners that scan barcodes almost every day, and use very many different codes while working, whether they are using the word processor, or using Gmail to write a letter to friends or a boss (Amuno, 2019).

Figure 4.6. *Coding is a part of our everyday lives. Even the smallest things are run by computers.*

Source: https://www.computersciencedegreehub.com/faq/what-is-coding/?amp.

Even our cars have different computers that help in controlling almost everything in the car including power management, oil, fuel, systems that are used in navigation, etc. The roads we drive one arm managed using computer cords. This is seen in the traffic lights that are all mostly little computers and all the traffic networks in the world are controlled by computers. Even elevators are run using a cord with the help of processors. This process normally enables them to move to the designated floor. Without any tiny computers in them, elevators would not be able to open the doors automatically, sense if the elevator has a problem, and also prevent the doors from closing if there is someone standing in their way (LaMarco, 2019).

Greenhouses have temperature control which is computerized so as to grow cucumbers, bell peppers, spinach, and tomatoes when they are out of season, so at to provide to the growing population. There are even experiments being done to develop plant factories that allow the crops to properly grow indoors.

Chores in the household are made easier due to computers that have been programmed or coded. The refrigerator is able to maintain its temperature due to programming. Washing machines are also powered by computers allowing them to save time and energy. The modern washing machines have computers that have been programmed to monitor the weight of the load, the amount of water that is being used, and also setting the speed depending on the stage of the cycle.

4.5. FOR COMMUNICATION

Technology plays at major role in the 21st-century. We use computers to gain access to information, for creating and expressing ourselves, for communicating and collaborating, and also tracking that shipment of our outcomes in learning. It is important to understand all the factors of it (Singh et al, 2016).

Some of the roles of communication technology include:

- *Information Access* – we use technology almost every day to search for information. Materials such as the online encyclopedia, Wikipedia, etc. are online reference materials that offer a wide amount of information being able to do this while including multimedia and links that are interactive. Collections of electronic books are able to offer hundreds and thousands of texts. In addition, the number of articles and journals that are found online, on almost every topic one can imagine, help in making research easier, efficient, and very rewarding. Information technology devil has a major role in ensuring the development of any person interested in learning.

Figure 4.7. *Mobile phones are used by almost everyone on the earth and are the main form of communication.*

Source: https://amp.theguardian.com/technology/2019/sep/27/best-mobile-phones-budget.

- *Creativity and Self-Expression* – Communication and information technology has helped in allowing people to express themselves. People are able to explain the world in their own eyes, as well as include their own perspective to factors that are already in the wealth of knowledge available, so as to invent work that is original, all these due to the recording functions that are digital and integrated into our smartphones, tablets and other devices that we use such as computers. Editing software's that allow us to edit audios, photos and videos have helped in the contribution of inventions and different creations. This allows for us to not only access information but also to contribute to the information on the Internet. Human beings appreciate it when their work is found to be significant and also affirmed, and this can be promoted by the ability of members of the community being active in building the learning community, whether it is just in a school social media page or on the World Wide Web.

- *Collaboration and Communication* – more opportunities for communication and collaboration are built due to information and communication technology. There are many courses that have participation of the public in discussions using threads, chat, and video conference. An example of such a forum is Blackboard, which is a learning management system. Feedback is normally relayed more efficiently due to the collaborative functions that are available in office applications. This is because they allow us to view any comments that are posted in real time. Computers are important in the fact that they promote information technology.

Figure 4.8. *WhatsApp is one of the main communication platforms used in this modern time.*

Source: https://www.whatsapp.com/download.

Computers are important in this sector because they are improving and promoting communication. During the 1990s households started using Internet which led to the common use of blogs, emails, social networking, websites and video chats. These days the traditional methods of communication seem obsolete such as postal mail and landline phones. Some of the communication means include:

- *Internet* – The Internet has helped in revolutionizing how people are able to maintain communication with each other. Instead of having to wait for a couple of days or weeks so as to receive information, it is now possible for people to view this information at a very high speed. Emails have helped to transform how individuals are able to send information from one person to another and also in the conducting of business when it comes to its advantage speed and flexibility. Computers are able to process information at roughly 21 million bytes per second and this makes it easier for them to provide instant downloads and display of any email or text.
- *VOIP and Video Chat* – Voice over Internet protocol has helped to replace the use of landline telephones for many people all over the world. They are able to help in providing communication using phones that is instant, over the Internet. They are also normally cheaper than the phone lines that have been fixed. They also make it possible for one to see who they are speaking to do to the ability to conduct video chats. This platform is also helpful for one to ensure storage of their contact details so as to access and dial easily. The main disadvantage of this platform is that from the year 2011, 911 operators are not able to trace the location of the calls.
- *Social Networking* – some of the sites that are used for social networking include Twitter, Facebook, etc. which allow individuals to create content, at a fast rate, for people who are subscribed to their networks to view. Instead of having to send notes to each individual, social networking has helped to provide a stream of information and updates that is constant. This mode of communication is more commonly used than emails due to its ability to have instant communication on life status and updates to a large number of people who can reply to these updates with comments or likes in real time. Despite the fact that emails are also able to do this due to the distribution list, which could also

have the transfer of information to a large number of people, social networking has an interface that is streamlined and user-friendly and helps in precluding the overload of data, that may happen due to tying the same functions in an email program.

- *Routing* – routers are computers that are used in directing communication traffic. They, however, are not personal computers. They help in ensuring that close, emails or other Internet traffic at efficiently and correctly distributed. The routers take electronic data that has been packaged and allows it to be sent in the direction that its needs to go to so as to connect with the person intended to receive the information. They can also be used in the household but are mostly used in central data warehouses where there is a large amount of traffic in the same area.

4.6. FOR PLAYING GAMES

Computers that are used to play games are called gaming computers which are also known as gaming rigs. It is a personal computer that is made specifically to play video games and it requires a large quantity of computing power. One can compare the modern gaming computer to the normal traditional computer with additional components that are performance oriented, such as central processing units that have a high core count (Singh et al, 2016).

Figure 4.9. *Computers are able to provide high definition video footage for gamers all over the world.*

Source: https://www.techradar.com/in/news/best-budget-gaming-pc-2018-top-gaming-desktops-for-less.

Computers used for gaming are often put in association with enthusiast computers because they may be used for the same interest, however, they are differentiated in that, a gaming personal computer is designed to ensure achievement of performance for actual game play, while enthusiast personal computers are designed to ensure maximum performance, using games as the benchmark for real application. In the market, enthusiast personal computers are all high-end, however, gaming personal computers can either be low end, midrange, and high end. Manufactures of video cards mainly get the profits from the low-end and midrange gaming personal computers.

Due to the fact that gaming computers can have a wide variety of components that can go into them, they are rarely preassembled and most of them are custom assembled, either by the enthusiasts for gaming and hardware, or industries that make it their main aim to produce gaming machines that are custom. So as to raise the interest of the individual that is buying the computer, manufacturers of gaming computers produce boutique models for the computers that they sell with complete systems. This allows them to provide competition on the basis of aesthetics in addition to the hardware inside (Amuno, 2019).

Gamers had started to make it a big deal for them to build their own custom PCs as of 2012. This promoted the control of budgets and also made it easier for one to upgrade. When building your own custom computer, it makes it easier for the individual to ensure that the performance is maximized for the best value. When building your own custom gaming computer, there are a couple of things that must be considered, and these include the motherboard, the central processing unit, the memory, the solid-state drive, the power supply, the video pad, and the case of the computer.

So as to select the hardware when building the custom-built gaming personal computers, the individuals normally look up to independent benchmarks. There are some organizations that help in providing these benchmarks and reviews on hardware. These include Tom's hardware guide. These organizations help in providing ratings for personal computer components that are important in building these gaming computers. The person building the computer also has to consider the cooling system of the computer, which will help in eliminating waste heat that is normally produce by the components of the gaming computer.

Figure 4.10. *Above is a PS4 console that is used by gamers all over the world.*

Source: https://grantech.co.ke/product/sony-playstation-4-pro/.

Despite the fact that there are many gamers who choose to build their own personal computers, there are others who prefer to go with those that are pre-built. These, however, can be much more expensive in comparison to building your own computer. For these pre-build computers, there are many different companies that offer a wide variety of customization. There are some companies that offer case designs that are unique and very little customization for the user before the computer is bought, while others allow for a higher level of customization as well as higher value for your money, almost similar to if one had chosen to build the gaming computer themselves (LaMarco, 2019).

There are some disadvantages to building your own computer. When one builds their own computer that means that the responsibility for any problems that may occur is theirs. These problems may occur during assembly of the computer and even after assembly when it has been used regularly. This is in comparison to buying a pre-built computer and having a hotline for technical support to help in covering the entire system. When you build your own computer, one will have to deal with manufacturers of individual components.

Complement manufacturers are often inconsistent regarding purchasing the components you need to build your computer, and due to this, it can be hard to get support if your computer gets any problems. This is one of the main reasons why gamers normally get the advice of a system integrator for their custom-built personal computers. Choosing to build your own computer system may have many advantages as well. One of these includes no longer having to follow specific configurations. It is also much cheaper to build your own computer in comparison to one that has been pre-built, allowing one to save quite a lot of money. When building your own computer, each individual piece of hardware has its own warranty in comparison to the pre-build system that has one warranty for the entire system which can only last between one and two years (LaMarco, 2019).

4.7. FOR DESIGNING

Designs that are aided by computers use computers to help in creating, modifying, analyzing, or optimizing designs. There are software's for computer-aided designs that are used in increasing the designer productivity, improving design quality, improving the level of communication due to enhanced documenting, and creating a database for the manufacture of these designs. Computer-aided designs are normally created in the form of files that are electronic, so as to be able to print, machine, or other operations for manufacture.

Figure 4.11. *Computers are used on a daily basis to design different works of art such as posters, graphic images, etc.*

Source: https://laptopshunt.com/best-laptop-for-graphic-design/amp/.

Electronically sign automation of the files to the designing of electronic systems. Mechanical design automation is used in mechanical design. It includes being able to create a technical drawing using a specific computer software.

Using computer-aided design software for mechanical design requires the use of graphics that are vector based, so as to allow the depiction of objects that are of traditional drafting, or also to ensure production of raster graphics so as to ensure the main appearance of the objects that have been designed. This, however, is much more than just the shapes. Computer-aided design must also give out information, such as the process that was used, the materials that were used, the dimensions of the design, and how much the design can tolerate, according to conventions that our application specific. This means that computer-aided design is more than just the shapes (Singh et al., 2016).

Computer-aided design can help in designing curves and figures that are in two dimensions or solids, curves and surfaces that are in three dimensions. Computer-aided design is highly used for many different applications, especially in industrial design. It has been used in architecture, the design of prosthetics, shipbuilding, aerospace industries, etc. It has also been used for the creation of computer animations for special-effects in advertising, movies, etc. This is normally referred to a digital content creation.

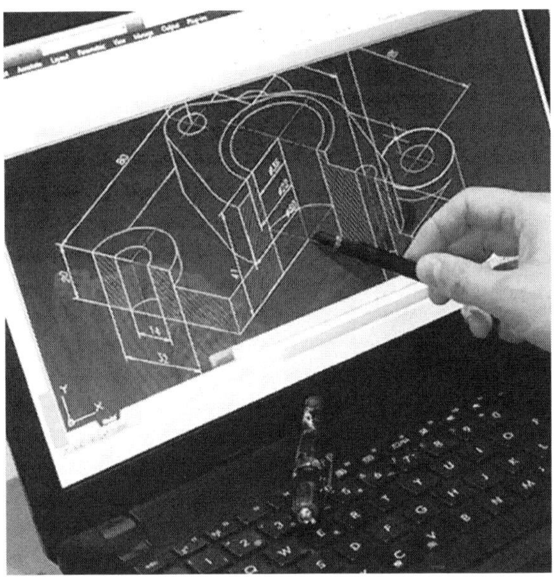

Figure 4.12. *Above shows a structure that has been drawn using computer-aided design.*

Source: https://www.mountainviewcollege.edu/cd/ce/cepgms/computer/pages/cad.aspx.

These days, computer-aided design has also been used to create and design perfume bottles and dispensers for shampoo. These are uses of the computer that many engineers from the 1960s may not know about. Due to the fact that the computer-aided design has shown a great economic importance, there is a lot of research that is being done by computer engineers on the hardware and software of computer graphics and competition geometry. This is actually more specific on their geometric model designs for the shapes of objects in particular (Singh et al., 2016).

Engineers and designers use computer-aided design almost every day of their lives in many different ways. This is dependent on the profession that the user is in and the different types of software's that are used. Computer-aided design can be used together with many other tools which have either been models that have been integrated or products that stand alone, because they are just a part of the whole digital product development activity that is used in different management processes. It can be used to give instructions to computer numerical control machines and manage document and control revision when using product data management. It can also be used to create photo simulations that are accurate and often required in reports on the impacts of the environment. This is done when simulations of building are superimposed into pictures of buildings that already exist, so as to see the consequences of these actions. Analysis of how view corridors can be blocked and shadow studies are done using computer-aided design.

Engineers have also found computer-aided design very helpful. Four of the properties that they use in computer-aided design include features, history, parameterization, and high-level constraints.

The history of any construction can be used to go back into their features of the model and also allow one to work on a specific area instead of the whole model.

Constraints and parameters can be used to ensure the size, shape, and other components of the different elements that were used in the model. Computer-aided design systems and also help in checking the measurement of certain tools that are used in engineering designs such as: electrical, tensile strength, your strength and electromagnetic properties. Computer-aided design can also help in creating simulations on how certain elements can affect different constructions such as stress, temperatures, humidity, etc (Singh et al., 2016).

4.8. FOR EDUCATION PURPOSES

Computers are now more than often used in education and this has been increasing at a steady rate and has greatly revolutionized traditional education. These days, teachers and students benefit greatly from computers in the classroom.

Of the many valuable resources in the education sector, computers have become one of them because they help in performing many different functions. Students have been able to a great wealth of information which they can access almost instantaneously due to computers and the Internet. This helps in developing their skills in communication and research while also helping them prepare for their careers in the future, where they will be having to work in a workforce that is greatly relying on computer technology (Singh et al., 2016).

Figure 4.13. *Computers are used widely in schools to make education more interesting for the younger generations that have grown up using computers.*

Source: https://www.gettyimages.com/detail/photo/serious-student-using-computers-in-school-computer-royalty-free-image/115616757.

Utilizing educational software and programs has become one of the most common uses of computers in the classroom today. This software's and programs have helped in facilitating online instructions that are personalized for students. Students can be assessed in reading and math using programs such as iReady. The students are then able to use these programs to do interactive reading and math lessons that have been designed in a specific manner, to allow the targeting of the students specific academic needs which have already been previously diagnosed using testing.

Search software helps in simplifying the method of differentiating instructions, so as to ensure that each students unique learning needs are met. Teachers are also able to maximize learning and working with the students in the class, due to these tools being able to provide a lot of data that is useful, as well as resources that the students can use to learn. Assessing the students using online tests is also much more efficient in comparison to paper testing because it allows for the teachers to get feedback and data that is almost immediate (Amuno, 2019).

Due to the development of computer technology, computers have now proven to be important in more than just a primary and secondary education classroom. Higher education is much more available now more than ever. There are many online classes that are offered by colleges and universities, and there are some that even allow for the students to complete a degree program all exclusively online. All this makes it easier for students with special needs such as single parents and those who are working, to proceed with their education from the comfort of their homes and even at their own pace.

There are many benefits of using computers in the classroom. These benefits are much more than efficiency and online learning opportunities. Being able to use computers in the classroom allows teachers to teach the students on citizenship skills that are digital and demonstrates the correct ways to use technology in a responsible manner. This is important considering the fact that many people own mobile devices and technologies, but this does not mean that they are able to naturally understand how to appropriately use these forms of technology.

Computers have also helped to improve and ensure maximum student engagement. Students of these days are exposed to a lot of technology even when they are not inside the classroom. They also enjoy using smartphones and other technology. The interest in technology can help in improving their engagement in the learning process as long as it involves subjects that they are accustomed to and enjoy doing (Singh et al., 2016).

Figure 4.14. *Teachers are now able to personalize their lessons with computers, also making the students much more engaged.*

Source: https://education.cu-portland.edu/blog/classroom-resources/6-strategies-for-teaching-special-education-classes/.

Computers in the classrooms not only help the students but also the teachers. They are able to use the computers to make it easier to do different tasks such as recording grades, calculating student averages, managing class attendance and also accessing student data on performance in programs and assessments that they do online. Teachers are also able to change their ways of delivering instructions due to computers. They are able to use technology in their lessons to ensure that the students remain engaged, instead of lecturing in front of the students for a full class period. This helps in providing a number of different learning styles which will then ensure that the students do not get bored. This can be done by creating presentations using visual media such as video clips and photos to add onto the lesson at hand. This also helps in making it easier for the students to understand the content.

Despite all these advantages there are some disadvantages in having computers in the educational center. Computers may cause distractions to the students because they allow the students to be distracted with applications such as games, chats, or videos which can prevent them from finishing their work. This, however, can be avoided using some settings that are available in educational computers that the teachers and parents can use to set restrictions so as to reduce the level of destruction (LaMarco, 2019).

Computers can also make the students over-rely on technology. There are many critics that states that some computer features such as spell-check and AutoCorrect can make students lazy to learn and ensure application of these rules on their own. But if you look at this in a positive way, these features may help students know when they are wrong and this helps to provides an opportunity for the student to learn and enhance the spelling and punctuation. There are much more advantages of using computers in the classroom compared to the disadvantages.

4.9. USES IN BUSINESS AND MARKETING

Computers of been able to speed up the processes and systems that as used in business. They are used in starting both online and offline businesses. Computers have become important in automating the process of manufacturing, marketing and distributing business facilities.

Computers have been able to help increase the productivity in the workplace at a cost that is lower, with lower times and much higher quality. They have helped in ensuring processes that are done in the business sector are done in a much more efficient manner including: producing, distributing, marketing, banking, researching, management of teams, management of employees, and automation of the business. Profits are generated and managed by the computer in the workplace or in any business (LaMarco, 2019).

Figure 4.15. *Online marketing has become a popular way to market products and services in the business sector.*

Source: https://www.tncedunews.com/2019/06/applications-of-computers-in-todays-area.html.

Computer applications such as Microsoft Excel, PowerPoint, MS Word, etc., have helped businesses in managing, calculating, arranging, and visualizing any data and information that is provided by the customers.

They have also helped in promoting fast communication with customers by using Internet phone systems, the Internet itself, and any other tools for communication that are found online. Management of resources and opportunities is also done by computers in any business.

Computers have also helped in creating materials that are used to market and advertise businesses by using applications such as Adobe Photoshop and other tools that are found online for designing marketing strategies. Businesses are also able to create websites so as to allow easier access to their customers. Business transactions are also made easier by computers due to methods such as online banking. This helps to automate business transactions.

Anyone who would like to start a business, always uses a computer. The computer can be used to decide on business ideas by using the Internet to search for these ideas and also facts on the business one wants to start. This is done on sites such as Google. There are over a million people who are always on the Internet daily for new business ideas, business opportunities, part-time business ideas, computer business ideas, etc. There are many other questions to do with business that are also searched on the Internet such as start-ups for different businesses. All this is done on the Internet because it is much easier and faster to find accurate information on all these questions (Amuno, 2019).

Figure 4.16. *Businesses can also advertise on online platforms such as YouTube.*

Source: https://www.oberlo.com/blog/youtube-ads-beginners-launch-first-campaign/amp.

Businesses have to market and advertise so as to remain relevant. Marketing and advertising is very important for owners who own small businesses and those who are bases at home, for them to be able to survive this hard market. They are required to market and advertise their materials almost every day. However, in order to create material that they can use to market and advertise, it is important for them to use applications that are found on the computer and are used in the designing of such material such as: Microsoft Office, Adobe Photoshop, etc. It is very difficult to accurately and efficiently create marketing material without a computer. By marketing materials one means business cards, images, billboards, slideshows, etc.

Business owners also use computers to hire employees. They have to use computers to be able to access the Internet, so as to run websites that they can use to advertise job opportunities to the public. Considering the fact that the generation of today mostly looks for their job opportunities online. It has proven time saving and convincing to hire employees and remote workers through online job portals and Freelance websites. Business owners have found it much more time saving to hire workers on the Internet on a price that is fixed, and hourly, which helps in also reducing the costs of conducting physical interviews (LaMarco, 2019).

4.10. FOR STORING IMPORTANT DATA

Technology has made it possible and easier to store our information and data. Advancements in technology equipment has also helped in providing methods that are much more systematic and improved on implementing and managing information that his computer related. Considering the fact that almost everyone uses a computer and relies heavily on them for many different tasks, development and research has been greatly considered and effected so. to improve the computer system. Computers are greatly used for process flow systems. They are used to store, process, protect, secure, transmit, receive, and retrieve information. For all these tasks to be done, the computer needs a couple of software and hardware back up procedures so as to efficiently work (Barry, 2015).

Figure 4.17. *Above are some of the common online data services that users can use to store data.*

Source: https://www.lemmymorgan.com/online-data-storage-services/amp/.

Data storage is one of the main components of a personal computer. It is used to store and read data or information. There are two main forms of computer duster age. This includes the primary storage in the secondary storage. The primary storage is directly accessible to the central processing unit and the secondary storage is referred to as the external memory. They hard disk drive is the main form of external storage that is used by many people right now globally.

Hard disk drives and portable devices have shown to be efficient for many people, as they can be connected to the computer using a fire wire cable. They, however, have a capacity and accessibility that is quite limited. Most small and medium scale businesses prefer to use a file-level computer data storage because they have a much bigger and demanding storage need.

One of the new methods of storing data that has gained a lot of popularity because it allows for there to be convenient sharing of data between different computers is the network attached storage. This is a storage device that is connected to a network of computers so as to be able to give data access to more than one client. Considering the fact that it is a network resource that is shared, all computers are able to fully access it. This means that the storage is used depending on their real time needs of each individual. As long as a device is recognized by the network, it is possible to add an expansion device to the system at any time. This storage drive is much more preferred over the other devices. It helps in providing the client with a storage that is efficient and flexible without having to depend on a data server that has to be added. Also helps in providing businesses with superior data protection (Amuno, 2019).

4.11. FOR GETTING INFORMATION USING THE INTERNET

This refers to being able to get information for research on the World Wide Web or resources that are Internet-based. The manner in which ideas are formed and knowledge undergoes creation has been impacted greatly by Internet research. Many people use the Internet to research on different issues such as personal questions (probably something heard on the news or from a friend), schoolwork, academic projects and papers, journalism, and even just researching for different stories. In other words, everyone looks up things on the web daily. It involves identifying a specific topic and putting in effort to find information on this specific topic so as to further understand it. It can also be done to improve the quality and synthesis of information.

Figure 4.18. *Above are some of the main online searching platforms. Google is one of the main and mostly used platforms.*

Source: https://sites.google.com/site/internet65658/zanimljivosti.

Searching on the Internet can allow for one to gain information on many different topics at a fast rate. This can be done by being able to also open different pages of the same topic at the same time and also search for different aspects of a specific topic. Individuals are also able to access different experts for information in different fields due to some facilities such as emails, online forums for discussions, and even other personal communication facilities such as instant messaging (Smith, 2013).

Being able to find information on the Internet has made it easier in comparison to doing research using library resources. The Internet allows one to access this information just by typing a few words and clicking search, in comparison to going to the library and finding a specific book so as to find specific information on a certain topic. The Internet can allow one to such on many different topics at the same time in a matter of seconds.

Despite the fact that results that are provided by the Internet after a search may be biased, the information provided is quick, immediate and very vast considering the fact that there are millions of articles on each topic. This, however, makes it hard to verify the credentials of any writer and this makes the accuracy of the information very debatable. Researching on the Internet also depends on the sufficient skills of a searcher to find results that are meaningful from the abundant material that is found on the Internet. The results that show up first on the Internet may not be the specific results that one may want to use to answer a particular question. Normally, the Internet structures results in terms of the popularity, however, the most popular opinion may not always be the correct one. There is so much knowledge and opinion on many other articles that may not be as popular (Smith, 2013).

When you compare all the different forms of research, library research may have hindrances due to access, commercial research may be expensive to carry out, while Internet research is able to provide high-quality and abundant information while being able achieve to avoid a biased opinion. This is because the information environment that occurs in Internet research is not quite mature. It is less sophisticated and not many skills and effort are required to organize the information. Despite the fact that library and commercial environments may be harder to use in research, they invest much more in ensuring that their information is well organized and vetted before providing it to the public.

The internet has many different search tools that can be used to find information. Some of the popular ones include Web search, web directories and Meta search engines. There is a software that the web search engine uses so as to be able to follow the links associated with the search, thus being able to connect the different pages of the World Wide Web. The search engine is the one that indexes and stores this information. Individuals use keywords in a search form so as to be able to access the information on the World Wide Web. The search engine then uses algorithms which consider where the individual is and how many times the keyword has been used on the web page and also the number of links that are pointing to the specific webpage (Smith, 2013).

The Meta search engine allows one to one search question, which it is then able to run against different search engines at the same time. This allows it to create a list of results that are aggregated. Because there is no search engine that can look for information in the whole web, this engine allows for there to be a much more comprehensive search. These engines are equipped with a software that allows then to get rid of results that are duplicate automatically. These engines have disadvantages as they do not include search engines such as Google due to some legal restrictions.

Figure 4.19. *Online research has made work easier for many students all over the world. The internet has a wealth of information.*

Source: https://www.practicweb.com/2015/07/research-on-internet.html.

Web directories are able to use hierarchy to organize information. This allows an individual to search the main keyword, and scroll down for any other links and content that may be important. Directories can use algorithms or handcraft to assemble their information. Those that are edited by humans have an advantage in that they are vetted making the provide information that is of high quality and reliable. Those that are edited by algorithms are much more comprehensive. Yahoo is an example of a Web directory (Smith, 2013).

Individuals are able to find information that is stored in databases using specialty search tools. These cannot be accessed by the other engines. Actually, most of the information that is found on the Web is found in databases which only allow users to access the information by going to a specific site and using a search form. This is normally referred to as the invisible or deep web, because the results of the search are hidden from search engines. Specialty search tools have allowed individuals to access information on the deep web. Technology such as the Virtual Private Library has made it possible for users to access the content on the deep web.

4.12. For Multi-Purpose Use Like Video, Songs, Photos, etc.

Computers are equipped with multimedia software that helps in achieving purposes such as videos, songs and photos. This is a type of software which helps in the combining of texts, audio, videos and image files. It helps to enhance any form of text document by adding photos that are interesting, chats, animations and also graphics. It gives the user an opportunity to use this software without having to have computer skills. This software can help in providing entertainment in addition to being useful.

It gives individuals the chance to listen to different songs, play music, add speech recordings and even make interesting sound effects. Computers that have this software make it possible for one to listen to legit pronunciations of phrases, listen to sounds from animals or songs from musical, see artwork from all over the world and even hear music from famous composers as well as watching movies (Amuno, 2019).

Multimedia allows one to choose from a wide selection of choices that the individual can enjoy, and this is one of its benefits. It can also be quite advantageous in different fields such as science and technology, history, geography, sports, arts, health and medicine, etc. This software normally requires a large storage and can be obtained in the format of a CD.

Figure 4.20. *Above are some of the devices that we use to achieve videos, audios, etc..*

Source: https://www.123rf.com/photo_111770329_stock-vector-electronics-computers-or-multimedia-and-smart-devices-icons-vector-pc-monitor-or-desktop-computer-wi.html.

Multimedia has been used to revolutionize the field of education. It has been able to ensure that education is much more attractive and efficient especially now in the modern terms. It has been used to provide information in either still or moving pictures, sound, etc. which makes students much more interested in learning. It has also allowed people to even learn more and more while staying in the house through different software's.

Multimedia technology has also helped in improving the field of entertainment. Many people all around the world watch television, listen to the radio, use record players, etc. almost on a daily basis. There are also many people who use computers to play games and draw pictures and this is also part of multimedia technology. These days, people are also able to online even using video calls (Amuno, 2019).

As mentioned above, computers have also been used to develop videos, pictures, radio presentations, etc. so as to increase sales in different companies which helps in marketing. They use this information to relay issues on the terms of sales, prices and discounts, usage, etc. of their products and services that they are promoting so as to be able to distribute to the end-user. what's up this is normally done on a compact disc ROM software. It pushes buyers to purchase these products because they are aware of the price, terms of sale, where the items are being sold, etc.

People are able to use audio and video-conferences to have meetings. Computers together with electronic bases communication has helped businesses and even other people socially, politically, economically, and internationally to communicate and ensure that different activities done.

Doctors have also been able to advise their patients when they are at home due to the use of multimedia through computers in videos, audio calls, etc. It has also made it easier to diagnose diseases and also prescribe medication.

Videos and audios have also made it easier for students to learn especially during research. There are many educational videos that are found on the Internet that can help a student do their research work without having to read a lengthy article or booklet.

These days we are able to interact with an environment that has been stimulated by computers due to virtual reality technology. This simulation can be very similar to the world that we know. It has helped in the medical field where doctors are able to simulate surgeries for training and even for pilots who use simulations to learn how to fly. It is based on multimedia bounder technology (Amuno, 2019).

Chapter 5

History of Computer Science

CONTENTS

5.1. INTRODUCTION

Computer Science refers to the study of digital computing and computational structures. Unlike electrical and PC engineers, computer researchers deal generally with programming and software products; this incorporates their hypothesis, plan, creation, and application. Some primary sectors of study in Computer Science are artificial intelligence, computer frameworks and structures, security, database units, human computer communication, and programming languages among other fields.

Although learning how to code is fundamental to computer science practice, it's just one component of the sector. Computer scientists plan and analyze calculations to solve programs, while pondering the execution of PC hardware and software. Some issues that computer researchers experience vary from the theoretical-- deciding what issues can be unraveled using computers plus the intricacy of the algorithms which unravel them – to the substantial – planning applications that work well on handheld gadgets, which are simple to operate, and that maintain security factors. Currently, computer science ranks as the third most prevalent study subject among international scholars going to the U.S. There are numerous reasons why computer science is widely popular, such as high job security, impressive beginning salaries, and various job prospects across industries.

Generally talking, computer science refers to the study of digital technology, both firmware and software. Nevertheless, computer science is a multifaceted field; some of its necessary skills are valid and in-demand across almost every industry in the modern digital world. Consequently, the sector of computer science is subdivided amongst multiple sub-disciplines, some of which are complete specialized disciplines by themselves such as bioinformatics, robotics, cryptography and memory systems to mention a few.

5.2. EARLY COMPUTATION

The earliest record of computation was a device known as Abacus, also called the counting frame. It's a mechanical gadget used to help an individual in performing numerical estimations and checking. Despite the fact that it's as yet obscure who fabricated the original device and when it got constructed. There is proof of the math device being utilized in Mesopotamia way back during 2700 B.C., for application with their sexagesimal numerical framework. The math device was likewise utilized in other early societies, including the Egyptian, Greek, Medo-Persia, and Roman empires. Before computer systems, calculators, and even arithmetic through paper and pencil, the abacus became the top superior tool for crunching numbers. Prior to it, the best strategies humans had to apply for their calculations was their palms and toes, and even stones within the dirt (O'Regan, 2012).

Figure 5.1. *The first computers were bulky and consumed a lot of power during operation.*

Source: http://bzupages.com/f185/brief-history-computer-eniac-1946-ti-ipad-2010-action-speaks-louder-than-words-9298/.

5.2.1. How to Use It?

Before learning to utilize the math device, realize there are distinctive sorts of abacus. For illustration, the classical math device or Chinese abacus consists of five globules on the base and a pair of beads at the apex. The present-day abacus, Japanese math device, or soroban has 4 beads at the foot and one globule at the apex. The upper beads are known as "Heavenly beads" and are worth 5 beads within the preliminary column. The lower beads, on the other hand, are known as "Earthly beads" which are each worth at least one bead within the first column. While moving a bead on to the central bar (reckoning bar), it is consider numbered and when there is no bead touching this bar then the column is akin to zero.

The separation between dots and rancid-colored beads will depend on the abacus, though they are always applied to split numbers into units of 3. These markers may also mark your original position if you no longer wish to start counting starting from the far-right. The beads values begin inside the right 1's column, these are beads valued from between 1 to 9. Moving from right-to-left, these beads values rise to the 10's position, 100's position, 1000's position, and so on (O'Regan, 2016).

5.2.2. Analytical Engines

These were invented by engineer Charles Babbage in 1834. He designed two categories of engine, Difference and Analytical Engines. The former engines are so-referred due to the numerical precept on which they're based, particularly, the technique of finite variations. The splendor of the technique is that it utilizes only effective arithmetical addition and gets rid of the need for multiplying and division that are much harder to execute automatically.

Difference engines are calculators. They decipher numbers the only means they know how – through rehashed addition agreeing to the strategy of limited contrasts. They can't be utilized for common arithmetical calculation. Instead, the Analytical Motor is way more than any calculator plus it marks the movement from the mechanized formula of calculation to full-fledged all-purpose computation. There were around three plans at distinctive phases of the advancement of his thoughts. Thus, it is entirely correct to allude to these Analytical Engines in plural form (O'Regan, 2016).

5.2.3. Binary, Decimal, and Fault Detection

Babbage's computing engines are decimal numerical machines. They're decimal because they utilize the commonplace 10 numbers '0' to '9'. Howeve, they are also computerized and hence entire numbers are perceived as legitimate. Numerical values are marked by a gear wheel, plus every digit of an integer has its unique wheel. In case a wheel stops in a position middle between entire number qualities, the figure is viewed as uncertain plus the motor is intended to stick to demonstrate that the respectability of the estimation has been undermined. Sticking is a type of blunder recognition.

Babbage considered utilizing number frameworks apart from decimal, such as parallel and numerical sets 3, 4, 5, twelve, sixteen and hundred. He went for decimal numbers out of engineering proficiency – to diminish the ratio of moving parts – plus for their ordinary familiarity.

With the construction assignment stalled, and was free of the hustles of any specific creation, Babbage discovered, in 1834, a greater system, later known as an analytical engine, an all-purpose programmable computing engine. The analytical engine has various crucial capabilities found in the present-day digital personal computer. It was programmable through punched cards, a concept borrowed from jacquard loom that is used for weaving complicated patterns in fabrics. The system had a 'store' whereby numbers and inter-mediate results might be held, plus a separate 'mill' whereby the mathematics processing was finished (O'Regan, 2016).

It had an inner catalog of the 4 arithmetical roles and could execute instant multiplication and division. It was further capable of functions that we have more modern names like: conditional branching, iteration, microprogramming, corresponding processing, and latching amongst others, even though Babbage never used these terms specifically.

There were also a range of outputs such as hard-copy printout, punched cards, graphics plotting and the programmed production of stereotypes – layers of soft material whereby results were impressed which could be applied as molds for creating printing plates.

The logical configuration of the Analytical Machine was essentially similar as that which did dominate computer design during the electronic period – the parting of the memory ('Store') away from the primary processor (the 'Mill'), sequential operation through a 'fetch-execute modus,' and amenities for inputting and exporting data as well as instructions. Naming Babbage 'the original computer pioneer' isn't a farfetched tribute (O'Regan, 2016).

5.2.4. The Hollerith Machine

It was invented in 1890 by Hollerith Herman, who was an engineer. Originally called upon by the press, Hollerith's tabulating apparatus integrated an electric sensing components that recorded the numerals of holes at particular locations in non-conductive material which do not carry any electrical charge.

Signals were transferred only when electrical wave passed through the hole inside the card, creating a closed circuit. Then rolls of punched tape were applied as the non-conducting substance, but later Hollerith swapped to cards which were the same dimension as dollar bills during that time; this adjustment allowed him to integrate cash storage cases into his apparatus later on. Patents and selling of his tabulating machine among other discoveries made Hollerith famous during his time. In 1911, the official Calculating-Tabulating-Recording Firm (CTR) was invented courtesy of his works (O'Regan, 2016).

5.3. ANALOG COMPUTERS

The analog workstation is a computer that is used to record analog data. These computers store information in a continuous system of physical quantities, plus perform calculations through the help of measurements. It's quite different compared to digital computers, which widely make use of figurative numbers to symbolize results. Analog processers are excellent for cases which require information to be measured straight without converting into numbers or codes. Analog processers, though available and applied in industrial and research applications such as control structures and aircraft, have mostly been replaced by arithmetical computers due to a wide variety of complexities involved (Tedre, 2014).

Figure 5.2. *Analog computers were rudimentary and only performed basic functions*

Source: https://hackaday.com/2019/09/23/secrets-from-a-1969-analog-computer/.

These computers were the original computer machines established and were among the most complex apparatuses for analog calculation and process control. Analog data is not a discrete, but rather a continuous process. Examples of such information are pressure, voltage, temperature, speed and weight. Furthermore, an analog computer utilizes continuous values though not discrete values. Due to this, processes involving analog computer cannot be repeated for precise equivalent results. Different from digital computers, analog ones are resistant to quantization sound. Some of the typical computing elements available in equivalent computers are system generators, integrators, and multipliers among others.

Reliant on the application, some specialized components might also be used. Encoding on an analog workstation involves conversion of the problematic calculations into the analog processer circuit.

There are various advantages associated with analog PCs. Real-time processing and simultaneous computation is possible with the help of analog computers. Analog workstations can also provide quick insight of the issues and errors in the case of a miscalculation by analog users (Tedre, 2014).

5.3.1. Precursors

Modern age analog computing machine was known as The Dumaresq and it was a mechanical computing device invented in 1902 John Dumaresq from the Royal Navy. Basically, it was an analog processer which paired vital features of the fire management problem onto the movement or operation of a targeted ship. It was frequently used together with other devices, like a Vickers range clock for generating range and deflection rates such that the ammo sights of the vessel could be constantly set. A wide variety of Dumaresq versions were produced of growing complexity as creation proceeded.

In 1912 Pollen had established an electrically run mechanical analog PC for fire-control structures, depending on the variance analyzer. It was applied by the Russian Navy during World War I. Moreover, beginning in 1929, AC system analyzers were built to solve calculation glitches related to electrical systems which were too big to solve using numerical methods during the time. They were essentially scale replicas of the electrical functions of the whole-size system (Tedre, 2014).

Since system analyzers could handle glitches too large for diagnostic methods or physical computation, they were further used to solve glitches in nuclear physics as well as in designing of structures. Well over 50 massive network analyzers were constructed by the finish of the 1950s.

Later in 1942 Helmut Hölzer constructed a fully-electronic analog device at Peenemünde Army Exploration Center, being as an implanted control system to measure V-2 rocket propulsions from the speeding up and orientations, plus for stabilizing and guiding the missile. Motorized analog computers were key in gunfire management in World War II, Korean War plus well past Vietnam War as well; they were developed in significant quantities.

In 1945 in the Netherlands, Johan Veen established an analog processor for calculating and predicting tidal currents once the channels geometry is changed. By 1950, this same idea was further assimilated into the Deltar, an analog workstation supporting the closing functions of estuaries found in the southwestern parts of the Netherlands (Tedre, 2014).

5.3.2. Electronic Analog

Electronic analog computers are also known as polish analog PC AKAT-1 EAI 8800. Physical computing systems were applied for certain hardware-in-the-loop simulations of Claas tractors. The resemblance between linear mechanical constituents, such as springs and dashpots, plus electrical components, like capacitors, inductors, as well as resistors is outstanding in regards to mathematics. These can be modeled through equivalences of the same nature.

Nevertheless, the variance between these structures is what essentially makes analog computing valuable. If one contemplates a simple mass–spring structure, assembling the physical system shall require making or amending the springs plus masses. This will be followed by fastening them to one another and a suitable anchor, gathering test equipment bearing the suitable input range, plus finally, taking measurements. For more complicated cases, like suspensions for race cars, experimental construction, adjustment, and testing can be both complex and costly. The electrical equivalent may be developed with only a few working amplifiers including some passive linear modules (O'Regan, 2016).

These measurements may be taken instantly using an oscilloscope. Within the circuit, the (virtual) 'spring stiffness,' for example, may be altered by regulating the capacitor parameters. The electrical structure is an analogy for the physical system, thus the name, but it's less costly to construct, normally safer, plus much easier to amend. Also, an electronic circuit may typically function at greater frequencies compared to the system that's being simulated. It allows the simulation a much faster run compared to real time that could, in some cases, be several hours, weeks, or much longer. Practiced users of electric analog computers commented that they provided a comparatively intimate management and comprehension of the problem, comparative to digital models. The downside of the mechanical-electrical equivalence is that electronics often are restricted by the range through which the variables can because of the stationary supply voltage. As such, each problem must be scaled down to its essential parameters and dimensions, for instance, the anticipated scales of the velocity as well as the location of spring pendulum. Poorly scaled problems may suffer from greater noise levels. Additionally, floating-point numerical calculations have a vast dynamic range though may also suffer from inaccuracy if small differences of vast values cause numerical instability (O'Regan, 2016).

The electric circuits might also easily implement a wide range of simulations. Case in point, voltage can mimic water pressure while electric current can copy rate of flow with regards to cubic metres a second. Furthermore, an integrator might provide the average accumulated capacity of liquid, through an input current relative to the potentially varying flow rate.

5.4. HISTORY OF ALGORITHMS

From early civilizations to modern cryptographers, algorithms have advanced meticulously, preserving the essence of procedures somewhat intact. Through definition, an algorithm may be termed as a pre-defined, autonomous set of instructions essential for executing diverse functions. These rules date as far back as 300 BC, where they were often found written on Babylonian tablets. Basic algorithms were often regarded as marking schemes which the ancient people used to maintain track of, with regards to their livestock and grain stock. It was followed by invention of the numerical system, plus a subsequent progression of abacus, algebra plus variables followed, opening way to the rise of symbols and procedures involved in developing evaluation systems (O'Regan, 2016).

Figure 5.3. *Persian scholar Al-Khwarizmi is regarded as the father of modern algorithms.*

Source: https://www.bbc.com/ideas/videos/why-algorithms-are-called-algorithms/p07gdlwf.

Algorithms get their place in PC programs and automated applications. The genesis of the word is credited to the Persian astronomer and statistician, Abu Abdullah Al-Khwarizmi (c. 850 AD). The scholar's works included presenting the decimal positioning in arithmetic structures to the West, alongside the first ever methodical formulation of direct and quadratic equations. Within its original, basic form, algorithms, also called algorism, was viewed as policies for computing calculations plus performing arithmetic using Hindu-Arabic numerals. Far along, with the Latin rendition of Al-Khwarizmi's name, the algorisms set fixed standards for doing computations for executing tasks.

Nevertheless, algorithms that are known today were just put into effect with the arrival and rise of automated engineering and processes. Within its original context, algorithms gave a foundation to the logic algebra, applying variables in calculations. Among the earliest examples of algorithms were Euclid's function of highest joint divisor in numeric, including Archimedes' estimation of Pi, plus Eratosthenes' estimation of prime numbers. Nevertheless, the first individual to use the original form of the word algorithm was twelfth-century English theorist, Adelard de Bath, he used the phrase algorismus when interpreting Al-Khwarizmi's Arabic workings.

A pivotal series of achievements for the progression of algorithms emerged during the 1800s, with the first one recognized by English statistician George Boole, he further coined Laws of Thought in algorithm and developed Boolean-Algebra. By 1847, Boole had integrated logic with arithmetic and developed binary algebra, which is the foundation of computing judgment of today. Moreover, in 1888, Giuseppe Peano founded the axiomatization of math. He applied equations using symbols to achieve results. These would thereafter go on to grow into rules which modern day arithmetic and algorithms are founded on (Tedre, 2014).

Years later, present algorithms came into effect with Alan Turing's calculation machine. It soon became the calculating correspondent of Turing Machines, whereby a variable was tied to specific tasks or executable equations for carrying out operations. Turing's PC model was based upon the concept of a human PC and "frames of mind" or situations, whereby functions inscribed down in symbols may find application. It was further divided down into simple squares, each contributing to certain operations.

All these plain squares would conceive a symbol, plus each symbol may be finite within its own form and relativity. A PC's action would rely upon the score of logic – with each of the symbols functioning as tads of data, with the computer's "frame of mind" serving as the condition or resolve of the function that's being executed. Turing further enforced a limit on the amount of symbols being calculated at the same instance, and calculating more complex logic shall require the device to execute same, successive operations. Every one of these processes, hence, shall be the most basic unit within the launch 'code.' An encryption would be the whole compilation of the class of functions, or algorithm, upon which an issue would be solved (O'Regan, 2016).

5.4.1. Algorithm as the Foundation of Modern Computers

Turing's algorithm logic also set down the groundwork for operations concerning variable factors, whereby a subsequent symbol could be altered depending on the computation system between two previous symbols. In basic terms, when a role between dual variables are executed, then the resulting would be the number that would be applied in calculating with the subsequent variable, thus giving rise to liberal algorithms that place into account shifting values to calculate a code. If necessary, these operations shall also define the result, shifting the "frame of mind" or precincts of a calculation.

In the meantime, the groundwork set by Alan Turing was refined upon by another American theorist, John Barkley Rosser. Describing an "effective mathematical process", Rosser claimed that each phase of an algorithm needs to be accurately defined, and not just left to variable consequence chances, with a fixed number of steps for obtaining the result. This, in agreement with the foundation effort put down by Turing, resulted to the necessity for a computing device that would work and execute functions without the requirement for human intervention (Tedre, 2014).

Later, this was trailed by the founding of Kleene's 'Algorithmic Theory' during the year 1943. Kleene mentioned, in developing a whole algorithmic principle, what is to be done is describing a procedure, executable for each group of values touching on the autonomous variables, which procedure essentially terminates and in a way that from the result there can be read a resolute answer, which is "yes" or "no," towards the question.

Kleene's model set up the policy that today's algorithms follow – autonomous, self-sustaining computer functions that would perform functions within a finite group of instructions. Later, this made computing a lot faster, plus with the arrival of private computers from the late 60s, algorithms have witnessed significant improvements (Tedre, 2014).

Current applications of algorithms can be found in almost every single instant of our daily lives. For example, on Smartphone devices, the color stability of photographs caught by its camera may be defined through a group of algorithms, which classifies colors and balances disparities based on a particular scene. With growing processing power, many algorithms have advanced in their complexity as well as levels of computational ability.

The current generation is focused on quantum computing as well as artificial intelligence. Mostly, machine learning relies on algorithms for purposes of "learning" from usage methods, plus to prepare actions depending on personal means of operations. The society is also at the brink of time whereby 'bots' are seeking to replace apps that we use on a daily basis (Tedre, 2014).

5.5. THE DEVELOPMENT OF BINARY LOGIC

5.5.1. Most Modern Computers

Even though Gottfried Leibniz has been credited with the invention of binary as it is known today, the original logic-based appliances were formed by Charles Babbage. The first Difference Engine to be made was a mechanical calculator constructed to formulate polynomial equations and display the outcomes on a piece of paper. However, digital logic as it is known today required association from 1000s of people spanning thousands of years. Prior to the creation of electronic devices, statisticians and philosophers were mistakenly generating the code of binary and setting up the basis for modern computing appliances (Reilly, 2003).

Figure 5.4. *Binary Logic relies on zero and one codes for command processing.*

Source: https://sites.psu.edu/historicalcharacters/2016/12/02/the-escapades-of-leibniz/.

These theories were later used in similar communication systems such as Morse Code plus the binary which we are accustomed with today. Statisticians like George Boole as well as Charles Babbage used these concepts in mechanical devices to mechanize them. While computing bears a rich past, the logic gates which allow PCs to function receive less attention.

5.5.2. Antique Logic and Binary

During the tenth century in China, a researcher named Shao Yong reorganized the hexagrams taken from I-Ching into a form that is similar to binary. There are scholars who even propose that the I-Ching was Gottfried Leibniz's motivation for binary code. Furthermore, there were truth tables during ancient Greece bearing YES and NO functions such as ON and OFF for the instance of transistors.

Leibniz probably found encouragement from Greek mathematicians since their works were quite accessible to scholars in Europe in the 17th as well as 18th centuries. There as well was the small, secluded Polynesian islet of Mangareva that used a binary number system to assist with mental arithmetic. A number of ancient civilizations had arithmetic systems with resemblances to binary like we know it currently. Whether Leibniz got inspiration from one of these ancient systems still remains one of the great mysteries of history. The study of primeval mathematics plus binary is quite interesting, though it also helps in tempering one's expectations as well as get prepared for information that's out there (Reilly, 2003).

5.5.3. From Mechanical Binary to Digital Logic

Even though Gottfried Wilhelm Leibniz has been credited with the invention of binary in a form that we know today, original logic based equipment were developed by Charles Babbage. The inventor's first Difference Engine was basically a mechanical calculator planned to tabulate polynomial balances and print out the outcomes on a rolling paper.

In Babbage's strategy, mechanical gears aided the role of logic gates. He invented another Difference Engine, commonly known as Analytical Engine, though could never get funding to actualize it. His designs later were noticed during the 80s and a wholly functional format was finally developed to his specifications (Reilly, 2003).The original widely used logic gates were electro-magnetic relays that were fundamentally ON-OFF controls. The electromechanical switch was designed by Joseph Henry during the year 1835, though the genius of his invention wasn't understood until later when the relays were applied in the telegraph. Following the creation of the rotary disc in 1890, other complex relays with a series of positions were invented.

Later in 1898, Nikola Tesla made a patent for the invention he termed "tele automation," whereby he confirmed with a radio-controlled small boat, the original remote control machine ever developed. The remote control unit contained a system for decrypting Hertzian waves.

The unit would toggle actions depending on different signals, working as a gate. The original digital, programmable electrical devices' logic circuitry was placed in vacuum tubes. It includes prominent computers such as Colossus, ENIAC and Alan Turing's classic Pilot Ace. These original digital computers were vast and carried 1000s of vacuum tubes. For purposes of making computing devices available to the public, basically logic circuitry would have to shrink (Reilly, 2003).

This required decrease in dimension came about in the 60s with resistor-transition logic (RTL) and dual transistor logic (TTL). RTLs became the primary logic gadgets to be integrated into coordinate circuits and were thereafter utilized in the Apollo command computer. The original TTL coordinate circuits were created in 1963 by a scientist called Sylvania and were made popular by TI's 7400 structure. From there, cutting edge logic circuitry has steadily been contracting these concepts and including extra Boolean gates.

5.5.4. Digital Logic Now

Years of development have triggered the development of minor and powerful logic gadgets such as FPGAs, Pico Entryways and PLCs, which permit little gadgets to have mechanical control and command functionality that shadows the gigantic computers of past times. Nowadays, there are minor logic bundles for almost each work possible, whether it arrives in a cluster or a concealed package. In case you would want to discover more on how discrete logic bundles are being miniaturized, you can search on computer websites.

A digital computer framework basically is a mix of double logic and storage components combined in a way that performs a particular valuable task. Any PC system, whether it is a microcomputer handled with one hand for information gathering, or a massive data-processing framework comprising of multiple cabinets of hardware covered in a uniquely built air-conditioned PC room, perpetually contains a blend of different parts working together to deliver optimal performance (Tedre, 2014).

The frame of logic most appropriate for executing electronically is a twofold logic. In double logic, we address as it were just two states. A matter may either be true or untrue: there aren't any half-truths. A number is 1 or 0: there aren't any divisions or alternative values. The transistor is either completely on (saturated) or completely off: it swaps quickly from one condition to the other, using a small amount of time in the middle states. A voltage can either be high or low: but middle values generally have no meaning.

The on-off, top-low features of double logic means that it's possible to plan electronic circuits which can demonstrate coherent statements with outright exactness. Users got to be worried with just two voltage levels, but not with every other conceivable levels which are there in (for illustration) sound circuits. These days, indeed sound circuits are primarily digital but, at the slightest, in their input plus output areas, they have a continuous run of voltage levels within the system (Reilly, 2003).

5.6. FOUNDERS OF MODERN COMPUTING

5.6.1. Charles Babbage

It might be contended that the original computer was called the abacus or even its follower, the slide rule, designed by William Ought red during the year 1622. However, the original computer that resembles present-day machines was called the Analytical Engine, referring to a gadget conceived and invented by UK statistician Charles Babbage between the years 1833 and 1871. However, before Babbage emerged a "computer" was literally an individual, somebody who truly sat all day in the office, calculating numbers and putting in the digits into tables. The tables later showed up in books, such that other individuals might apply them to complete assignments, like propelling artillery shells precisely or calculating taxes (O'Regan, 2016).

Figure 5.5. *British mathematician Charles Babbage is considered the originator of modern computing.*

Source: https://www.britannica.com/biography/Charles-Babbage.

It was, in reality, a huge number-crunching venture that motivated Babbage originally. Napoleon Bonaparte started the venture in 1790, by requesting for a switch from ancient royal frameworks of estimations to the fresh metric framework. For around 10 years, a number of rudimentary computers made the fundamental conversions and finished the tables. Bonaparte wasn't able to distribute the tables, nonetheless, and they laid gathering dust in the libraries in Paris.

In 1819, Charles Babbage visited Paris and checked the unpublished document with consecutive pages of tables. He worried if there was some way of producing such tables much faster, with less effort and fewer errors. He thought of various marvels brought about by Industrialization. If creative and diligent inventors could invent the cotton gin as well as steam engine, why not an instrument to do calculations Campbell thought (O'Regan, 2016).

Babbage came back to Britain and settled on building just such an equipment. His original vision was something that he named the Difference Equipment, which functioned on the rule of limited contrasts, or developing complex scientific calculations through rehashed addition without utilizing duplication or division. He secured state subsidy in 1824 then went through 8 full years rearranging his thoughts. In 1832, he created a working model of his table-matching machine, as it were only to find his financing had been finished. But, as you may have speculated, the story doesn't conclude there.

Some individuals may have been disheartened, but not Babbage. Rather than simplifying his plan to create an easier version of the Difference Engine, he focused his attention towards a grander thought -- the Analytical Machine, a modern type of mechanical device that makes more complicated calculations, plus multiplication and divisions.The fundamental sections of the Analytical Machine resemble the parts of any computer available on the market nowadays. It included two trademarks of any cutting-edge machine: a focal handling unit, or CPU, plus memory. Babbage, definitely, didn't utilize those terms. He named the CPU "mill." On the other hand, memory was termed the "store." He further had a gadget -- the "reader" -- for putting in informational, and a means to record, through paper, outcomes produced by the device. Babbage named this output gadget a printer, being the forerunner of inkjet and digital printers that are so common nowadays (O'Regan, 2016).

Babbage's fresh innovation existed nearly completely on paper. He maintained voluminous notes and outlines around his computers -- roughly 5,000 pages' worth --plus although he never developed a single replica version of the Analytical Equipment, he had a coherent vision around how the machine shall look and function.Borrowing the same innovation applied by the Jacquard machine, a weaving device created in 1804-05 which made it conceivable to develop a range of cloth designs mechanically, information would be included on punched cards.

Around 1,000 50-digit numerals might be held within the same computer's store. Also, punched cards might carry the information, which the device seems execute out of consecutive order. One specialist would supervise the entire operation, though steam would still control it, turning wrenches, transferring cams and poles, plus spinning gearwheels (O'Regan, 2016).

Shockingly, the innovation of the day didn't convey on Babbage's master plan. It wasn't till 1991 that his specific ideas were at long last deciphered into a working computer. It's when the Research Gallery in London finally built, to Babbage's precise details, his Difference Machine. It stood 11 ft long and 7 ft tall, containing 8,000 moving sections and weighing 15 tons (13.6 tons). A duplicate of the device was built and dispatched to the Computer Museum in the region of Mountain View, California, where it stayed on show until December 2010. Not one or the other gadget would work on a desktop, though they are no question the original computers and forerunners to the present-day PC. Plus, those computers impacted on the creation of the Internet as we know it today.

5.6.2. Alan Turing

Turing was an English statistician, computer scientist, theorist, cryptanalyst, logician and theoretical environmentalist. Turing was prominent in the advancement of theory-based computer science, giving a validation of the notions of algorithm and calculation with the Turing device, which may be regarded a prototype of an all-purpose PC. Turing is broadly regarded as the originator of theory-based computer-science as well as artificial intelligence.

In spite of these achievements, he wasn't fully acknowledged back home during his lifetime, since a lot of his inventions were covered by Official Secrets Act and many people weren't aware of them. In World War II, Turing was employed with the State Code and Cypher College at Bletchley Park, the UK's code breaking institute back then that created Ultra intelligence (O'Regan, 2016).

For a while he oversaw Hut 8, the unit responsible for overseeing German naval cryptanalysis. During this time, he devised various techniques for fast-tracking the cracking of German ciphers, as well as advances to the pre-war bombe technique, an electromechanical instrument that was useful in finding tunings for the Enigma equipment. Alan played a key role in breaking intercepted coded communication that allowed the Allies to overthrow the Nazis in various crucial engagements, such as the Atlantic Battle, and by so doing facilitated in winning the war.

Because of the glitches of counterfactual history, sometimes it might be hard to approximate what outcome Ultra Intelligence, which Turing invented, had on the battle. However, it's estimated that his invention helped save well over 14 million people in Europe. Following the war, Turing worked with the National Physical Research Centre, where he developed the Automatic Computing Machine (O'Regan, 2016).

5.7. THE ANALYTICAL ENGINE

Figure 5.6. *Developed by Charles Babbage, this is one of the earliest computers to be invented.*

Source: https://www.ssplprints.com/image/90371/babbages-analytical-engine-1834-1871.

The Analytical Machine was a technical general-purpose processor outlined by English mathematician Charles Babbage. This machine was first portrayed in 1837 where it was marketed as the follower to Babbage's difference machine, a model for a less complex mechanical computer. The Analytical Machine included a numerical logic unit, control stream in form of temporary branching and circles, and integral memory, making it among the original designs for an all-purpose computer which could be portrayed in modern terminology as Turing-complete.

Meaning, the consistent framework of the Analytical Machine was basically similar as that which ruled computer plans within the electronic phase. The Analytical Machine is among the primary accomplishments of Charles Babbage. While he wasn't able to finish the development of his equipment due to misunderstandings with his engineer and insufficient financing. It wasn't until 1941 when the primary all-purpose computer, Z3, got built, around a century after Charles Babbage had suggested the pioneering Analytical Machine in 1837 (O'Regan, 2012).

5.7.1. Design

There are two forms of punched cards applicable in programming of the machine. The first are 'operational cards,' used for entering instructions; and 'variable cards' which are applicable for entering data. Babbage's initial attempt towards developing a mechanical computing system, the Difference Engine, became a special-purpose equipment designed to organize logarithms and trigonometric features by assessing finite differences to develop approximating polynomials.

During this program, he recognized that a much more all-purpose blueprint, the Analytical Machine, was possible. The task of designing the Analytical Engine began in c. 1833. The input, comprising of programs and codes was to be offered to the machine through punched cards, a technique being applied at the moment to determine mechanical looms like the Jacquard loom.As for output, the machine might have a printer, a curve plotter or a bell. The device was also be capable of punching digits onto cards that can be read in much later. It utilized typical base-10 set-point arithmetic. There was supposed to be a storage (that is, memory) able to hold 1,000 numerical of 40 decimal units, with each carrying a capacity of 16.2 kB (O'Regan, 2012).An arithmetic component (the "mill") could be able to achieve all 4 arithmetic operations, including comparisons and temporarily square roots. Originally (1838) it was regarded as a difference machine curved back onto itself, in a rather circular sequence, with the wide store going off to one point. Later drawings (1858) showcase a regularized grid plan.

Just like the CPU in an advanced computer, the mill shall rely upon its unique internal processes, to be kept in the context of pegs implanted into rotating drums known as "barrels," for carrying out a couple of complex commands the user's program may specify. The programming code to be applied by users was similar to present-day assembly communication. Loops and conditional structuring were possible, plus so the dialect as conceived shall have become Turing-complete as consequently described by Alan Turing.There were 3 different kinds of punch cards which were used: arithmetical operations, numerical constants, and another for both load and store processes, moving records from the store over to the numerical unit or back. Using three different readers for different forms of cards, Babbage was able to construct 3 different types of cards. He established some two dozen systems for Analytical Engine technology between 1837-and-1840, with one additional program later. These systems make use of polynomials, iterative formulations, Gaussian exclusion, as well as Bernoulli numbers (Schäfer, 2013).

5.7.2. Instructional Set

Babbage isn't known to have composed any expressive set of directions for the engine similarly to an advanced processor manual. Rather he revealed his projects as records of states amid their execution, revealing what operator system was utilized at each stage with small signs of how the management flow shall be guided. Some researchers have proposed that the slot deck may well be examined in forwards as well as in reverse bearings, as a role of conditional structuring after testing for circumstances, which shall make the motor Turing-complete (Schäfer, 2013).

The introduction initially, in 1845, of operator systems for a range of service models including, most vitally, a viable framework for operator management of looping in controller programs. There's no sign how the course of revolution of the activity and variable slots is indicated. In the nonexistence of other evidence some researchers have had to embrace the negligible default presumption that either the direction and variable slots can as it were be turned in reverse as is vital to actualize the circles used in Babbage's test programs. There won't be any mechanical or micro-programming problem in setting the course of movement under the direction of the operator.

The Engine's Slot Reader isn't constrained to only process the slots in a sequence one after the other from beginning to end. It can, additionally, by coordinated by the very slots it reads and prompted by whether the Mill's revolving lever is actuated, card chain progressed forward, skipping the mediating cards, or in reverse, causing past-read slots to be reworked once again. There are emulators that do provide a composed symbolic instruction manual, even though it's been built by its inventors instead of based upon Babbage's unique works (Schäfer, 2013).

5.7.3. Construction

The development of Babbage's Analytical Machine was finished in 1910, as recorded by the Science Museum in London.

Much later in his life, he sought methods to build a basic version of the appliance, and developed a small portion of it prior to his demise in 1871. Thereafter in 1878, a committee from the UK Association for Development of Science defined the Analytical Machine as "a device of mechanical ingenuity," though recommended against fabricating it.

The committee recognized the practicality and worth of the machine, however, it couldn't appraise the cost of developing it, plus were unsure on if the device would work properly after being developed. Additionally, from 1880 up to 1910, Babbage's son Prevost Henry Babbage began forming a section of the mill plus the printing apparatus. By 1910, the engine was capable of calculating an (estimate) list of manifolds of pi. This comprised of just a small portion of the entire engine; it wasn't programmable plus had no storage though later improvements were made to add these functions.

5.8. BEGINNINGS OF COMPUTER SCIENCE

Figure 5.7. *The earliest computers were used for science and military work.*

Source: https://engineering.case.edu/eecs/about/history.

The modern computer-science era started with Alan Turing's formation of the Turing Device, and triple Bell Labs scientists' discovery of the transistor, that made modern-age computing feasible, and won them the 1956 Physics Nobel Prize. Though the current computing-machine age began with Turing's invention, it was the latter technology by Bell Labs researchers that made present-style computing possible.

For years, computing technology was select to the state and the military; afterward, scholarly institutions came online, plus Steve Wozniak developed the circuit board used for Apple-1, ensuring domestic computing was practicable. As for the network side, Tim Berners-Lee made the World Wide Web, while Marc Andreessen formed the browser, which is how we eventually came to stay in a world whereby a pair of glasses can show us what we're watching. Through wearable devices, embeddable chips, smart apparatuses, and other progresses in technology into the future, the journey towards developing smarter, quicker and more proficient computers is really just starting (Shelly, Freund, &Vermaat, 2010).

Turing was an established statistician and computer researcher. He's frequently presented as the pioneer of computer science—even though it is without a doubt an unsuccessful endeavor to exclusively pinpoint such a pioneer to something which was made collectively. He is known for immense contributions to initial computer science. During the 30s, he developed among the original precise descriptions of a calculation. His point was to research what was "calculable." Duplication, for instance, is calculable since it can be done in a particular number of steps. However, what are calculable issues? It's quite a troublesome question, which was a prevalent theme of research in the 30s, while Turing centered particularly on it. While examining the issue, he developed a theoretical machine—or a device that wasn't planned to be truly built—though which he would utilize to develop his thinking. Envisioning how it worked empowered him to efficiently consider what was calculable plus what wasn't.

This engine was portrayed rather in a very basic manner. It utilized a tape that contained a sequence of boxes which stored information (0s and 1s). The device was able to examine what was inside the boxes, transfer from left to right upon the tape, and type in a box. Through this device, Turing proved that it was conceivable to supplant any other machine, through composing the "code" of the supplanted device on the tape (such as, duplication) then by the "information" to which this project would be applied. The strategy of merging program and information in a computing device was a major step and nowadays exists in almost all computers (Shelly, Freund, &Vermaat, 2010).During the Second World War, Turing played a significant role in developing electromechanical machines which could decrypt the clandestine codes utilized by the Germans without recognizing the key. Following the war, he assisted in designing the original UK computing machines in the Physical Research facility, then later the University of Manchester.

5.8.1. Grace Hopper's Contribution

Grace Murray was a U.S. statistician, born in 1906. In her childhood, she demonstrated incredible interest in research and innovation (for instance, by dismantling the alarm clocks found in her home one by one, until she was able to reassemble them back together by the time she was 7yrs old. Her parents nurtured her liking for the sciences whereas ensuring that her wishes were supported, instead of taking after tradition in regards to the learning of young American ladies. Grace subsequently got to be among the few ladies of her time to learn at Yale College and get a doctorate degree in mathematics.

By the time of World War II, Grace joined the naval force as a lieutenant, then later joined the group commanding Mark 1, the original computer in U.S. Grace Hopper became a part of the original group which could program the machine. Later Mark 1 got instructions and information from punched cards, like was intended for Babbage's machine, plus the Jacquard loom around two centuries previously. During the 50s, Hopper believed emphatically in the notion that computer science must be open to as many individuals as possible, and not only computer scientists and mathematicians. She contended that punched slots were hindering the advancement of computers and started developing a programming communication venture, which would be near to English and ensure program computing was simpler. The trouble was to create a program able to change top-level instructions (within a dialect comparative to English which would be effortlessly understood by a person) into low-range instructions (the PC's dialect) (Schäfer, 2013).

Today, this kind of program is known as a "compiler," while its innovation is somewhat thanks to Hopper. Her coding dialect, called COBOL, got to be the most far-reaching between 1960 to 1980. Grace isn't just popular for ensuring computers are more available to non-specialists. In a certain day, when programming her machines with punched cards, there's one in particular that failed.

Upon going to discover what really happened, she detected a moth lodged inside the gaps of a certain punched card. She wrote it down in her report, commenting that the bug was to blame for the breakdown. Henceforth, the word "bug" began being used by researchers, like Thomas Edison, to distinguish errors caused by the unwanted obstructions by some of them within their tests. Through applying it to the unsuccessful launching of the computer system, Grace turned it into a household term to portray this technical situation. In essence, she invented the word "computer bug" in 1947 (Schäfer, 2013).

5.8.2. Invention of the Internet

The notion of linking multiple computers into a single network stared from the U.S. during the 60s. Particularly, in 1961 scientist Leonard Kleinrock established a method of sharing data between workstations by breaking down the data being transferred into packets, relaying them along a range of different paths, plus piecing them back harmoniously in the correct order at the recipient's end. This is the code behind the process still used nowadays to send data—like emails—on the Web. The subsequent year, Licklider promoted the device as a message and resource-sharing implement, and proposed development of a system of interconnected computers. Soon afterwards, Licklider enlisted with the Advanced Research Programs Agency (ARPA), to provide the U.S. military and technological support.

5.9. HISTORY OF MODERN COMPUTER HARDWARE (PRE-1960S)

Figure 5.8. *The Pascal's machine is among the earliest forms of computer hardware.*

Source: http://www.cs.uah.edu/~rcoleman/Common/History/History.html.

The history of computing machines dates back to earliest technological developments that aided in basic calculation. Prior to the 20th century, the majority of calculations were carried out by humans. Some ancient mechanical tools to assist humans with numerical calculations, such as the abacus, were referred to as "calculating machines," by proprietary names, or simply as calculators. Later on the operating machine was referred to as the computer.

During the 1920s, already electromechanical tabulating devices could add, deduct, and print accumulated sums. Machine operations were directed by inputting dozens of cable jumpers into detachable control boards. When the U.S. introduced Social Security numbers in 1935, IBM's punched-card were already being used to update the records of close to 26 million workers. These punched cards soon became popular in industry and state for bookkeeping and administration (Dasgupta, 2016).

Publications on Punched Card Systems in Technical Computation in 1940, defined punched-card systems as sufficiently applicable in solving some variance equations, or completing multiplication and division processes through floating point depictions, all recorded on punched cards as well as unit record devices. These machines were applied during the Second World War for cryptographic arithmetical processing, including a vast range of administrative roles. The Columbia University's Astronomical Computing Bureau, further conducted astronomical calculations highlighting the progress in computing.

5.9.1. Earliest Records of Computer Hardware

German polymath and inventor Wilhelm Schickard first developed a calculating device in 1623 that combined a mechanized system of Napier's rods through the world's initial mechanical addition machine structured into the base. Since it utilized a single-tooth equipment, there were still conditions where its transmit mechanism would jam (O'Regan, 2016).

In 1642, while still a youngster, Blaise Pascal began some pioneering research on calculating devices, and after a few years of effort developed 50 prototype models of the mechanical calculator. He constructed 20 of these devices in the subsequent 10 years. Some of his inventions have survived up to date and are on show in various European museums. An ongoing debate persists on whether Pascal or Schickard should be considered as the "originator of the technical calculator."

A short while afterwards, Gottfried Wilhelm devised the stepped reckoner including his popular stepped drum machine in around 1672. He sought to build a machine that may be used not just for adding and subtracting, but also apply a transferrable carriage to allow for long multiplying and division processes (Dasgupta, 2016).

Nevertheless, Leibniz didn't incorporate a totally successful data transfer system. He also defined the binary numerical system, a primary component of all contemporary computers. Until the 1940s, many successive designs (such as Charles Babbage's devices of earlier times) were centered around the decimal system. However, in 1820 Charles Xavier produced what would rise to become the first effective, mass-produced automated calculator, commonly known as the Thomas-Arithmometer.

The machine could be applied for basic addition and subtraction, and with a transferrable carriage, the operator may also do multiplication and division by a procedure of long calculations. It applied a stepped drum unit similar in design to that conceived by Leibniz. Mechanical calculators still stayed in use up to the 1970s (O'Regan, 2016).

5.9.2. Punched-Card Data Processing

During the year 1804, Joseph Jacquard established a loom whereby the pattern being woven was done by a paper tape made from punched cards. This paper tape was able to be swapped without changing the automated design of the loom. It was a landmark accomplishment in programmability. The machine was an enhancement over comparable weaving looms. Punched slots were preceded by the punch bands, like in the machine brought forward by BasileBouchon.

The bands would later inspire data recording for automated pianos and even recently numerical regulator machine devices. By the late 1880s, American Herman Hollerith had invented data storing on punched cards which could then be deciphered by a machine. In order to process the punched cards, Hollerith developed the tabulator as well as keypunch machine. His equipment used electromechanical transmissions and counters, and thereafter Hollerith's technique was utilized in the 1890 U.S. Census (O'Regan, 2016).

That particular census was processed around two years quicker than the previous census had been, in fact, Hollerith's firm eventually became the precursor of IBM. As of 1920, electromechanical tabulating apparatuses could perform basic addition, subtraction, and generate accumulated totals. Basically, machine functions were done by inserting a number of cable jumpers into transferrable control panels.

However, earlier in 1912, UK engineer Arthur Pollen built the first electrically run mechanical analog workstation (commonly known as Argo Clock). This machine was applied by the Russian Navy during World War I with some considerable success. The other substitute, Dreyer Table Mechanical appliances were also used to assist with the pinpoint precision of mid-air bombing.

It measured the wind velocity from the within and applied that measurement in calculating the wind's properties on the route of the bombs. The structure was later enhanced with the Course Structure Bomb Sight, and attained a peak with the Second World War bomb sights, as well as RAF Bomber Command. The technology of mechanical analog calculation reached its peak with the variance analyzer, constructed by Vannevar Bush and H. L. Hazen as from 1927, which improved upon the automated integrators of Thomson, James and the rotation amplifiers devised by Nieman H. W (O'Regan, 2016).

A number of these procedures were developed before their undesirability became evident; the most prevailing was built at University of Pennsylvania's and in particular Moore College of Electrical Engineering, in which the ENIAC was developed. A wholly electronic analog workstation was fabricated by Helmut Hölzer during the year 1942 from the Peenemünde Army Research Institute. By 1950s, the apparent success of virtual electronic computers had brought an end to most analog computer machines, though hybrid analog computers, regulated by digital electronics, continued in considerable use during the 50s and 60s, then later in various specialized applications.

Around the same time, the Harvard Mark I machine was built at IBM's Endicott labs, it was a unique all-purpose electronic computer that was more powerful than the Z3, even though it wasn't really Turing-complete. A short while later, the phrase digital computation was developed by George Stibitz denoting where a voltage isn't applied to straightly represent a value. (Schäfer, 2013).

5.10. THE TRANSITION FROM ANALOG TO DIGITAL

5.10.1. Analog Computer

During the initial half of the twentieth century, analog processers were considered by most people to be the ultimate future of computers. These machines utilized the persistently changeable factors of physical properties such as electrical, technical, and hydraulic factors to demonstrate the issue being tackled, different from advanced computers that showcased shifting amounts typically, since their numerical values alter. Since an analog processor doesn't utilize discrete values, but instead continuous values, procedures can't be dependably repeated with accurate comparability, in as way they do with Turing equipment. The original modern analog processor was a tide-predicting appliance, designed by Sir William-Thomson, afterward Lord Kelvin, did some improvements in 1872. It utilized a framework of pulleys and cables to naturally calculate anticipated tide functions for a given period at a particular area and was of incredible help to navigation in shallow waters. The gadget became the basis for additional improvements in analog computers (ITL Education Solutions Limited, 2011).

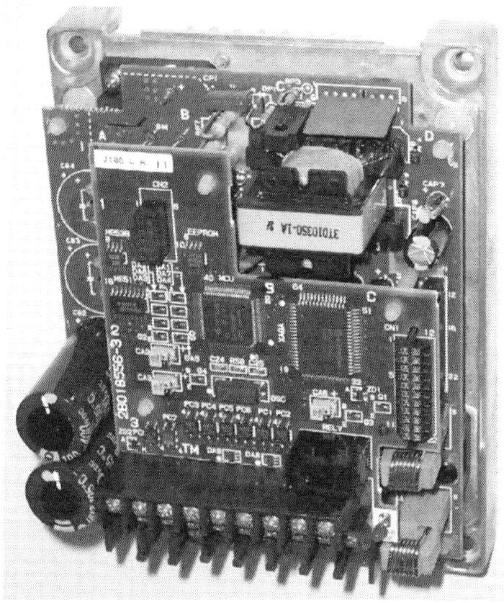

Figure 5.9. *Digital computers are more powerful than their analog counterparts due to superior processors.*

Source: https://en.wikipedia.org/wiki/Digital_electronics.

The differential analyzer is a mechanical analog processer designed to process differential equations by assimilation through wheel-and-disc appliances, was hypothesized in 1876 by Thomson James, whose brother to a more renowned inventor Lord Kelvin. James explored the various construction of these calculators, but was hindered by the narrow output torque that the round-and-disk integrators had. In a variance analyzer, the productivity of one integrator propelled the transfer of the subsequent integrator, or a display output. Analog analyzers were further used for the Mk. I Drift-Sight machine that was used in World War I. The lever found right ahead of the missile aimer's fingertips helped set up the altitude, the wheels around the knuckles also set the wind as well as airspeed. A significant advance in analog processing was the construction of the first fire-control units for long range vessel gun-laying.

When gunnery ranges improved dramatically during the late nineteenth century, it wasn't just a simple issue of calculating the appropriate aim point, considering the shells flight times. Different spotters aboard the ship would transmit distance measures, plus observations to a core plotting axis. There the fire bearing teams fed into the position, speed and course of the ship as well as its target, and various alterations for Coriolis Effect, climatic effects on the atmosphere, and other adjustments; then the processer would provide a firing solution that would be dished to the available turrets for laying (ITL Education Solutions Limited, 2011).

5.10.2. The Advent of Digital Computers

The invention of modern processors was first defined by computer researcher Alan Turing, he initially set out the notion in his thesis 1936 publication on Computable Numbers. He restructured Kurt Gödel's 1931 outcome on the restrictions of proof and calculation, replacing Gödel's collective arithmetic-based official language with the proper and basic hypothetical devices which became referred to as Turing engines. He showed that some such equipment would be able to perform various conceivable mathematical calculation, as if it were shown as an algorithm. Godel went ahead to demonstrate that there wasn't a resolution for the Entscheidungs issue, by first revealing that the stoppage issue for Turing engines is undecidable (Shelly, Freund, &Vermaat, 2010).

Generally, it's not conceivable to decide numerically whether a particular Turing appliance will ever halt. The inventor also presented the model of "universal machine" (currently referred to as the collective Turing engine), with the impression that such a device could do the functions of other machines, or alternatively, it's provably able to compute anything that's computable through executing a sequence stored on tape, permitting the engine to be programmable. Commenting on this invention, Von Neumann admitted that the core concept of the present-day computer was directly attributed to this research. Turing machines are up to date a core aspect of studies in hypothesis of computation. Apart for the restrictions imposed through their fixed memory stores, contemporary computers are believed to be Turing-filled, which is to mean, they have algorithm implementation capability similar to the universal Turing engine (Shelly, Freund, &Vermaat, 2010).*Electromechanical workstations:* The era of contemporary computing started with an increment of improvements before and after World War II. A majority of numerical computers developed during this duration were electromechanical – power switches drove motorized relays to do the calculation. The devices had a minimal operating tempo, and were ultimately succeeded by much quicker all-electric computers, initially using vacuum tubes. Also, Z2 became one of the primary models of an electromechanical transmission computer, plus was developed by German researcher Konrad Zuse during the year 1940. This became an enhancement from his earlier invention the Z1, even though it operated using a similar mechanical memory, the device substituted the arithmetic and regulator logic with mechanical relay circuits.

Around the same time, a copy of Zuse's Z3 was also introduced, becoming the first wholly automatic, electromechanical computer. Around the same period, electro-mechanical appliances known as "bombes" were developed by UK cryptologists to assist in deciphering German Enigma-device-encrypted secret communication during the Second World War.

The bombes' original design was developed in 1939 from the UK Government Encryption and Cypher School at Bletchley Square by Alan Turing, through a vital refinement formulated in 1940 by Welchman Gordon. The engineering program and development was the task of Keen Harold of the UK Tabulating Machine Firm. It was a significant development from an engine that had been developed in 1938 through Polish Cipher Agency cryptologist Marian Rejewski, commonly referred to as the "cryptologic bomb."

By 1941, Zuse was already following up with his previous machine the Z3, which became the world's original functional electromechanical programmable, wholly programmed numerical computer. The Z3 got developed with 2000 relays, executing a 22-bit phrase length that functioned at a clock ratio of around 5–10 Hz. Sequence code and information were reserved on punched film.

The system was rather similar to contemporary machines in multiple respects, pioneering different advances like floating point statistics. Replacement of difficult-to-implement fractional system was also used in Babbage's former design, however, the basic binary structure meant that Zuse's engines were simpler to build and possibly more reliable, considering the technologies that were available during that time. Probably, the Z3 was a Turing-whole machine. In dual 1936 patent submissions, Zuse also expected that machine commands could be reserved in the similar storage system used for data—a key intuition of what soon became to be called the von Neumann design.

5.11. HISTORY OF COMPUTER HARDWARE (POST-1960S)

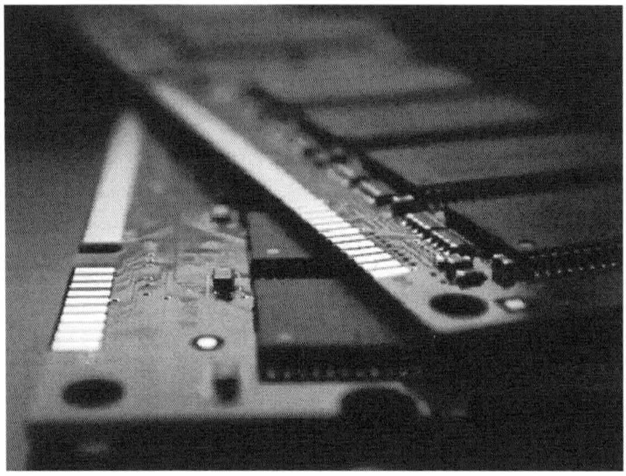

Figure 5.10. *RAM (Random Access Memory) is a modern computer hardware used to store data.*

Source: https://www.lifewire.com/types-of-ram-4150713.

The initial aids to technical computation were merely mechanical devices that required the operative to establish the original values of a fundamental arithmetic operation, then tweak the device to attain the result. Afterwards, computers represented statistics in a continuous format, for example, distance across a scale, shaft rotation and voltage. Figures could also be characterized in form of digits, mechanically operated through an automatic system. Although this approach typically required more advanced mechanisms, it highly increased the accuracy of results.

The creation of transistor equipment and later the assimilated circuit chip triggered a series of innovations, beginning with transistor processers, and then later integrated circuit workstations, making digital computers to essentially replace their analog counterparts. The metal-oxide-semiconductor, also known as (MOS) as well as large-scale incorporation (LSI) then triggered semiconductor memory plus the microprocessor, triggering yet another major breakthrough, in form of a smaller personal computer (PC) during the 70s. The overall price of computers gradually became so affordable that personal home computers by the 90s, and later mobile computers also known as smartphones or tablets became available by the 2000s (Shelly, Freund, &Vermaat, 2010).

5.11.1. Calculators

The Curta calculator is considered amongst the very first machines to do perform multiplication and division equations. Later in the 20th century, versions of mechanical calculators, currency registers, and accounting appliances, were redesigned to utilize electric motors, whereby gear position acted as the symbol for the form of a variable. The term "computer" was basically a job title given to mostly women who utilized these calculators to do mathematical calculations (Page & Gamboa, 2019).

Also, around the same time British researcher Lewis Fry Richardson's captivation in weather forecast led him to suggest human computers and arithmetic analysis as models of predicting weather; up to today, the most equipped processors on Earth are required to adequately shape its weather through the Navier–Stokes calculations. Businesses like Marchant Calculator, Friden and Monroe further developed desktop motorized calculators from the 30s which had capacity to add, deduct, multiply and divide.

However, the globe's original all-electronic portable calculator was known as the UK Bell Punch ANITA, which was launched in 1961. It incorporated vacuum ducts, cold-cathode pipes and Dekatrons within its circuits, using 12 cold-cathode "Nixie" ducts for showcasing. The ANITA became popular because it was the exclusive electronic desktop computer available at the time, plus it was quiet and fast in operation. The tube innovation was succeeded in 1963 by the American developed Friden EC-130 machine, which featured an all-transistor scheme, a combination of four 13-figure numbers exhibited on a five-inch CRT, and presented reverse Polish notation or RPN (Page & Gamboa, 2019).

At around the same time, U.S.-based electronic developer Claude Shannon as well as Soviet Statistician Victor Shestakov both revealed a close resemblance between the notions of Boolean arithmetic and some electrical circuits, now referred to as logic gates that are now quite common in digital computer systems. They revealed that electrical relays and controls can discern the languages of Boolean algebra. The thesis basically initiated practical computerized circuit design.

5.11.2. Further Advancements

Generally, the history of computer hardware beginning in 1960 is characterized by the transformation from vacuum pipe to solid-state appliances like transistors, plus later integrated circuit (IC) slots. This triggered the primary movement from computer memory to magnetic-core storage devices to physical-state static and vibrant semiconductor memory, that greatly minimized the cost, dimension and power utility of computers. The advances led to various other technological improvements in computers like those mentioned below:

Semiconductor memory: The MOS transistor was developed by DawonKahng and Mohamed Atalla from the Bell Labs Company in 1959. Apart from information processing, the MOSFET allowed the practical usage of MOS transistors in storage cell storage features, a function formerly availed by the magnetic cores. Semi transistor memory, commonly known as MOS data, was cheaper and took less power compared to magnetic-core storage. MOS random-access memory, presented in form of fixed RAM, was created by Schmidt John at Fairchild Semi transmitter in 1964. Later in 1966, Dennard Robert from IBM created the MOS dynamic RAM. Later on, Simon Sze and DawonKahng in 1967 came up with the floating-door MOSFET, the foundation for MOS nonvolatile storage like EEPROM, EPROM and flash memory.

Microprocessors: The primary building block of all microprocessors is a metal-oxide semi transistor field-effect switch. The microprocessor has beginnings in the MOS assimilated circuit (MOS IC) chip. This machine was first conceptualized by Mohamed Atalla in 1960, later improved by Steven Hofstein and Fred Heiman from the RCA in 1962. Because of swift MOSFET scaling, the MOS IC slots rapidly grew in complicacy at a pace forecasted by Moore's law, eventually causing large scale integration (LSI) with multiple transistors on one MOS slot by the late 60s. The utilization of MOS LSI slots to enhance computing was the foundation for the original microprocessors, since engineers began noticing that a whole computer processor might be stored within one MOS LSI slot.

The original multi-chip microprocessors consisted of IV-Phase Structures AL-1 and were developed in 1969, a year later they were already being fitted with MOS LSI chips. On November 1971, Intel launched the world's foremost single-chip microprocessor, called the 4004, based on just one MOS LSI chip. This device's development was overseen by Federico Faggin, through silicon-gate MOS innovation, alongside other inventors like Stanley Mazor, Ted Hoff, and Masatoshi Shima.

The appliance was made for a Japanese computer company known as Busicom, acting as a substitute to hardwired circuitry, though soon afterwards computers were designed around it, whereby most of their processing functions were done from a single tiny microprocessor chip.

The versatile RAM (DRAM) slot was reliant on the MOS-DRAM storage cell invented by Robert Dennard from IBM, providing kilobits of storage on a single chip. Intel fortified the RAM chip using the microprocessor, thereby permitting fourth-generation processors to be slighter and quicker than previous computers.

Essentially, the 4004 was capable of achieving 60,000 commands per second, even though its successors introduced ever-growing tempo and power to processors, such as the Intel 8008, 8086/8088 family and other powerful computer processors. This paved way for the production of other more efficient microprocessors used in specialized computers.

5.12. THE ADVENT OF THE HOME COMPUTER

Figure 5.11. *Early home computers made it possible for people to work from anywhere.*

Source: https://www.inexhibit.com/case-studies/computer-design-commodore-pet-2001-1977/.

The history of portable computers as popular consumer electronic machine started with the microcomputer uprising of the 1970s. Generally, a home computer is that which is intended for collaborative individual use, rather than a mainframe processor where the final user's requests are sieved through operating staff, or maybe a time-sharing structure whereby a single large workstation is shared by multiple individuals. Following the invention of the microprocessor, individual home computers were affordable enough in price that they ultimately became accessible consumer goods. Early home computers – commonly called microcomputers – became popular in electronic kit package and in limited ratios, plus they were of particular interest to computer hobbyists and technicians (Henderson, 2009).An early application of the word "home computer" was found in the November 1962, New York Times editorial by John W. Mauchly, where he described portending future of computing as captured by a particular meeting by members of the Institute of Mechanical Engineers. In 1968, a computer company took upon themselves the risk of calling their product the home computer, this happened when Hewlett-Packard marketed their new launch the "Powerful Computing Genie" as a home use computer. Even though this advertisement was considered too controversial for the potential audience and substituted with another rather flat ad, the point had already been put across.

Throughout the following seven years, the word had gained immense popularity that Byte magazine gave its readers the initial page of "home computing field," while Creative Computing defined the home computer as a "private computing system holding plenty of processing power and data storing abilities," meant to satisfy the wishes of the individual user. By 1977, there were three fresh pre-assembled mini-computers that had hit the market, dubbed by Byte magazine as "1977 Trinity" home computing. These brands included Apple II and PET 2001 which were marketed as home computers, whereas the TRS-80 got the description of a microcomputer applied for domestic errands like "personal financial management." In 1979, around half a million micro-computers had been sold and most youth had developed a new perception of the home computer (Henderson, 2009).

5.12.1. Early Beginnings

The emergence of personal computers as mass-market electronic devices essentially began in 1977, following the introduction of micro-computers, but some mainframe and smaller computers had been used as single-operator systems much earlier. A home computer is the one meant for interactive personal use, rather than a larger processor where the ultimate user's requests are first passed through the operating staff for processing, or even a time sharing processor whereby one large processor is used by several people (O'Regan, 2016).

The previous models of home computers were foreshadowed by how the first, pre-commercial, experimental processors were used, whereby one user had sole access to the processor. In regions like Carnegie Mellon University as well as MIT, learners with access to a couple of the original processors experimented using applications which would today be ranked as a typical home computer; for instance, computer-assisted drafting was the forerunner of T-square, a computer program developed much earlier in 1961, and the precursor of many of today's home computer applications.

5.13. IMPLICATIONS

Figure 5.12. *Computers have made knowledge transfer and learning much easier.*

Source: https://smallbusiness.chron.com/five-positive-effects-technology-education-31222.html.

Computing technologies, just like many other types of technology, aren't socially neutral. They have great impacts and are themselves influenced by society. Processors have changed how people associate with one another, as well as their surrounding environment, including how people arrange their work, communities, plus time. On the other hand, society has impacted on the advancement of computers via the needs users have for processing data. In fact, the study of these connections has grown to be referred to as "social informatics."

Computer technology has steadily evolved from a means of resolving certain issues in human society. The first models of computational machines were the automated calculators designed by Blaise Pascal in 1645, used for solving directional and scientific issues that started to arise when Europe entered a fresh and vibrant era of scientific growth and global commerce. By 1801, Joseph-Marie Jacquard had developed perhaps the first form of programmed machine, known as Jacquard's Loom, for purposes of automating the weaving of fabric with patterns. He was inspired by the need of manufacturers in the first Industrial Age, who were looking for a way of decreasing the cost of making their products through large-scale production in factories (ITL Education Solutions Limited, 2011).By the twentieth century, there was heightened development of technical research and engineering systems which needed progressively complex computations. Pressing military needs occasioned by the Second World War prompted the creation of the first automated computers; the appliances in use nowadays are direct progenies of these small-scale early efforts to rationalize military formation and calculation. The requirements and needs of modern society have consequently influenced the creation of a massive range of computing technologies, such as supercomputers, games, graphics processors, audio and digital video, portable computing devices as well as telephones.As for the twenty-first century, computers have grown to be used in nearly every fabric of society, such as agriculture, art, architecture, international trade, commerce, education, governance, and science just to mention a few. In general, these modern computing technologies fall into either one of two groups. The first class covers applications which require the arrangement, storage, and recovery of large volumes of data like bank records and library catalogs. The other category comprises of applications which require the arrangement of complex processes, such as control of machines involved in manufacturing of vehicles or the publication of books and daily papers (ITL Education Solutions Limited, 2011).

5.13.1. Influence of Computers on Daily Work

Among the ways that modern-day computers have impacted society, depends on how people have structured themselves into workplace groups as it relates to computers. The first work computers were designed to perform very specific roles in science, research, engineering, and military which had formerly been carried out by hand.

Sooner than later, general-purpose processers were capable of automating almost all information processing tasks needed to run an organization, like payroll processing and file management. Nevertheless, since early generation processors were relatively affordable, all of the company's information processing duties were typically centered around a single large processor computer that the organization could afford. Specific departments and people within such groups would similarly be organized within a centralized context to ease their access to the central computer; that, however, changed when computers became more common and each employee could have their own unit at the office (ITL Education Solutions Limited, 2011).

Chapter 6

Principal Areas of Study with in Computer Science

CONTENTS

6.1. INTRODUCTION

Computer science refers to the studying of computers and its operational systems. Different from electrical or computer technicians, computer scientists for the most part deal with application and software systems; including aspects such as their modeling, design, development, and usage. Experts in this field often use algorithms to adjust, record, and communicate virtual data.

The subject can be categorized into theoretical and applied disciplines. Computational complexity model is rather abstract, whereas computer graphics give emphasis to real-world uses. Programming language system covers strategies used for description of computational systems, whereas computer programming itself includes the usage of programming codes and complex structures.

Human-computer communication considers the roles in making these machines valuable, usable, and available. Some primary fields of study within discipline include computer systems and frameworks, security, artificial intelligence, database systems, numerical analysis, software engineering and bioinformatics among others.

Even though learning how to code is fundamental to the studies of computer science, it's just one aspect of the field. Experts in this field plan and analyze algorithms for purposes of solving programs and studying the activity of computer equipment and programs.

The matters that computer scientists explore vary from the theoretical--deciding what issues can be addressed with computers plus the intricacy of the algorithms which solve them – to the substantial – planning applications that do well on handheld appliances, which are simple to apply, and that maintain security measures.

The term "computer science" was initially coined in 1956 by Louis Fein, who was remarking on the formation of a Computer Sciences Graduate School at Harvard Business School.

6.2. ARTIFICIAL INTELLIGENCE

Figure 6.1. *AI is quickly becoming part of our everyday lives since it helps to improve human activities.*

Source: https://bluumi.net/inteligencia-artificial-2/.

Artificial intelligence (AI) is a branch of computer science which emphasizes the development of intelligent systems that work and respond like people. A few of the activities that processors with this ability are developed for include: voice chat, recognition, learning, structuring and problem solving. Studies related with artificial intelligence are quite technical and focused in approach. The main issue with artificial intelligence comprises programming processors for certain characteristics like those specified above (Barry, 2015).

Knowledge engineering forms a central aspect of AI research. Computers can sometimes act and respond like people only in the event that they have plenteous data relating to the society. Artificial intelligence should have access to items, categories, properties and relationships between these factors in order to implement data engineering. Initiating common sense, logic and problem-solving qualities in machines may be a hard and monotonous task, but skilled computer scientists can still do it. Machine learning forms a central aspect of AI. When learning occurs without any form of supervision, it typically requires some capacity to distinguish designs in patterns of inputs, while learning with sufficient supervision incorporates classification and arithmetical regressions.Classification determines the class that a programmable object is placed to, while regression addresses the obtainment of a set of arithmetical input or output factors, subsequently discovering capacities allowing for the generation of appropriate yields from particular inputs.

Numerical analysis of ML calculations and their execution is a well-defined department of hypothetical computer science regularly alluded to as computational knowledge theory.

Machine recognition deals with the capacity to utilize tactile inputs to infer the distinctive attributes of the world, whereas computer vision refers to the ability to detect visual inputs using a couple of sub-classes like facial, object and motion recognition. Robotics is additionally a major subject related to AI. Most robots require intelligence in order to accomplish tasks like object control and navigation, besides sub-problems of localization, movement planning and mapping (Barry, 2015).

6.2.1. Branches of Artificial Intelligence

Algorithm: An algorithm refers to a set of commands for fulfilling a task. In case you need a computer to discern how to perform something, you must first provide it with an instructional algorithm. We typically use algorithms in everyday life, the control of the algorithm arises from the reality that, most computers actualize the steps rapidly and accurately. Algorithms are applied for information processing, calculations, and mechanized thinking.

Machine Learning: ML is among the most commonly used AI algorithms. Its learning process includes the improvement of modern explanatory information, the improvement of mental and motor abilities through recitation or instruction. Since the advent of the computer age, analysts and scientists have been attempting to embed such functions in computers. Solving this matter has been, plus remains to be, an interesting and far-reaching long-term objective in AI.

Deep Learning: This is a subfield of ML and among the most effective and quickest developing applications of Artificial Intelligence. Deep Learning is often applied to solve issues which are already considered too complex and include an expansive range of information. Deep learning happens through the application of neural systems that are layered to identify designs and complex connections in information. The application of deep learning needs a vast dataset, as well as compelling computational control to work.

Natural Language Processing: NLP refers to a strategy whereby computers are programmed to understand, implement and interpret human dialect. To achieve this objective, the computer must be able to "comprehend" a vast quantity of information – from grammar sentence structure and policies to different accents and colloquialisms. While a speech acknowledgment system, for instance, manual speech gets to be sound information, which consequently changes into content information, a rather complicated process itself.

This textual data may be executed in an "intelligent" form for diverse applications like monitoring devices or translators.*Computer Vision:* This refers to the process of scientifically manipulating or interpreting videos and pictures. It has various applications, consisting of augmented reality, independent driving and mechanical inspection.

The application of deep-learning for processor vision can be distinguished into various categories such as; identification, generation, division and classification, which are both in tapes and images.

6.2.2. Social Impact of Artificial Intelligence

Technology experts have described AI and deep learning as the new frontier in science.

They believe that the technology will soon drive majority of our undertakings in society as well as daily business, radically changing how we work and live. Learning how this technology works and comprehending its implications in our daily lives is of great importance, just like learning how to read or write. In the current digital era, recognizing that artificial intelligence will soon be a part of our daily existence is vital (Barry, 2015).

6.3. COMPUTER SYSTEMS AND NETWORKS

Figure 6.2. *Computer networks allow for easy communication between different computers and across vast distances.*

Source: https://www.plymouth.ac.uk/student-life/new-students/induction/bsc-hons-computer-systems-and-networks-stage-2-returning-students-induction-information.

Among the earliest models of a computer system was a grid of interactive computers, which operated as a branch of America's army Semi-Automatic Ground Ecosystem (SAGE) radar grid. By 1969, institutes like the University of California, Stanford Research Institute, and the University of Utah had already successfully connected computer systems, being part of their computer connectivity research project. It's this network which later progressed to become the internet as we know it today (Barry, 2015).

6.3.1. Local-Area-Network (LAN)

LAN refers to local-area-network, meaning a computer network found within a tiny location like a home, computer laboratory, school, office structure or cluster of buildings. It consists of inter-linked workstations and PCs which are capable of retrieving and sharing information and devices, like printers, scanners and information storage devices, from whichever position on the LAN.

Typically, these systems are marked by greater communication and information transfer rates, plus the absence of any requirement for hired communication lines. During the 60s, universities and large colleges benefited from having the original LAN systems. By mid-70s, Ethernet was created by Xerox PARC and officially launched in 1976. New York's Chase Manhattan later became the first commercial organization to use the LAN system in December 1977 (Dasgupta, 2016).

During the late 70s and early 80s, it was typical to have several hundreds of personal computers found in the same location. Most users and directors were enticed to the notion of multiple workstations sharing an otherwise costly disk space, plus laser printers. As from the mid-80s up to 1990s, Novell's Netware had most control of the LAN program market. With time, competitors like Microsoft released other similar items to the position where today, local networking is regarded as base functionality for most operating systems.

6.3.2. Topology

When computers are connected on a particular network, this is usually referred to as nodes. The link between computers may be done through cabling, oftentimes the Ethernet cable, or remotely through radio waves. Linked computers can share various resources, such as Web access, printers, file programs, and others. A network refers to a multipurpose network that allows a particular computer to perform exceptionally.

Computer networks may be broken down traditionally into topologies, this referring to a technique of linking processors. The most popular topology currently is the collapsed ring. Mainly due to the effectiveness of a network structure called the Ethernet. It's a protocol, or computer language that supports both the Web, Wide Area Networks (WAN) and Local Area Networks (LAN) (Dasgupta, 2016).

- *Ring Topology:* In this arrangement, computers are linked through a single cable, though the terminal nodes also are linked to each other. For this design, the signal flows through the network till it finds the planned recipient. In case a network node isn't configured appropriately, or it's down momentarily for another reason, it means the signal shall make a variety of efforts to find its location. The collapsed ring, in particular, is a topology in which the middle node is a system device known as the hub, router, or switch. The device operates a ring topology within and has plugins for cables. Also, each computer features an autonomous cable, which connects into the device. A majority of present-day offices comprise of a wiring closet, or a space comprising a switch device which links up the network. All processors in the office attach to the wiring closet as well as the switch. Even in cases where a system plug is close to a desk, the socket is connected through a cable onto the electrical closet.

- *Star Topology:* Generally, a star topology refers to a network design where the central node stretches a cord to each processer on the network. For the star network, computers are linked autonomously to the epicenter of the network. In case a cable gets broken, then other computers will continue operating without any problems. However, star topology needs lots of cabling to function.
- *Bus Topology:* This is yet another form of network design where one cable joins all computers, including the information required for the terminal node on the system must move through each linked computer. In case a cable is damaged, then all computers attached down the line won't reach the system. The main advantage of this topology is that very minimal cabling is required.

6.3.3. Wide Area Network (WAN)

Somewhat more complicated than LAN, the WAN connects processors together across broader physical distances. This permits computers and low-voltage equipment to be remotely attached to one another over a single large grid to communicate, even in the situation where they're quite far apart. The Web is the simplest illustration of a WAN, joining all computers mutually around the world. Due to WAN's immense reach, it's normally owned and sustained by several administrators or members of the public (Barry, 2015).

6.4. SECURITY

Figure 6.3. *Adequate data security is necessary for protecting youth information from cybercriminals.*

Source: https://www.cs.vu.nl/en/research/computer-systems/Systemsandnetworksecurity/.

Computer security is also referred to as IT security or cyber security. Essentially, it refers to the protection of network systems from robbery or destruction to the firmware, software, and any data stored on them, including from interruption or misdirection of services that they provide. It may involve regulating physical admission to the hardware, or protecting against damage that could arise from network access, information and code injection, plus due to misuse by operators, whether deliberate, unintentional, or because of them getting tricked into omitting secure procedures.

Generally, this field comprises of four key areas: I) Confidentiality - Whereby only approved users can gain access to available data assets and information. II) Integrity - Only approved personnel should be in a position to modify the stored data when required. III) Accessibility - Data must be available to operators when needed. IV) Authentication - these are systems that ensure you are indeed communicating with whoever you think you're interacting with (Tucker, 2004).

6.4.1. The Importance of Computer Security

First, it's essential in the deterrence of data theft like bank account figures, credit card details, PINs, work-related brochures or sheets, and so on. Network security is vital in today's communications as many of our daily actions rely on the security that these data paths provide. The data available in a computer may also be misused through unapproved intrusions. An intruder may modify and alter the program command codes, or use your photos and email accounts to develop offensive content like obscene images, deceptive and invasive social accounts.

Similarly, malicious intents could be a factor in IT security. Intruders regularly use your processors for attacking other vulnerable computers or sites and networks for purposes of causing havoc. Resentful hackers might also crash someone's network system to intentionally create data loss, plus DDOS attacks may be triggered to inhibit access to websites through crashing of the server. For your data to remain secure and confidential, it's essential that you safeguard your computer and thus the need for having Computer Security arises (Tucker, 2004).

Firewalls: A firewall refers to a security-conscious bit of firmware or software which sits between the Web and your network focusing one particular task: which is preventing malware from reaching over to us. This firewall serves as a security barrier between the Web and your Local-Area

Network. Every network traffic moving into and out from the LAN should go through the firewall, and it consequently prevents unlawful access to the computer network (Tedre, 2014).

There are different types of firewalls that exist. The first one is packet-filtering which inspects each packet crossing the firewall and examines the packet based on a set of guidelines that you establish. In case the packet succeeds in this test, it's permitted to pass. But if the packet fails to pass, it's excluded.

Packet filters seem to be the least costly form of firewall. Therefore, packet-filtering firewalls are quite common.

The second one is Stateful-Packet Inspection (SPI), whereby there's a setup in aptitude from basic packet filtering. This form of packet looks at packets existing in groups instead of individually. It traces up which packets have gone past the firewall and may detect patterns which indicate unauthorized access. Likewise, Deep-Packet Inspection (DPI) is the tangible aspect of the packets that's inspected so that viruses, spam, and various other risky content can be jammed. DPI further allows practices, like data mining, content censorship, and eavesdropping which make its application a controversial matter (Tedre, 2014).

Antivirus: An antivirus is a software that detects malicious programs, files or software that may compromise your processor, either from being executable or through exploiting a particular susceptibility in the program commonly utilized to process them. It distinguishes these types of harmful programs which are already fitted on your processor, or about to get installed. The antivirus can perform different protective measures depending on the security features in the Anti-virus application, like separation, permanent removal or fix. It also looks for possibly harmful files which are downloaded.

Lastly, whereas the Internet has altered and greatly enhanced our lives, this broad network and its related technologies have unlocked the gates to an ever-increasing amount of security risks from which persons, families and business should protect themselves. The results of attacks may vary from the somewhat inconvenient to the wholly debilitating. Crucial files can be lost, confidentiality can be violated plus your computer may even be utilized by an external attacker to infiltrate other computers connected to the Internet. The security systems available vary in terms of sophistication, it can be a basic program safeguarding one or two home computers, or a complex program used by organizations like banks (Tedre, 2014).

6.5. DATABASE SYSTEMS

Figure 6.4. *Database systems are normally used to store large amounts of information within the computer.*

Source: https://www.edx.org/course/database-systems-concepts-and-design-2.

A database refers to a group of data which persists for a lengthy period of time. A number of structures fit this particular definition, for instance, a file system, digital notebook, including cloud storage which has recently come up. A Database Management Structure (DBMS) is simply a system which gives an interface to databanks for material storage and retrieval. People are usually more fascinated by software systems instead of manual systems since they can perform the work more efficiently. Some popular features of the DBMS include: multi-user support, effective retrieval mechanisms, ability to hold large portions of data, effective retrieval mechanisms and ease of using interface language, which are also known as SQL-structured request language.

The DBMS program additionally covers the key facilities applied to manage the database. The overall volume of the database, including the DBMS and related applications may be known as a "database system." Oftentimes the phrase "database" is also applied to loosely signify any of the available DBMS, the database structure or software linked with the database (Barry, 2015).

Scientists may categorize database-management structures based on database models which they support. Later relational databases became prevalent during the 1980s. They model information in form of rows and columns within a sequence of tables, plus the greater majority utilize SQL for writing and probing data. During the 2000s, non-relational digital files became popular, where they were known as NoSQL since they use varying query languages.

6.5.1. Context

Historically, a "database" is a group of similar data and the means it's structured. Access to this information is typically provided through a "database managing system" (DBMS), comprising of an assimilated set of program software which allows operators to interact with each other, or more databases while providing access to every data comprised in the database (even though restrictions could exist that restrict access to certain data. The DBMS offers various attributes which allow for entry, storage and recovery of large amounts of information, plus provides techniques to determine how that material is organized.

Due to the close relationship existing between them, the word "database" is typically used informally to denote both a catalog and the DBMS applied to operate it. Outside the realm of specialized information technology, the phrase database is typically applied to refer to a group of related data like a spreadsheet, since size and usage needs typically require the use of a database managerial system. Present DBMSs provide different functions which allow for administration of a database as well as its data, often classified into different functional groups (Barry, 2015).

Both the database and related DBMS relate to the philosophies of a specific database arrangement. "Database system" refers jointly to the database configuration, database management structure, and database. Essentially, database servers are devoted computers which hold the particular databases and operate only the DBMS, plus its related software. Mostly database servers are multiprocessor devices, with considerable storage and RAID disk arrangements used for solid storage. RAID is applied for data recovery in case any of the available disks fail.

Hardware catalog accelerators, linked to one or several servers through a high-speed network, are also utilized in large volume operation processing settings. DBMSs can be found at the core of most filing applications. DBMSs can be developed around a custom multitasking kernel having built-in networking assistance, even though modern DBMSs normally rely on a typical operating system for providing these functions.

Since DBMSs cover a considerable market portion, PC and storage vendors often take into consideration DBMS necessities in their individual development arrangements. Databases and DBMSs may be categorized based on the database model(s) which they support (like relational or XML), including the form of computer that they operate on varying from a server group to a Smartphone, query language(s) applied to gain entry to the database like SQL or XQuery, plus their internal engineering, that affects output, scalability, flexibility, and security (Barry, 2015).

6.5.2. Database Management System Functions

According to scholars, Database Management System is defined as an application that allows users to describe, create, maintain and regulate admission to a database. Sometimes, it's extended to implicate the core database structure, whereby RDBMS is for relational, ORDBMS and OODBMS for object (orientated) structure and ORDBMS for Item-Relational. Other extensions may indicate some other functions, like DDBMS which stands for detached database management systems.

The functionality presented by a DBMS system can vary immensely. The central functionality is the data storage, recovery and update programs of a computer. It's also normally to be expected that the DBMS shall provide a number of utilities for these purposes as would be needed to manage the database effectively, including import, export, assessing, defragmentation and analysis assets (Barry, 2015).

6.6. HUMAN-COMPUTER INTERACTION

Figure 6.5. *Human-computer interaction is an interactive and intuitive process*

Source: https://www.njit.edu/academics/degree/bs-human-computer-interaction.

Human-computer interaction, or simply HCI, refers to a multidisciplinary area of study that focuses on the structure of computer technology, particularly, the relationship between people and computers. Though initially concerned with processors, HCI has since grown to cover nearly all types of IT design.

6.6.1. Beginnings

HCI first surfaced during the 1980s with invention of portable computers, just when machines like the Apple Macintosh, Commodore 64 and IBM PC 5150 began turning up in houses and offices in large numbers. At long last, complex electronic systems were accessible to typical consumers for uses like word processors, accounting assistance and games units.

Accordingly, since computers were not room-sized any longer, or expensive appliances exclusively built for specialists in controlled environments, the requirement to build human-computer communication that was also simple and effective for less experienced operators became progressively vital. From its roots, HCI would develop to integrate multiple disciplines, like computer science, human-factors engineering and cognitive science (Barry, 2015).

It soon became the topic of intense academic analysis. Those who researched and worked in this discipline viewed it as a vital instrument in popularizing the idea that collaboration between a processor and its user must resemble a person-to-person, open-ended dialogue.

Originally, HCI scientists focused on enhancing the applicability of desktop computers.

Nevertheless, with the introduction of technologies like the internet and smartphones, computer usage would gradually move away from desktops to include the mobile world as well.

It's no longer feasible to regard human-computer interaction as merely a branch of computer science, the field has grown broader, wider and more widespread than even computer science itself.

The sector has expanded from previously focusing on personal and generic user experience to comprise social and administrative computing, improving accessibility for the physically impaired and a wide range of other human-related experiences and activities (Page & Gamboa, 2019).

It further expanded from basic desktop office apps to include games, commerce, emergency planning, learning and education, and systems for support association and community. The field grew from initial graphical operator interfaces to include a variety of interaction procedures and instruments, multi-modal interactions, equipment support for prototype user interface features, and a wide range of emergent live chat and contextual interactions.

6.6.2. Fields of HCI

HCI is a rather broad sector which directly overlaps with other sectors like user-interface (UI) design, user-focused design and user experience design which bear a resemblance to it in many ways.However, HCI specialists often seem to be more knowledge focused. They're focused on technical research and creating empirical understandings of those who use this technology. Alternatively, some designers are mostly invariably industry-focused, plus involved in developing products or services—such as, smartphone applications and sites. Despite this divide, the typical considerations for products which manufacturers concern themselves over have direct correlation with the findings of various HCI specialists concerning users' mindsets (Page & Gamboa, 2019).

6.6.3. Short History of Human-Computer Interaction

Generally, human computer interaction has been mistaken by many people to be a field of UI design. Since it focuses on how people and computers cooperate to ever increasing points of both sophistication and simplicity.

It is easy to notice that till the mid-to-late 70s this field wasn't particularly significant. The few individuals who had easy access to workstations were scholars or professionals, including a few exceedingly dedicated (and affluent) hobbyists also in the mix. Lacking a broad base of operators, it wasn't essential to concentrate on how those individuals interacted with computers – however, they just utilized whatever was available or created the things that they required themselves (O'Regan, 2016).

Later on with the onset of private computing; things became clearer. Most people wanted computing though they did not want to pass through complex rigmarole to perform what they needed with a computer. The developers weren't prepared to develop and program their individual joysticks for the online apps which they bought, for instance, they didn't anticipate developing the mouse before coming up with a word-processor.

According to statistics from the Labor Statistics Bureau, human-computer interaction will grow by approximately 12% between 2014 and 2024, which is quicker than average expansion levels for most other occupations. This shows the vast market demand for experts who will have the appropriate computer and IT aptitudes. Interactions between workstations and humans must be as instinctive as conversations happening between two people—and yet a whole lot products and services still fail to accomplish this. So, what's required in order to create a more dynamic user experience? Well, human psychology, emotional design and specialized design procedures are just some of the factors needed to formulate effective human computer interaction programs. Cognitive engineering is also a field that developers are increasingly delving into (O'Regan, 2016).

6.7. COMPUTER VISION AND GRAPHICS

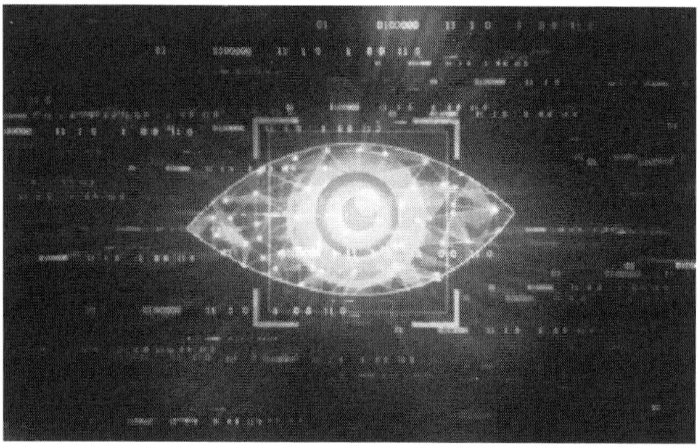

Figure 6.6. *Computer vision/graphics allows for improved visual content output.*

Source: https://skywell.software/blog/top-6-computer-vision-techniques-and-algorithms/.

Computer graphics renders 3D visuals from available lists plus scene descriptions, whereas Computer Vision looks is where users can envision a typical camera and co-processor, such as a GPU, which can generate an item list and scene depiction from constantly captured camera casings involving depth map, textures and segmented/recognized objects. Therefore, in a way making computer-vision is just the reverse of graphics translation. The 3D scanner as well as printer are now a reality. The question is at what point they merge, so that image capture to display is inseparable from a virtual video stream. Moreover, both disciplines must should work together closely just like all the others working with models plus simulations, including those that use experiments to gain new insight and new knowledge. Including various similar tandems in physics of experimental and theoretic nature.

In its most basic form, vison tasks can be quite parallel, whereas performing these tasks the GPU usually is a natural fit. The issue with the present innovation, may be a reasonably long transport: one needs to thrust the captured pictures to a GPU, prepare them there, and then pull these back again to the CPU system for further preparing. In a more advanced world, a person will conduct all IP/CV errands on a GPU-like gadget, where the captured photos are set straight from the device's sensor(s), which calls for executing such precise equipment and some few SDKs (like, by amplifying CUDA operations. To create parallels along with the bio-phrase: the vision portion would correspond to seeing, whereas the design portion would generally compare to dreaming. If tried out today, such complex gadgets could be very costly, but still innovatively conceivable. The genuine address is among the primary inspirations: before trying any usage, ponder on what you're aiming to do with such results (Tucker, 2004).

Generally, computer graphics can create images which humans consider indistinguishable from a photo of the scene, even though a pixel level image difference would show considerable differences in sections of the image, which the human eye or brain simply overlooks. However, both graphics and computer vision disciplines must work closer together and the process is expected to pick up speed in studies since with recent progresses in physically accurate rendering, CG processes and the vastly growing GPU processing power, CG produced images and video streams may become a worthy input to modern computer vision.

During the early 80's, Apple perceived the request for a GUI based text and graphics. Being among the first companies to utilize this innovation in doing a few of the primary computer-based graphic systems, most apple users did not require advance persuading of its possibilities nor did most online businesses or competitors. Presently, we do not think of that any longer but the demand coming from marketplace and Apple largely recognizing the technology and reacting to it is likely what spared Apple from getting overrun by Microsoft. Eventually, where there's a will then there shall always be a way (Tucker, 2004).

6.7.1. Future of the Two Technologies

There's a more particular zone where scholars believe graphics and computing vision shall combine. A quickly growing research field on robotic vision is the synchronous posture estimation and reproduction of a video scene. By tracing points within the video, users will be able to calculate camera postures, as well as the 3D posture of the points through strategies like SLAM or PTAM. Instead of following points, you may do a solid reconstruction for various pixels or for a given volume – for the most part known as DTAM.

Basically, DTAM methods make exceptionally basic presumptions around the surface properties – expecting just Lambertian reflection then you may just anticipate the assumption of a similar 3D point to bear the same shade in nearly all video views. Be that as it may, if you consolidate other properties, like specular reflection, then you must have some idea concerning what the scene lighting is. Many analysts are already looking into factor. Basically, you can say the more precise the graphical model then the more accurate its reconstruction will be (ITL Education Solutions Limited, 2011).

An area which interests many people is registration/tracking/pose estimation for surgical cases, where certain highlights are a noteworthy aspect for strategies like PTAM/DTAM. You'll as of now have some model of the model that you're checking from preoperative pictures. In other areas like camera-based route you will moreover have progressively accurate predefined renditions of the scene. For this case a conceivable way to unravel the issue is coordinating renderings of the copy to every video outline. Again, the more precise the rendering the greater the pose estimation shall be.

6.8. NUMERICAL ANALYSIS

Figure 6.7. This method is all about improving research capabilities for numerical analysis and other daily work-related activities.

Source: https://www.strath.ac.uk/research/subjects/mathematicsstatistics/numericalanalysisscientificcomputing/.

Numerical analysis is mostly concerned with the scientific derivation, portrayal and examination of strategies of obtaining numerical arrangements for scientific issues. Scholars are more curious about valuable strategies in arithmetic; which are strategies that reveal how to develop solutions of research problems. For instance, a useful verification of the presence of a solution towards the issue not just as it were shows that the finding exists, though too depicts how a structure may be decided. A verification which reveals the presence of a solution through a procedure known as reduction ad absurdum† however, may not be applicable in all cases (ITL Education Solutions Limited, 2011).

6.8.1. Case Study

Numerical analysis and logical interests have propelled the advancement of processors long before electronic computers indeed existed. Starting from the abacus up to Napier's bones, up to the difference as well as analytical engines, the acknowledgment that huge portions of math seem to depict nearly everything which encompasses us—to basic accuracy—fostered the advancement of procedures and devices which may perform these fundamental numerical operations dependably, rapidly, and with full precision.

The role of logical computing for the advancement of the computing sector at large has barely reduced in the present-day world; supercomputers are designed for climate simulations, fabric testing, and investigating the universe as well. The microchips which power supercomputers, portable workstations, and also smartphones are themselves gauged by their capacity to "crunch numbers" within contexts inferred from logical computing (Tedre, 2014).

The recurrent role that logical computing has played towards the advancement and improvement of computing, by and large, is due to the unmitigated requirement for bigger and more complex models and issues. Considering the resources, chemists would readily include more particles to their atomic flow re-enactment through this technology, whereas an oceanographer shall joyfully utilize more lattice cells to portray the sea, and an astrophysicist doubtlessly has no problem in envisioning more stellar bodies within their model. Even though the universe might be finite, still it's exceptionally large.

6.8.2. The Correctness Challenge

Apart from requesting massive computational assets, any designer of arithmetic codes is definitely mindful of the issue of guaranteeing that their task is being done as expected. Advanced arithmetic is particular, and numerous ideas that build upon various numerical constructs within the theoretical context require cautious shepherding into the tangible world to be valuable, whereas multiple others are totally unsuitable (Tedre, 2014).

There are various "moving aspects" to a logical code, which with considerable persistence and discipline can be worked out to guarantee correctness all through: Some of the elements to consider is whether the numerical aspect of the phenomena is appropriate at the first place? Whether it's numerically steady? Were the right parameters selected? Is the code which executes it correct? Is the firmware reliable?

In some instances, the buggy code shall still create the proper answer, though much slower compared to a correct program would—anathema to the catalyst!

6.8.3. Specialized Tools

Program developers have for long understood the advantages of standardized instruments that convey correct behavior and (ideally) performance, though software libraries should by nature be optimized. Whereas LAPACK/BLAS is also a valuable device, not all codes (for instance, those for specialized tools) are appropriate for expression in regards to their operators.

Luckily, compiler innovation (probably the most widely applicable of all software instruments) has proceeded to advance with continuously sophisticated hardware. Progressively, it is adequate for a designer to communicate how parts of the code ought to act with regard to different structural features, plus the low-level highlights—for illustration, what vector formalities are utilized, how strings are marshaled—plus are managed automatically (Tedre, 2014).

6.8.4. Modern Computing Environments

The compiler is among the most important aspects of today's "computing environment" which consists of the codes that we develop.

This system includes:

- Firmware: the micro/macro architecture of a processor, I/O, and contact interfaces with cluster-level considerations
- Runtime: the operating network and runtime program which oversees the firmware's resources and gives some form of abstraction to operators.
- Development instruments: The compiler, debugger, and examination instruments that assist the programmer to interpret their thoughts into accurate and productive codes.

Each aspect of the computing system features a great aspect of how the code is created, maintained, plus how it works. New technologies plus concepts continue to arise and be embraced in the look for improved performance and rather expressive tools.

6.8.5. The Scientist-Programmer's Predicament

Scientific codes are typically inscribed by domain specialists who comprehend the theory of programming well. These research-coders are typically familiar with the recurrently evolving state of computing systems, though not always cordially so. Progress of a particular scientific codebase may span either a decade or several, and the task of either adapting to fresh methodologies, or continuing to back legacy users may be nearly impractical but there's still hope for programmers.

6.9. PROGRAMMING LANGUAGES

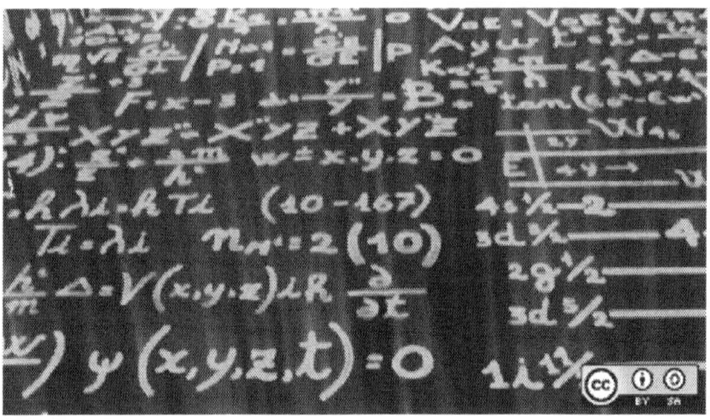

Figure 6.8. *Computers typically use programming language to interpret data.*

Source: https://opensource.com/alternatives/matlab.

Programming language refers to a formal computer communication, which consists of a group of instructions which produce different types of output. Generally, programming languages are applied in IT programming to execute algorithms.

A great deal of programming languages comprises of guidelines for processors. There is programmable equipment which use a list of specific instructions, instead of overall programming languages. The earliest ones preceded the creation of the digital computer, with the first possibly being the mechanical flute player depicted in the nineteenth century during the Arabic

Golden Age. Ever since the 1800s, several programs have been applied to determine the conduct of machines like music boxes, Jacquard looms and artistic pianos. The structures for these machineries (like the player piano's spools) didn't, however, produce varying behavior in reaction to various inputs or circumstances (Tucker, 2004).

All programming languages consists of a few basic building blocks for the depiction of information, including the procedures or changes applied to them (such as the addition of dual numbers or the determination of an object from a collection). These basic components are characterized by syntactic as well as semantic rules that depict their form and meaning respectively.

6.9.1. Syntax Programming

The Syntax programming code is regularly applied to assist programmers in identifying components of source code. A programming language's structural frame is called its syntax in computer language. Most coding languages are largely textual; meaning they utilize groupings of text such as words, numerical digits, and punctuation, more so like written everyday languages. To the contrary, there are a few other programming languages that are more visual in nature, utilizing visual connections between images to describe a program.

The syntax system of a language depicts the conceivable combinations of images that shape a grammatically correct program. The significance given to a set of symbols is addressed by semantics (in either formal mechanism or hard-coded using a reference system. Since a majority of languages are text-based, the emphasis is largely on syntax. In addition, programming language syntax is typically characterized using a set of standard expressions (for general lexical structure) as well as Backus–Naur shape (for syntactic structure) (Tucker, 2004).

C++: C++ is an all-purpose programming language developed by Bjarne Stroustrup, mostly as an expansion of the C range programming medium. The program has grown considerably over time, whereby present-day C++ has item-oriented, nonexclusive, and utilitarian functions apart from facilities for low-range memory manipulation. It's nearly always actualized as a compiled language, plus most merchants provide C++ compilers, as well as Free Software Establishment,, Microsoft, Intel, LLVM, Oracle, and IBM, such that it's accessible on multiple platforms. C++ was developed with a predisposition toward structural programming and implanted, resource-constrained program and massive frameworks, with execution, efficiency, and adaptability of use like its design models. C++ has moreover been found valuable in various other settings, with key qualities being computer program infrastructure and resource-constrained matters, such as desktop applications, and servers (for example, e-commerce, internet search, or SQL servers, plus performance-critical systems like phone switches and space probes.

C++ is regulated by the International Organization for Standardization (ISO), in which the most recent standard revision confirmed and distributed by ISO was in December 2017, known as ISO/IEC 14882:2017 (or casually as C++17).

The C++ programming system was originally standardized in 1998, being referred to as the ISO/IEC 14882:1998, and which was at that point revised by the C++03, C++14, and C+++ 11 protocols. The present C++17 standard largely supersedes these with modern highlights and an extended standard library. Prior to the introduction of standardization within the year 1998, the C++ program was originally created by Danish computer researcher Bjarne Stroustrup in 1979, while working for Chime Labs as an expansion of the C code; he needed an effective and adaptable language comparative to C which too gave high-level highlights for program organization. C++20 is the following intended standard, going by the current system of a fresh version being introduced after every three-year period.

Templates: For the most part, C++ templates allow for generic encoding. The program supports function, group, alias, as well as variable templates.

Moreover, templates can be parameterized based on forms, compile-time parameters, and other such templates. These templates are usually implemented through instantiation at the compile-time. To launch a template, compilers first substitute particular arguments for the template's parameters in order to produce a concrete feature or class instance. But a few substitutions aren't possible; which may be eliminated through a surplus resolution policy defined by the term "Substitution failure isn't an error" or (SFINAE). Templates are a vital tool which can be utilized for generic programming, code optimization as well as template meta programming, though this power may imply a cost.

6.10. SOFTWARE ENGINEERING

Figure 6.9. *Software engineering promotes the development of new and advanced computer programs.*

Source: http://www.mzcltd.com/software-engineering/.

Software engineering refers to the method of analyzing client needs and planning, building, and testing final client applications which will fulfil these needs via the use of application programming languages. It's the use of designing principles to software improvement. Different from basic programming, software designing is commonly applied, for bigger and more complex application frameworks, which are utilized as basic IT systems for industries and companies (Shelly, Freund, &Vermaat, 2010).

A software engineer typically considers the software requirements of final users, and subsequently creates or designs modern applications that meet their needs. Furthermore, this field may include the method of analyzing existing computer programs and altering it to meet modern application needs. As computer equipment gets to be affordable, the focus moves to software programs. Huge software systems might be more complicated than the equipment used to run them, therefore there's growing demand for best practices, as well as engineering procedures which can be used for software improvement.

6.10.1. Application

There should be discipline and management during software development, much like in every complex engineering process. In present-day customer gadgets, devices in straight competition regularly have comparable equipment and handling control, though the client experience will differ significantly based on the program being used. Software development is a point by point study of engineering for the purpose of designing, improving and maintenance of computer programs. Software designing was presented to address the problems of low-range software ventures. Issues emerge when an application by and large surpasses timelines, budgets, and current cutting-edge specifications. This guarantees that the software is built reliably, accurately, in a timely way and within budget while meeting the user's necessities. The demand for an emerging app may exceed consumers' expectations. A software product can be rated by how simply it can be applied by the end-user, including the features that it provides them. A good application should score in these areas:

- *Operational:* This focuses on how well an application works on operations such as budget, efficiency, correctness, usability, functionality, reliability, security and safety.
- *Transitional:* It's vital in cases where an app is moved from one point to another. Therefore, portability, reusability and flexibility come in this capacity.
- *Maintenance:* This stipulates how effective a software functions in the ever-shifting environment. Furthermore, maintainability, flexibility, standardization and scalability play a key role in maintenance.

In most cases, software designing starts with the initial phase as a user-request launch for a particular duty or an output. The client first submits his needs to a software provider organization. The app development group isolates client requirements, structural requirements, and utilitarian necessities. The need is collected by doing interviews with a client, referring to a database, examining the existing framework, etc. Following requirement gathering, the group examines if the computer program can be set to satisfy all the necessities of the client. The engineer at that point chooses a guide of his plan. Systemic analysis moreover incorporates an understanding of application product restrictions. According to the requirements and existing examination, a software plan is developed. The execution of software plan begins in terms of composing program codes in a reasonable programming language. Application testing is performed during coding by the designers and exhaustive testing is performed by testing specialists at different ranks of code like module testing (Shelly, Freund, &Vermaat, 2010).

6.10.2. Impact of Globalization

The original impact of outsourcing, plus the generally lower price of universal human assets in improving developing nations drove to a large movement of software improvement activities from organizations in North America, Europe, India and afterwards to China, Russia, and various other emerging nations. This method had a few flaws, basically the distance/time zone distinction that avoided human interaction between users and designers, plus the enormous job transfers. This dealt a negative effect on different viewpoints of the program designing profession. For instance, a few students in the developing countries omit education related to computer program designing because of the apprehension of offshore outsourcing (bringing in software items or services from different nations) and of being substituted by foreign visa operators. Even though statistics don't presently show a risk to program designing itself; a similar career, software programming does seem to have been influenced (Dasgupta, 2016).

Nonetheless, the ability to make use of offshore and local software programs has largely been made possible through software engineering. It has allowed for global outsourcing, whereby individuals from different time zones can share work and interact with their peers from different countries. Software engineering has brought the world much closer to us so to say.

6.11. BIOINFORMATICS

Figure 6.10. *Bioinformatics is a new field of computer science that concerned with gene modifications.*

Source: https://www.cancer.gov/research/nci-role/bioinformatics.

Bioinformatics is a multidisciplinary field that creates methods and computer programs for understanding natural data. Being an interdisciplinary branch of science, bioinformatics integrates science, research, data engineering, science and insights to analyze and translate natural information. Bioinformatics has been applied for in silico investigations of biological inquiries using scientific and statistical methodologies. Bioinformatics incorporates biological research which utilizes computer programming being part of their strategy, including a particular analysis "pipelines" which are repeatedly utilized, especially in the sector of genomics. Typical uses of bioinformatics incorporate the distinguishing of candidate genomes, plus single nucleotide polymorphisms or (SNPs). Regularly, such identification is developed with the goal of better comprehending the genetic context of disease, special adaptations, desirable qualities (especially in agriculture), or disparities between populations. In a more casual way, bioinformatics further seeks to understand the structural principles found in nucleic acid, as well as protein sequences known as proteomics (Dasgupta, 2016).

Bioinformatics has grown to be a vital aspect of different aspects of science. In research molecular science, bioinformatics procedures like picture and signal processing permit extraction of valuable results from huge portions of raw information. In the sector of genetics, it helps in sequencing as well as explaining genomes plus their observed transformations. This plays a part in the content mining of biological writing and the advancement of biological and genome ontologies to arrange and query biological information. It too plays a part in the examination of genetic and protein expression plus control. Bioinformatics devices help in comparing, assessing and translating of hereditary and genomic information, plus more generally in the comprehension of developmental perspectives of atomic science. Within a more integrative level, it assists in analysis and recording the natural pathways and systems which are a critical aspect of systems science. In structural science, it helps in the recreation and shaping of DNA, RNA and proteins also biomolecular exchanges (Barry, 2015).

6.11.1. Scope

To study how ordinary cellular activities are modified in different malady states, the biological information must be gathered to make a detailed picture of these functions. Subsequently, the sector of bioinformatics has advanced such that the foremost pressing duty now includes the examination and translation of different kinds of information. This incorporates nucleotide and amino groupings, protein spaces, and protein derivatives. The actual procedures of analyzing and deciphering information is alluded to as computational science. Some crucial sub-disciplines within bioinformatics as well as computational science are:

- Development and execution of software programs that allow effective access to, administration and utilization of, different sorts of information.
- Development of various calculations (numerical equations) and statistical measures which survey connections among groups of massive information sets. For instance, there are techniques for finding a genome within a grouping, and to anticipate protein arrangement and/or purpose.

The essential objective of bioinformatics is increasing the understanding of organic processes. What separates it from other approaches, nevertheless, is its concentration on developing and utilizing computationally intensive methods to attain this objective. Cases include: pattern recognition, information mining, robotic learning codes, and visualization. Major research endeavors in the sector include grouping arrangement, genome finding, genome gathering, medication design, drug finding, protein structure arrangement, protein structure forecast, prediction of genome expression and amino–protein interactions, genome-wide relation studies, the shaping of evolution and cell multiplication/mitosis.

Bioinformatics presently involves the creation and progression of databases, algorithms, computational and measurable procedures, and hypothesis to unravel formal and viable issues emerging from the administration and investigation of natural data. Within the past few years, massive improvements in genomic as well as other atomic research factors have been achieved (Henderson, 2009).

Basically, bioinformatics as a field refers to the name that's given to these arithmetical and computing methods used to gather understanding of biological procedures. Some common undertakings in bioinformatics comprise; mapping and examining DNA and protein chains, matching DNA and protein structures to contrast them, and developing and observing 3-D copies of protein structures.

In the perspective of genomics, annotation refers to the procedure of marking genomes and other organic features within a DNA structure. This process must be automated for efficacy since most genetic chains are too immense to interpret through hand only, not to forget the wish to annotate as numerous genomes as possible, since the frequency of sequencing has so far ceased to posture a bottleneck. Annotation is made conceivable by the reality that genes have a recognizable beginning and stop points, although the precise grouping found in these points can shift between genes. The earliest description of an all-inclusive genome annotation structure was publicized in 1995, with help from the Institute for Genomic Research which implemented the original complete sequencing and genome exploration of a living cell (Henderson, 2009).

6.12. Theory of Computing

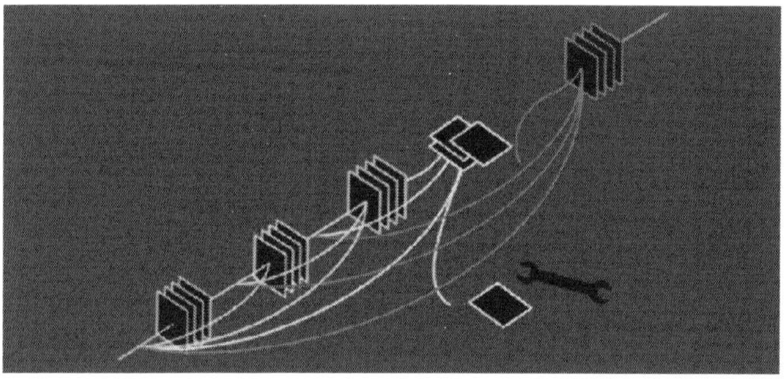

Figure 6.11. *Theory of computing is based upon the scientific models of Alan Turing.*

Source: https://simons.berkeley.edu/programs/past.

The computation theory is a field of computer sciences and arithmetic together that addresses how effectively issues can be unraveled on the basis of computation, utilizing an algorithm. It studies the overall features of computation that in turn, assists us to increase the proficiency at which processors illuminate issues. Typically, this is done upon estimating the legitimacy of the solutions provided by the computer via the model of computation, later alternating the algorithms such that users can get a more solid solution. This is a quickly-growing department that has assisted in understanding issues in various areas beside computer science, including Physics, Commerce, and Biology among other sectors. Before any introduction into the basics of the hypothesis of computation, it's important to learn more about the Turing machine because it plays a significant role in clarifying this theory (Tucker, 2004).

It is a hypothetical abstract equipment that is applied as a structure of computation. It utilizes a boundless memory tape whereby the data derived are saved, plus it analyzes this data to decide whether the process is feasible or otherwise. This device was developed by Alan Turing during the year 1963, where he applied it to demonstrate computation properties that are similar and reply to these questions: "Does a device exist which can decide whether any subjective machine on its spool is "circular" and "Does a device exist which can decide whether any self-assertive equipment on its tape does indeed print a particular symbol." As for computational theory itself, it can be read through 3 main fields which include:

6.12.1. Automata Theory

Each state has data around what needs to be do once an input is obtained by the machine (once more, rather like what happens once you arrive on Jail spot of a well-known board game). When the machine gets a new input, it typically checks the state and chooses a modern spot depend on the data on what to perform when it gets the input at that condition. In there aren't any more inputs, then the automaton ceases and the position it's on when it finishes decides whether the machine accepts or rejects the specific set of inputs.

Automata philosophy is very closely linked to formal language hypothesis. Generally, an automaton refers to a finite depiction of an official language which could be an infinite set. In most cases, Automata are classified based on the group of formal languages which they can recognize, normally exemplified by the famous Chomsky hierarchy, this describes the relationship between different languages and types of formalized logics. Mostly, Automata plays a crucial role in the compiler construction, computation theory, artificial intelligence, formal verification and parsing (Tucker, 2004).

6.12.2. Computability Theory

This is when users are able to frame the problem through a Turing machine effortlessly, but sometimes find it difficult to resolve it. Basically, it's when the workstation is able to tackle the problem though unable to arrive at a solution.

Also referred to as recursion model, this is a field of arithmetic logic, computer science, and the model of computation that rose in the 1930s through the study of calculable functions and Turing degrees. The sector has since grown to include studies on generalized computability as well as definability. For these areas, recursion philosophy overlaps with the proof hypothesis and the practical descriptive set theory. Even though there's considerable overlap with regards to knowledge and methodologies, mathematical recursion philosophers research the theory of comparative computability, reducibility models, and degree structures; whereas those in computer sciences field concentrate on the principle of formal methods, formal languages and sub recursive hierarchy (Tucker, 2004).

Kolmogorov complexity: The theory of Kolmogorov complexity including algorithmic randomness was first developed in the 1960s and 70s by Kolmogorov and Solomonoff among other researches. The key idea is considering a Turing machine and measuring up the intricacy of a number, where x is the dimension of the least input (p).

This technique revolutionized former ways of determining when an infinite structure is random or otherwise, by invoking a concept of randomness covering the finite items. Kolmogorov complexity turned to be not just a topic of independent study, though is also practical to other fields like a tool for attaining proofs. But there are still various open setbacks in this area.

6.12.3. Computational Complexity Theory

This theory delves into the efficiency whereby a problem can be solved. It's typically done by considering two key aspects: which are both time and space complexities, which serve as the measures of numerical steps necessary for analyzing and solving the problem, therefore determining the average memory space and resources required to solve the issue.

Chapter 7

The Relationship between Science and Technology

CONTENTS

7.1. INTRODUCTION

There's a quite deeper association between science and technology. This is because all innovation – from mobile phones to therapeutic scanners to vehicles – is intimately associated with science. If their scientific underpinnings are lacking, these inventions wouldn't exist. Generally, science is an exploration of the natural environment by collecting information through an efficient procedure called the scientific strategy. And innovation is where we use science to make gadgets that can unravel issues and do certain tasks. Innovation is actually the appliance of science. Therefore, it truly is impossible to detach the two.

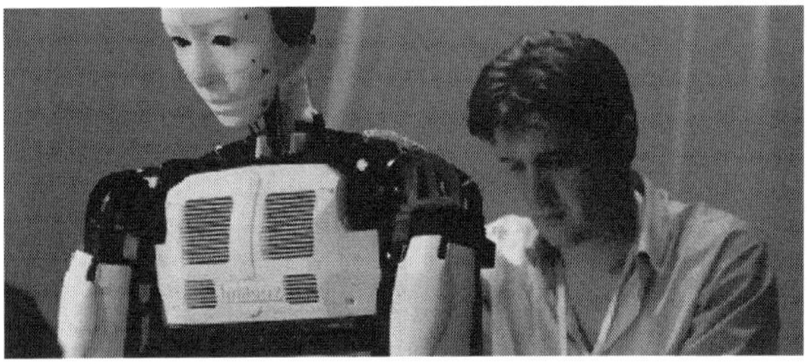

Figure 7.1. *Robotics is a modern-day example of how science is influencing technological advancement.*

Source: https://www.weforum.org/agenda/2015/12/how-can-we-improve-technological-innovation/.

By far the greatest association is what has already been touched on above: technology is the actualization of science. As a matter of fact, all through history, natural science has opened the way for different sorts of astounding progresses in the society. In the times of agrarian revolution, the way people lived changed forever. Going from mere hunter gatherers who wandered the earth, to starting to down in specific points. This is because they acquired the scientific knowledge essential for developing crops.

All of a sudden, these early people didn't have to be wanderers anymore. Technology allowed people to make sufficient food for nourish their families where they were. Then shelters stopped being simple and basic to more advanced permanent structures and buildings. All this was made possible due to advancement in technology. In the modern age, this same principle continues to play each day. For instance, technologies like Smartphone's and TVs wouldn't have been possible were it not for advanced sciences such as quantum mechanics.

7.2. INFLUENCES OF SCIENCE TO TECHNOLOGY

7.2.1. Science as a Direct Source of New Technological Ideas

Science, innovation and development each depict a progressively larger class of activities that are greatly interdependent but unique. Science contributes to innovation in different ways. First, it allows for new knowledge that provides a basis for new innovative possibilities. Also, it's a source of instruments and strategies that allow for an effective engineering plan and information base for the assessment of feasibility of projects. There are both indirect and direct links between science and innovation, the research benefits and potential social value is much wider and varied than would be connoted by checking only the direct relations between science and innovation. Moreover, nowadays many firms have operations which are based upon a set of specialized innovations which are frequently planned in close contact with potential clients. This approach helps in creating products that are user-focused and practical (Smith, 2013).

The relationship between science and innovation is multifaceted and depends mostly on the specific field of innovation being examined. For mechanical innovation, for instance, the input of science to innovation is generally weak, and it is regularly possible to form rather vital innovations without any deep knowledge around the fundamental science. In contrast, electrical, molecular, and atomic technology are highly reliant on science, plus most innovations are developed only by individuals with significant training in science.

The determination of a suitable level of effort, plus the development of an organizational structure that will promote the best possible identification of innovative opportunities, without a lot of limitation on the research plan is an ongoing matter in research planning with regards to this specific field of science and technology interaction. Science as a basis of developing design tools and methods. Whereas the process of designing is rather unique from the procedure of coming up with fresh knowledge of environmental phenomena, the two forms are exceptionally personally related. The relationship has grown to become increasingly critical as the price of experimentally testing and assessing complex model technological structures has grown. Hypothetical forecast, modeling, and recreation of large frameworks, regularly was accompanied by estimation and observational testing of subsystems as well as components, and has progressively substituted for holistic observational testing of absolute systems, and this needs design tools, as well as analytical methods founded in phenomenological understanding (Smith, 2013).

Social impact of information science and technology: Advancements in information science as well as innovation, which represent people's mental and imaginative items, are increasingly triggering changes in different areas of society. Focusing on computers and systems, the rather recent advancement and globalization of information science and innovation are empowering more individuals to utilize data in larger amounts, at quicker speeds, in highly advanced ways, quite effortlessly, at reduced costs, and over broader distances than previously. This will induce not only quantitative but even subjective changes in the usage and role of data in society, prompting the development, in the current century, of a community that relies on information science and innovation in every aspect, from social structures to personal ways of life and how the occupations of science are conducted. It's necessary first to keep up with the diverse range of differing social possibilities of improvements in IT science technology, plus the ongoing efforts to realize those possibilities. Similarly, the readiness to wholly recognize and correctly respond to emerging issues that come about from the communication-induced variations in society is required (Smith, 2013).

Different possibilities of IT and technology: Advancements in information science, as well as innovation will to begin with significantly improve the ratio of flexibility of personal choice and action, plus make more dynamic lifestyles possible. By growing the extent of communications progressively over time, the popularity of network connected computers shall improve the interactions among people, allowing the person not just to obtain data (from the different data accessible) but moreover to spread data and assist the person to engage in exercises beyond regional, physical or any other limitations.

As information science innovation progresses, it will lead to more efficiency, permitting individuals to engage in creative works and demonstrating them in real life for improved living standards.

In different aspects of a person life, the application of information science and innovation will trigger new activities and greater comfort, subsequently providing a wide range of alternatives including varying beliefs and values. Additionally, information science and innovation have incredible potential for improving the economy and community at large in useful ways; whereby the application of information science as well as innovation will considerably improve the efficiency of existing businesses and also promote the formation of new businesses through commercialization of new innovations and the combining of different areas (Smith, 2013).

7.2.2. Science as a Source of Engineering Design Tools and Techniques

Figure 7.2. *Science is continuously being applied in mechanical engineering to tackle various engineering challenges.*

Source: https://ocw.mit.edu/courses/mechanical-engineering/.

Engineering refers to the applied scientific research of obtaining and applying information to design, examine, and/or development of works for viable purposes. The U.S. Engineers' Board for Professional Advancement defines Engineering as inventive application of logical standards to plan or create structures, machines, device, or fabricating processes, or works applying them separately or jointly; or to build or operate similarly with complete recognition of their plan; or to estimate their behavior within particular working conditions; largely as regards an intended role, economics of operation plus security to life and assets. The wider discipline of engineering envelops a broad range of particular sub-disciplines which focus on the matters related to creating a particular form of item, or applying a particular type of technology. This, consequently, should speed up the move to a maintainable technological system that actualizes even greater value and which doesn't depend on the utilization of mass amounts of material assets. Moreover, information science and innovation will too bring around critical changes in strategies of research and improvement, subsequently accelerating the rate of scientific and technical progress (Moreira, 2016).

Context: Engineering new instruments for scientific advancement in the natural sciences still bears great promise, particularly in the field of imaging of small solids on nano-range scales and in different measurements (extending from for zero, to four for both time and range.) Two illustrations include (1) interaction-mode or dynamic space AFM whereby the tip isn't at the conclusion of a wavering cantilever pillar but rather the periphery of a few other mechanical systems, plus (2) NMR recurrence and relaxation-period spectroscopy strategies where the test model is purposely moved consistently to launch NMR access to (power) polarization and hence inner endogenous electric areas of any multipole arrangement. Both approaches, though, shall require unique thinking by young, free-thinking PhD-level researchers and engineers who don't necessarily believe researchers' claims that there aren't any new major advancements presently to pursue in these areas.

Nevertheless, by delving more deeply and profoundly into the fundamental physics, it shall become obvious that there are hypothetical physics frameworks through which to put hope that someday models of innovative new imaging microscopes shall be invented, developed, used in the laboratory, and recorded in popular peer-reviewed engineering as well as scientific research journals (Moreira, 2016).

DNA Synthesis: During the last few years, there have been considerable innovation progresses in this field, especially with regard to the de novo union of progressively longer DNA sequences. The molecular union and ligation of expansive fragments of a DNA layout, followed by enzymatic translation of RNA drove to the de novo development of poliovirus gene in 2002 (approximately 7,500 nucleotides in scope), from which the contagious, harmful infection was rescued taking after its transfection into tolerant cells. A short while later researchers reported the effective gathering of a microbial infection genome, a finding that was made possible thanks to scientific tools and techniques. Other endeavors in industry as well as academia drove to the blending and gathering of expansive fragments of the hepatitis C viral genome, from where replication competent RNA atoms were protected (Smith, 2013).

Impact of technology on modern development: Progresses in science and innovation drive the advancement of data systems. Logical, operational, and, progressively, business requirements decide what perceptions to form, how the data ought to be analyzed, plus what items to make. The logical understanding generated by creating and utilizing these information and items, together with enhancements in instrumentation and computer have led to a fresh set of prerequisites. The fresh capabilities arising from these advancements can alter what the divisions are doing or need to do—at times dramatically—and hence specifically influence open, private, and scholarly partnerships. Despite sharp decreases in the broadcast communications industry and Web start-up companies, new innovations and products proceed to be launched at quite a fast rate. Rapid innovative changes, strong competition, plus the development of new marketplaces are anticipated to continue or indeed escalate within the coming decade.

The history of innovation shows that technological advancements come in two primary forms: those which can be sensibly predicted and those which can't. Predictability falls off quickly with time, therefore the concentration here is on innovative changes in the business enterprise that are happening presently or which shall happen over the following few years. There are various computer and communications innovations which will have an effect on both modern enterprise and the connections among businesses. Some examples include simulations, communication innovations, visualization, human-computer interfacing, and innovations for storing, organizing, and exchanging information. Generally, predictable technological changes are expected to have some major impacts on private, public and academic sectors (Moreira, 2016).

7.2.3. Instrumentation, Laboratory Techniques, and Analytical Methods

"Laboratory instruments" is a broad term referring to all forms of instruments, vessels, as well as other devices required for operations in different laboratories, synthesis, and examination. Lab Instruments are usually exposed to a few extreme compounds and physical impacts and should at the same time give precise estimation results, should have long life plus ensure safety for users. Hence, laboratory instruments must have a great quality and be solid in form to meet all the benchmarks in laboratory technology. Modern laboratory devices feature certain interfaces and can in this manner be utilized not just by experts but even by untrained faculty because of user-friendly program operations. Approved and equipped with ISO certification, laboratory instruments provide significant results in the briefest possible time. These tested lab instruments may be delivered or be availed together with calibration certificates (ISO) (which are optionally accessible). ISO is accessible either with the original order for recalibration, such as on annual basis.

Scientific instruments found in the laboratory

- Conductivity Meters: Users have access to both common and waterproof conduction meters. There are too conductivity meters accessible for running water or freshwater (suggested for relevant businesses), including those Conductivity Meters used for flowing water or freshwater plus those with diverse conductivity measurement ranges. A critical factor in modern conductivity meters is the fact that they ordinarily measure electric conduction in μS/cm, in any case they can furthermore take estimations in mg/l (for precise reading of matter in dissolved solid matter). The connection is established in the following way: 2 μS/cm = 1ppm (fractions per million) is equal to 1 mg/l. Compensated heat levels in conductivity meters may be programmed or by hand.

- Hygrometers: Nowadays, you can find hygrometers which are capable of measuring relative air moisture, or combined gadgets that can moreover measure temperature. The hygrometers measure diverse aspects of humidity based on the particular model. Average air moisture is a vital component in measurement taking. These Hygrometers measure diverse aspects of humidity, some of the models are used in sectors like industry, transportation and gardening. The appliances are of flexible use. A few of the models give a data logger utility for around 60.000 estimation values which make durable estimations possible. Following the estimations, the decided data may either be kept on an inner storage tool like for illustration a memory card, or exchanged to a processor through interfaces like a USB.
- Further documenting and analysis may occur at that point. A good number of these appliances further include software programs, with which it's feasible to have your gathered information shown on your computer, and with the assistance of a table or even as a chart which can assist you to check the results of your testing series. By basically saving the information on your computer, it is additionally made conceivable to create long-term measurements within a long duration of time. Furthermore, it's possible to compare the ongoing of the test arrangement in particular time scales like months, quarterly and indeed even years. Through this storage you can compare the data with the past year and future as well. Since these items are moreover made to measure climatic conditions within the room, you'll see the moisture content which is within the room. There are also calibrations for the equipment which makes it feasible to ensure that calculations are done accurately (Moreira, 2016).

Analytical Methods

- Descriptive Analytics: This is among the most common aspects in analytics. In business, it gives the researcher a set of vital metrics and measurements within the organization. A good example of this may be a month to month profit or loss document. Likewise, an analyst might have information on a huge number of clients. Understanding statistic data on their clients, for instance, would be rated as "descriptive analytics." Using valuable visualization instruments improves the impact of descriptive analytics.
- Coefficient of Variation Calculator: This instrument calculates the coefficient of different groups of information. The variation coefficient is basically a measure of spread which tends to be applied when it is essential to contrast the distribution of numbers in multiple datasets with quite distinct means.
- To do the calculation, basically enter your information into the textbox provided, either a single score for each line or in form of a comma-delimited list, determine whether your information represents a particular populace or sample, then push on "Calculate."
- Pooled Variance Calculator: This machine will produce an appraisal of a populace variance through calculating the pooled fluctuation (or mutual variance) of double tests within the presumption that the tests have been derived from a single populace or two populaces with a similar variance. Only include your test scores into the content boxes provided, either one score for each line, or in form of a comma delimited catalog, and then press Calculate.

7.2.4. The Development of Human Skills

Advancements in science and innovation are drastically changing the way that individuals live, interact, and transact, with significant impacts on financial advancement. To promote tech development, advancing nations should contribute in quality education for youngsters, and persistent abilities training for labourers and managers.

Science and innovation are main drivers to improvement, since innovative and scientific transformations support financial progresses, advancements in health structures, education and infrastructure. The innovative revolutions of the modern 21st century are developing from totally new segments, depending on micro-systems, tele-communications, bio-scientific and nano-technology. Technology items are changing business practices all across the economy, including the lives of those with access to their impacts. The most momentous breakthroughs will arise from the blending of bits of knowledge and applications emerging when these innovations converge (McClellan III, & Dorn, 2006).

Through improvements in health and education, the innovations have the ability to enhance the lives of underprivileged individuals in developing nations. Removing diseases like malaria, a tribulation of African for many centuries, is presently possible. Cures for other infections which are endemic in emerging nations are moreover now conceivable, allowing individuals with weakened health conditions to remain healthy and lead productive lives.

Access and utility are essential: Service and innovation are the key differentiators between nations that are capable of handling destitution effectively by developing and growing their economies, as well as those that aren't. The degree to which developing countries rise to be financial powerhouses will vary based on their capacity to grasp and apply bits of knowledge from science and innovation plus utilize them creatively. Innovation is the key driver of technological development and promotes higher standards of living.

Being an engine for growth, the future prospective of technology is limitless, and still mainly untapped in developing regions across the world. Underdeveloped countries don't just lack expert labor and capital, but instead use these less proficiently as well. Inputs account for fewer than half of all the differences in yearly income across nations. The other half is because of inability to embrace and adapt technologies for improving productivity (McClellan III, & Dorn, 2006).

Computing for instance, through unlocking structural backlogs and management of integrated supply chains, technology can transform financial performance by allowing affordable and accessible services in education plus healthcare. The interaction of processors and internet, plus smartphones and "cloud computing," has improved human experience, empowering communities through access to information and markets, altering the relationship between people and those in positions of authority, while allowing new groupings to appear in virtual worlds spanning the whole globe.

According to UN International Telecommunications Union, by the conclusion of 2010 there existed a projected 5.3 billion smartphone subscriptions universally, plus 940 million registrations to 3G services. Around 90% of the globe's population can access smartphone networks, with around 3/4 of mobile subscribers currently found in developing economies. Likewise, cellular technology has permitted Africa to fast-track the age of stationary line telephony, providing affordable accessibility to millions of individuals (McClellan III, & Dorn, 2006).

Nevertheless, the sustained and equitable growth of Information Communications Technology (ICT) will be influenced by electricity. The actual gap over the coming 20yrs shall be between those having access to reliable electricity to run these devices and those who do not.

The other technologies being developed are programs for cognitive enhancement, proton cancer rehabilitation and genetic engineering. Furthermore, revolutionary inventions include local underground nuclear power modules called nuclear batteries, which shall be extra-safe and maintenance-free; other forms of photo-voltaic compounds will be able to generate cheaper electricity from sunlight compared to coal include; a variety of nano-technologies that reduce the cost and promote the reliability of various products – even in poorest communities of developing countries.

Managing innovative transformations poses certain challenges. Some innovations and discoveries may raise full bio-ethical issues, like genetic alteration of food plants and cloning of embryos which have been debated by scholars. There's a hazard that their cost, especially in the preliminary stages of improvement, will decline the present imbalance by restricting access to affluent people.

This as of now happens in health care sectors of the G7 nations, whereby the request for exceptionally high-cost demonstrative gear and surgical mediations promoting longevity and superior quality of life to more seasoned affluent individuals overstretch public wellbeing care budgets, plus lowers benefit quality in low class neighborhoods. At last, resource-intensive innovations, centered on fulfilling high utilization demand, such as holidays overseas in beach resorts, wilderness zones, or iconic cities, induce carbon emissions plus ecological damage (McClellan III, & Dorn, 2006).

To promote scientific advances, developing countries must invest in empowering their youth through education, continual skills training for employees and managers, plus ensuring the knowledge gained is shared widely across the society.

7.2.5. Technology Assessment

Figure 7.3. *Technology assessment is essential for maintaining high-quality standards in science and innovation.*

Source: https://www.executivegov.com/2019/12/gao-seeks-to-expand-science-technology-assessment-team.

Technology assessment (TA) is a discipline that endeavors to foresee future improvements of technologies, including projects plus their foreseeable impacts, and avail the assessments to appropriate decision arenas. TA has been updated (with textbooks and courses) and is presently a publicly acknowledged activity. The reality of its institutionalization demonstrates how present-day risk society is getting to be flexible. Vulnerabilities aren't diminished by TA, instead made manageable.

Technology Evaluation Agencies: Technology evaluation is the practical procedure of deciding the value of a fresh or emerging innovation by itself or set against present or competing innovations, utilizing security, viability, adequacy, result, risk administration, strategic, budgetary, and competitive criteria. Innovation evaluation too considers morals and law, including health needs and affordability compared to other competing innovations. A "technology" is described as instruments, equipment, computer program, drugs, biotechnologies, procedures, and treatments; plus systems applied to analyze, treat, or screen patients. The innovation evaluation procedure should be done professionally, so as to yield accurate results (Arnaldi& Bianchi, 2016).

Technology assessment isn't similar as innovation acquisition/buying or technology planning. The final two are procedures for determining gear traders, requesting offers, and methodically deciding an organization's technology-related requirements based on matters like strategic, financial, and management. The informational needs vary significantly between innovation appraisal and the procurement or structuring processes. This area focuses on the assets that are crucial to innovation assessment. Globally, there are about 400 companies (private, academic, and administrative) that avail technology evaluation data, databases, or counseling services. A few are entirely data clearinghouses, others perform innovation appraisal, while some do both.

For those who perform appraisals, the quality of data produced changes significantly from superficial studies to in-depth, denoted expository reports. Language impediments are also a critical matter in assessment. In the ultimate examination, the capacity to undertake innovation evaluation requires acclimatizing endless amounts of data, most of which persist as it were in the English language (Tedre, 2014).

Technology assessment research available with the Global Society for Technology Appraisal in Health Care (ISTAHC), together with other umbrella bodies are normally written in English. Apart from healthcare, others sectors like agriculture also use English for assessments of technological devices.

Technology Assessment: Technology appraisal includes examination of issues relating to item innovation and production innovation. Product innovation appraisal is especially vital for therapeutic items in the hospital environment. Of course, security matters are incredibly important as well. The technical plan of a therapeutic instrument must comply with present national and universal benchmarks and directions. Acknowledged design standards must be applied also.

The inclusion of outside people who aren't familiar with the program is a vital aspect of innovation evaluation. Such people are important for conducting tests as well as giving clientele input. Such an association frequently results in key changes in the plan and usefulness of a device. Innovation evaluation of a certain number of gadgets will influence the ultimate design of the object in a definitive way (Krohn, Layton, & Weingart, 2012).

Nevertheless, the involvement of "external" individuals in product assessment should include some form of protection in regards to secrecy declaration, or agreement whereby the concerned person is barred from revealing or applying the knowledge acquired during their assessment work.

The appraisal of invention technology problems is significant before mass production begins. The choice of appropriate production technologies may strongly influence the product's market price. If fresh production equipment is set up, then massive investments may be necessary. Additionally, they might impact the entire project's economy (Krohn, Layton, & Weingart, 2012).

If a massive production run of multiple devices is anticipated, a manufacturing technology-oriented design shall result in huge savings, especially for a developer in a university or clinic environment, who typically doesn't have wide experience in business production techniques. The origination of close and primary collaboration between the designer and final (industrial) creator of the appliance is strongly suggested. Such partnership often reduces the journey to market substantially and may reduce production costs as well.

Constructive Test Analysis: This model of technology testing was first developed in the Netherlands, though is applied and deliberated elsewhere in an attempt to improve the design of fresh technology through the feedback of Technology Analysis activities into the specific construction of technology.

Different from other types of TA, CTA isn't directed toward affecting regulatory practices by evaluating the effects of technology. Rather, CTA addresses social issues pertaining to technology influencing design practices.

The process seeks to mobilize perceptions on co-evolutionary aspects of science, technology and community for anticipating and evaluating technologies, instead of being predominantly focused with evaluating societal effects of quasi-given innovation. This assessment prompted the value of including users in development and innovation procedures, allowing for the development and inclusion of new technologies in daily life (Krohn, Layton, & Weingart, 2012).

7.2.6. Science as a Source of Development Strategy

Many companies today have pursued a policy called "Shots on Goal," whereby the goal is maximizing the number of products in market pipelines to increase the odds that hopefully a few shall prove successful. This method is intended to address the still partial knowledge on consumer needs, though in practice it typically results to higher product development costs and minimal productivity.

A better strategy instead is relying on development to identify and expedite promising programs. Ultimately, the goal is prioritizing programs resulting from targets which have been validated in humans, especially through genetic inquiry which shows a target's particular influence on product development and risk (Moreira, 2016).

While this approach doesn't guarantee that every designated program shall prove successful, scientists are optimistic that it can increase the general ratio of success for product trials, accelerate development timelines, minimize costs, and enhance returns on research and development investment.

When a company discovers itself with more projects than it can provide for clients with their own resources, they may move more forcefully to partner or out-license the overflow resources. The resulting assertions give incomes that can be utilized to back key programs within their pipeline, plus they serve the needs of clients by ensuring that more useful products get developed. They must also be dynamic in their pursuit of outside innovation which can complement their internal capacities and programs. This readiness to embrace development wherever a company is able to discover it is showcased by the acquisitions that it makes later on (Moreira, 2016).

Case Study: With multiple numbers to crunch when doing research, indeed specialists find it difficult to measure the advantages of research for community, especially when we take into consideration that innovation, and more specifically science, spreads quickly and universally from segment to segment and region to region.

Nevertheless, it's similarly vital to keep in mind that scientific improvement not only enhances financial development and technological competitiveness, but is additionally key to developing a country's riches and enhancing long-term and life quality of its citizens. However, later choices influencing the scientific division have not been very empowering, and some countries such as Spain are going back to a circumstance that many thought was consigned to history.

The mechanical division (53.0% of Research & Development investing, 0.69% of the GDP) has been greatly hit by improvidence plus the outcomes of the current financial emergency. Whereas most department diminished their R&D investing in 2012 as compared to the past year, the lessening within the industrial field was 4.1% (Moreira, 2016).

This shows that financing for scientific inquiry in Spain must proceed to arise from a continuously weakened public division that can't compete without comprehensive public–private union. Added onto this is the past overdue reforms of the college system, a key contributor in science and information exchange, subsequently guaranteeing the smooth operation of "Triple Helix" models shaped by academia (investigation, technology exchange offices, etc.), the state (legislation, grants, copyright, etc.) and business (development, investment, production, etc.), plus the integration of mechanical, innovative and scientific policies. To promote research toward Spain's actual interests calls for prompt action to assess and prioritize particular aspects and goals, whereas making concerted efforts to develop a vital competitive mass. The public must moreover realize the truth that the administrative and authoritative system underlying Spanish public research is unable to meet current market demands (Moreira, 2016).

Implications: In light of the increasing disenchantment and frustrations among scientists appealing for a range of measures which include legislative amendment, structural enhancements, investment and political contracts, there should be a way to unite community, political and business forces in the principle that science forms the foundation for a solid future and progress. Fresh ground rules must be established, like the description of a well prioritized scientific strategy, with a stable perspective capable of appealing to investors. At a certain stage, this looked to be easy to grasp, but only to be pulled away by the present economic situation plus subsequent budget restrictions that affect science and research departments.

It shall only again become factual if the reforms required to promote the growth and subsidy of competitive systems are set put. A critical aspect of this method is to rethink the obsolete human resources policies, while providing a clear career structure for scholars and researchers who presently find it hard to access influential positions in universities, as well as public research institutions. Yet another priority is identifying strategic sectors where scientists can be helpful right now, including others areas that may be potential targets of development in the near future, covering both public and private aspects (Moreira, 2016).

7.3. CONTRIBUTION OF TECHNOLOGY TO SCIENCE

7.3.1. Technology as a Source of New Scientific Challenges

The technology that scientists are using is becoming increasingly powerful by the day. Though in many regions of the world, consistent electricity and Web access, including supercomputing power continues to be elusive. There are various things which scientists can do, nevertheless to enhance their technological capabilities, such as pulling all their data needs together in a common place.

Significant technological progresses are being done over a wide sector of fields, such as data communications, and artificial intelligence (AI), especially in regards to machine learning and automation, nanotechnology, space innovation; biotechnology; as well as quantum computing just to mention but a few these breakthroughs are anticipated to be exceedingly disruptive and trigger some major transformative revolutions in how societies work (Moreira, 2016).

The innovative progresses are largely driven by advancements in insurgency that started around four decades back. These developments are centered around the gathering, preparation, and analyzing of massive reams of data rising from the information sciences and with suggestions for incalculable zones of inquiry and advancement. These progresses guarantee critical social and financial benefits, expanded productivity, and enhanced efficiency over a variety of sectors (Moreira, 2016).

Technology's disruptive ability: There are increasing concerns that technological innovations, plus how they're applied will posture serious challenges, such as labor force separations and other related marketplace disturbances, heightened imbalances, and fresh dangers to public security as well as national security. The innovations are generally dual use, such that they may be utilized as much to dish malicious or deadly purposes since they can be saddled to improve social and financial improvement, rendering endeavors to oversee them more complicated. Generally simple to access and utilize, a majority of them are intrinsically helpless to misuse and disturbance from both close and far.

In contrast, geopolitical pressures around the globe are increasing, and most nations progressively see these innovations as central to countrywide security. The probability for misuse is momentous (Smith, 2013). And greater financial integration and network mean that the impacts and results of innovative progresses are much less localized than previously and are prone to spread to nations and businesses worldwide. Technological advancement is generally happening past the realms of governments. In numerous cases, the pace of development is even outpacing states' capacity to keep in touch with recent improvements and their probable societal impacts. Plus indeed if one or several of national governments plan approaches for overseeing these impacts, the international reach of most developing innovations plus their impacts requires fresh approaches to multifaceted administration that's much more troublesome to concur on. A more prominent number and diversity of characters should be included to start, design, and actualize both technical and basic research programs.

However, just like governments, most of these other players don't have (or basically don't contribute to) the strategy to look at the broader, widespread societal implications of their investing, investigation, and advancements. When they perform so, recognizing the most important or viable policy-based or normative-focused places to talk about these implications can be tasking, not slightest since existing platforms oftentimes don't consider the diverse players involved, the cross-border access of the innovations in question, plus the diverse value and political structures at play. Especially the case when innovations are planned for profit-making only, and their directions are totally subordinate on community influences (Smith, 2013).

Today's innovative advances are regarded disruptive not just in market terms, though in terms also of the sense they're "provoking disturbances of lawful and administrative orders" plus have the ability to "disturb the profound values upon which authenticity of existing social structures rests, plus on which acknowledged lawful and administrative systems draw inspiration. Complex, dynamic systems already control a few areas of innovation. For instance, the internet is administered by a combination of existing worldwide laws; including an ever-growing, complex mix of political assertions; specialized guidelines and protocols; commerce, trade, and human rights policies; research standards; national controls; and self-management in the private field.

Engaging stakeholders in science and technology sectors: Lawmakers, regulators, private commerce leaders, analysts, and civic players must be prepared to react more dependably and viably to the impacts and consequences of innovative progresses and the likely societal hazards that they posture. Continuous tests with fresh rules, standards, and conventions to deal with solid pertinent arrangement issues are definitely essential, one case being the WEF's "flexible" administration initiative. However, executing these responses at scale plus applying them amid financial and security concerns still remains to be a complex issue (Smith, 2013).

This assignment likely will need a mix of systems, improved investing in public research programs, and the inclusion of various actors apart from the fair states. To this conclusion, it is crucial that pertinent actors portray residential and universal roles to decide which technology-based challenges should be addressed promptly.

7.3.2 Instrumentation and Measurement Techniques

Measurement is the practice of determining a particular target's weight, dimension, capacity, measurement, or other physical measurements. It's common to mistake the phrase "measurement" for words like "quantify" or "calculate" though as a policy of thumb, simply think of estimation as a basic activity within the word instrumentation. To gain a comprehensive understanding of this topic, this piece will look at the description of both estimation and instrumentation: Instrumentation can be described as a collective terminology for measuring certain instruments utilized for demonstrating, measuring and cataloging physical quantities. Estimation – to show measured outcomes utilizing values and signs. Be careful that the field of estimation is done when a person employs measuring devices or an estimation system or Instrumentation.

Historically, our capacity to measure has assisted humankind to improve and advance in different sectors of development like innovation, science, trade, as well as quantitative research. All through history, there have existed 100s of measuring structures that existed for each kind of field and occupation. For illustration, a shoe producer would have a distinctive measuring framework at that point a baker shall have a simple stone cutter, and would have a broad measuring framework then craftsmen will follow (McClellan III, & Dorn, 2006).

Differences between Measurement and Basic Inspection: Inspection is an allusion to the values attained through measurement using the existing references at hand whereas determining whether an item is acceptable. Alternatively, measurement is the amount of results discovered through the application of measurement tools. Usually, there's no need to apply the descriptions of measurement together with inspection separately. Nevertheless, it's still a great thing to understand that there's indeed some difference between these two.

Measuring techniques; There are two forms of measurement systems: which are direct and indirect measurement

- Direct Measurement: These are ascertained through using a tool to directly capture the height, length and other aspects of the object to decide its measurement. The model of direct measurement permits the measurement to be recognized as it is, nevertheless errors might ensue depending on the ability of the individual doing the measurement. Samples of direct measurements comprise measuring your height through a measuring tape, finding the temperatures of your oven by the use of thermometer, and calculating the overall length of your daytime exercises by using a stopwatch. In the realm of physics, among the more common instances of direct measuring is current. When trying to measure current passing through a wire, oftentimes you use an ammeter linked to the circuit for directly measuring it. This technique is regarded to be a direct measurement since the tool being applied, the ammeter, gauges the current passing in the cable without the need of knowing any data prior to that measurement.
- Indirect Measurement: Direct measurements might be what you're most accustomed to, but indirect measurements also have their uses. These measurements happen when you take a measurement of a particular unit/object then transform it such that it matches with the characteristics of another object. The notion of indirect measurement might be a bit challenging for some individuals to comprehend, because to the fact many individuals don't have any use for it within their ordinary lives. Let's check at an example. In case you were to have a dial gauge for measuring the height differences between a measurement object and a meter block you shall then, utilizing the indirect measuring method, use your calculation for indirectly estimating the target's height.
- – *Taking Measurements:* Imagine you're seeking to find out the weight of an elephant. You're quite sure that it weighs much, but you still don't know the precise number. Therefore, you ask your tutor, and she says that an elephant weighs similarly as three rhinos. That's good to know, however, how much again does a rhino weigh? Again, you inquire from your teacher, then she tells the rhino weighs same as around five alligators. That's some cool fact to recognize, but you still do not understand how much the

elephant weighs since comparing elephants and alligators may be confusing.

- – *Matching Measurements:* To avoid such confusion when taking measuring, scientists use the shared structure of measurement, known as the Universal System of Units or (SI). 'Unit' here is the term used to define how an object is measured. When studying a scientific question, we typically collect data, understand it then share the results together with other researchers. A common measurement structure allows people to make direct assessments rather than having to distinguish stuff like how much some particular animal weighs. For instance, when taking measurements for weight, the standard unit applied by researchers is kilograms or tons.

7.4. THE POSITIVE EXTERNALITIES OF INNOVATIVE ACTIVITY

Marketplace competition can sometimes offer an incentive for noticing new technology since a firm may earn more profits by discovering a way to produce items more affordably or to develop products with features that consumers want. As noted by a leading smartphone company CEO, "Persistent pursuit of new technology is the main principle of business and allows consumers to discern a world of possibilities through technology." An inventive firm realizes that it will typically have some edge over its key competitors, and therefore a capacity to earn beyond-normal proceeds before the competitors can reach up (Krohn, Layton, & Weingart, 2012).

In some cases, however, competition may discourage fresh technology, particularly when other companies can swiftly copy a new concept. Consider a pharmaceutical company wanting to develop some new drug. Averagely, it will cost around $700 million-plus several decades to notice a new drug, conduct the required safety tests, and carry the drug over to market. In case the researching and development effort flops—and every project within its scope has a probability of failure—it means that the firm shall incur losses and might even be taken out of business. In case the project succeeds, it means the firm's competitors might figure out methods of adapting or copying the fundamental idea, though without needing to pay the hefty costs themselves. Consequently, the innovative company shall bear the much greater costs of research and development, while enjoying at best just a small, provisional advantage over their competition (Krohn, Layton, & Weingart, 2012).

Several inventors through the years have learnt that their developments gave them less profit, as compared to what they may have reasonably anticipated. Consider the following examples:

- Thomas Edison still maintains the record of having most patents given to a person. His original invention was called the automatic voter counter, but despite its potential social benefits, Edison couldn't find a government which wanted to purchase it.
- Gordon Gould also invented the idea behind laser technology back in 1957. He delayed applying for patent technology besides, from the time that he applied, other researchers had laser discoveries of their own. Protracted legal battle ensued, whereby Gould spent a lot on attorneys, before he ultimately received a laser patent in 1977. In comparison to the vast social benefits that lasers provide, Gould got relatively minimal financial reward.

A range of studies by scholars have established that the original inventor gets around one-third to a half of the overall economic advantages from innovations, whereas other businesses and fresh product users receive the remaining bit.

7.4.1. Impact of Positive Externalities of Innovative Technology

If a company builds up a factory or purchases a set of equipment, then it receives all financial benefits resulting from the investments. Nevertheless, when an organization invests in fresh technology, then the private benefits, and profits, which the company receives are just but a fraction of the general social benefits. Typically, the social benefits that come with innovation consider the value of various affirmative externalities of the fresh idea or invention, whether appreciated by other firms or society in general, including the private benefits attained by the company which formed the new technology. These positive externalities are valuable spillovers to the third party, or other related parties.

Consider the case of pharmaceutical business that's planning its Research & Development budget for the forthcoming year. Economists and researchers working for this firm have gathered a list of possible research and development programs and assessed rates of return. (Referring to the amount of return that's payoff from the particular project.) (Krohn, Layton, & Weingart, 2012).

Suppose that the firm's outlay in researching and development causes a spillover benefit towards other companies and households. Considering most new innovations trigger other creative activities which society also values. In case the spill-over benefits which society enjoys are added to the company's private request for financial capital, then a benefit can be drawn which is derived from the original proceeds. Moreover, if there was some way for the company to wholly monopolize these social benefits through somehow making them inaccessible to others, then it means the company's private demand curve shall be similar as general society's demand curve.

7.4.2. Reasons to Invest in Human Capital

Investment in any project, whether it's developing a fresh power plant, or doing research for a new cancer facility, typically requires some upfront rate with an undefined future benefit. The outlay in education, and human capital, isn't any different. Through the span of several years, a scholar and his family invest considerable amounts of time as well as resources into that pupil's education. The impression is that greater levels of educational achievement will ultimately serve to improve the student's future output and successively their ability to earn (Smith, 2013).

Chapter 8

Benefits of Computer Science

CONTENTS

8.1. INTRODUCTION

We live in a world where technology is everything. We are dependent on technology in our day to day lives which is so evidently seen as we are so dependent on our phones. The world has evolved around technology. Technology is even incorporated in our education system and business institutions. This has brought about computer science. Computer science is the study of ways in which data can be presented in form of programs. It involves use of various algorithms to facilitate manipulation, communication and storage of information in digital format. This is to enable us to keep up with the recent adjustments in technology (Barry, 2015).

As technology revolves around computers, computer science seeks to give more information on computer languages and complex systems usually used in computer programing. With this knowledge, it has been used to create new software and software systems used in various institutions. Computer science has core principles which include human computer interaction, vision and graphics, numerical analysis, networks and computer system, software engineering and computers systems. It is therefore the work of a computer scientist to design and identify algorithms to solve problems concerning computer programs and poor performance in hardware and software.

Computer science has many benefits not only to and individual, it has had positive effects in the society as well. Majorly the fact that it has enabled people to improve their standards of living as they are able to work to gain income enabling them to support their families and themselves (Barry, 2015).

8.2. BENEFITS OF COMPUTER SCIENCE TO AN INDIVIDUAL

8.2.1. Increases Job Employment Opportunities

As people are trying to keep up with current trends when it comes to dealing with computers, this has prompted many to head back to learning institutions to learn on computers science. This has created a large demand for computer science lectures, teachers and tutors. This creates and employment opportunity for youths who have degrees in computer science and have not yet found jobs to offer their services as teachers in the learning institutions. Most times, those that are still about to graduate studying computer science often get the employment opportunities from the universities that they studied in.

Individuals with knowledge on computer science have a wide variety of choices to select on in terms of job opportunities. They have knowledge on programming and networks among others. They can therefore seek employment in various slots in a company for full time or part time employment. Employment opportunities include working as computer graphics artists, computer programmers, computer systems engineers, IT managers, technicians, or web designers. These professions typically earn high starting salaries.

It is also advantageous in that they don't necessarily have to look for employment, they can also decide to venture into private practice and start their own companies. They can offer services as consultants, financial analysts, network administrators, technical writers or as research scientists. This way they are able to earn and support themselves. They can also create employment opportunities for other individuals.

8.2.2. Creates Opportunities for Creativity

This is one of the main reasons why most young people would want to pursue computer science. They are more on being fulfilled and achieve. They are more on innovative job opportunities that will allow them to be creative and thinking outside the box. Computer science gives them this opportunity. It is more on creativity oriented not just programming. It entails identifying problems in various things such as software and creating possible solutions to these problems. For instance, it is the challenges that were experienced in the first-generation computers that prompted researchers to come up with better software (Schäfer, 2013). The first-generation computers had a problem of low processing speed and it took up large amounts of power.

They had to be creative to come up with the second-generation computers that had a much higher processing speed and use up much less amounts of power. A computer scientist therefore is more of an innovative minded person. In the spirit of creativity, they invent new software and programs to meet growing demands for various things. For instance, there has been a growing demand for a variety of social cites as people wants to express themselves more (Schäfer, 2013).

The youth take advantage of the knowledge in computer science to make the social cites such as Facebook and Twitter among others. It also encourages team work among the youth as they work together to create the programs. They gain more experience and ideas as they continue working giving room for innovation.

8.2.3. Strengthening Primary Careers

As always, some careers are considered competitive. Careers such as medicine, engineering, and architecture were considered very competitive. Many individuals would tarmac for years to get jobs and some people would even give up thinking on getting employment in such fields of work opting them to do other casual jobs. All this changed with advancement in technology. Even in those fields of work, there is use of technology that includes machines. In industries, there has been automation of machines and this requires the computers to be programmed to carry out these processes (Anderson, Ferro, & Hilton, 2010).

Computer science has been taken up by individuals in the health care and education sector. It is advantageous for them as it enables them to gain more skills. It has also increased their chances of getting employment or internship opportunities. In a scenario whereby two candidates apply for a job opportunity. One has only a degree in health care while the other not only has a degree but has a degree in computer science, there is more likely that the candidate with the degree will be more eligible for the job opportunity. This is because they will be more beneficial of the company as they have a variety of skills to offer the company. Knowledge in computer science gives individuals a large range of skills that can be incorporated and applied in a variety of careers and gives them an added advantage in a crowded job market ensuring they do not lack employment (Anderson, Ferro, & Hilton, 2010).

8.2.4. Engage in Making Positive Difference in the World

While technology has vast benefits to society, it also has several downfall. One of the major downfalls is cybercrime which is becoming more and more common in the common world. Cybercrime is the use of computers for illegal and selfish gains. It involves acts such as fraud, violating privacy, trafficking intellectual property and stealing of identities among others, the most common being cyber bullying which involves online harassment of people. Majority of the people carrying out such practices have knowledge on computers some of them having learnt computer science but they do not use the knowledge for good.

But not all individuals are evil minded. Some individuals use their knowledge on computer science to counteract these vices. For instance, if a virus is developed, they are able to come up with programs such as antiviruses that counteract the viruses produced. Hackers are very keen on obtaining peoples information so that they can use it to exploit them for financial gains. This has challenged many computer scientists to come up with solutions to these problems. They have been able to create software that enable users to identify whether or not their devices have been hacked.

They keep on improving on the security of devices by coming up with security update to counteract security breaches. They also create awareness to both adults and children on cybercrime and how to counteract it. By so doing, they are positively impacting the society and thus creating a sense of self-fulfilment.

8.2.5. Helps Individuals to Gain Civil Liberty Protection

In the current day and age, individuals are more focused on posting pictures or criticizing people on social media platforms. Some of them do not think of the dangers that are possible. Some individuals flaunt their properties and assets on social media and revealing their locations. This makes them vulnerable to theft and people disrupting their privacy for their gains. This is common as much of our information floods the internet. This is made possible as we give plenty information to sites so as to access their services. It is beneficial but the risk is that not all the cites are genuine. Some of them are created by hackers to gain peoples information making most internet users vulnerable to hacking. Some of them use this information to publicly shame people as revenge or to just meet their pleasures. This is illegal as everyone has a constitutional right to enjoy their privacy. With such information being easily accessible by hackers, may lead to several cases of privacy violations whereby crucial information of a person such as their salary and financial transactions may be exposed to people whom it does not concern them.

Computer scientists help in bringing about civil liberty protection by creating ways of safeguarding people's privacy while they use the internet. Some have come up with solutions such as configurations to enable the right owner to access their information. For some such as Google, there is a confirmation emails whereby if the owner's account is accessed by another party the owner is notified (Barry, 2015).

8.3. BENEFITS OF COMPUTERS SCIENCE IN THE BUSINESSES

8.3.1. Brings About Team Work

For a business to prosper, teamwork plays a crucial role to its prosperity. Teamwork enables the employees to share ideas, give insights concerning various things and also, in the long run, create a good relationship between the employees.

The interactions during company events where they are able to create bonds is beneficial for the company. More so the companies that are more oriented towards technology or the products that the company sells majorly revolve around computers or anything to do with technology.

In these companies, their projects are required to come up with new software or programs that are better and more efficient for the user's experience. In the course of the projects, the employees meet to discuss. For instance, what program or software they would like to develop and since they are several employees, there will be a variety of ideas and afterwards they decide which idea that they will actualize.

They then come up with components that they will incorporate into the program and the possible downfalls of the project and how they can counteract it. They are able to share various insights and probabilities concerning the program or system. During this process, they create bonds and teamwork is much emphasized on which the company productivity increases.

8.3.2. Improve Productivity

In the current business trends, various technologies are being incorporated into the business environment. There is automation of various processes and machines being used and many organizations embracing the use of computers to carry out various processes. For many of these companies, the machines are custom-made with programs that fit the business environment (Reilly, 2003). For instance, in banks, the companies' computers are custom-made to carry out processes that deal with calculations. This is made possible by computer scientists who come up with the various programs for the various companies.

The computer scientist come up with the programs or instructions that will facilitate the automation of machines. For instance, in factories, the computers are programmed such that at a certain time various processes occur. Like in an automated car wash, from the wetting of the car to the scrubbing of the car to the rinsing and finally the polishing. The computer is programmed so that the processes occur at the right time and also reduces wastage of water and electricity.

The automation of business institution has been advantageous to the employers in that they are able to replace manpower with machines thus the money that would be used to play and train employees are incorporated back into the business and are used to increase the company's profits. It has also saved on time in that machines are able to work and process faster than manpower. This is as a result of knowledge on computer science (Reilly, 2003).

8.3.3. Broadening Business Opportunities

Computer science due to the various principles it contains creates a large scope for business ideas for entrepreneurs and businessmen who want to expand their businesses. There is a wide field when it comes to computer science and the major advantage being that with the current advancements in technology, there are more and more business opportunities being created. Computer expertise is used to develop new types of internet-based devices. For instance, the current appliances that were generated are in excess and it is taking much space on the earth.

Therefore, the computer scientists are thinking of new ways on how to make new appliances that will assist in the reduction of the number of appliance thus saving space and making it efficient for use as the appliances are able to carry out various activities in other wards it is able to multitask. They are working on ways to transform the internet to fit various processes efficiently. This will create more job opportunities and fields for companies to venture into.

More businesses are getting into production of equipment for various uses therefore it's a potential business opportunity. Even for those for who have studied computer science are able to form consulting companies that are able to merge with the private consultants for a period of time under a contract specified by the company.

This is among other opportunities that can come about in the field of computer science broadening the chances of business opportunities in different sectors.

8.4. BENEFITS OF COMPUTERS SCIENCE FOR PEOPLE WITH DISABILITIES

8.4.1. In their Education

For a long time, people with disabilities have been looked down on and are not considered to be valuable members of the society. This has caused some of them to lack self-value and self-esteem. Therefore, they opt not to engage with other people, which is not right. They have a right to mix and interact with people in various areas including the work industry and also in education. For this reason, computer scientists have been able to come up with programs and software to cater for their needs depending on their disability.

For instance, for the blind, they have been able to come up with braille keyboards so as to enable them use computers and other devices. This among others is also used in their education system to that they are at par with other students. The braille keyboard enables them to enter data into the computer by feeling the words on the keyboard. For those that are partially bind, there is a software created for them where the graphics used in the computer enables them to work and also interact with others on the network there by assisting them in their education (ITL Education Solutions Limited, 2011).

To the lame, they have been able to come up with programs whereby they can use voice input to enter information in the computer. It is also useful for them during the examinations as it enables them to answer questions easily by use of data entry by use of voice.

8.4.2. In locomotion

The issue of locomotion is majorly experienced with people who are lame. For some of them it is a challenge to use public transport more so in developing countries. It is seen to be time consuming and tiresome to load and offload wheelchairs on the buses so many tend to be neglected when it comes to boarding the various public transports. The knowledge on computer science has been useful in that they have been able to work with automotive engineers to come up with buses that will enable them have efficient transport.

The computer scientist program the buses so that once the bus reaches the bus stop, the inbuilt ramp releases itself allowing them to board or alight buses easily. The buses are specially made so that there are spaces for the wheelchairs and they are able to be connected to the buses for a much safer traveling experience.

The major challenge with this is that it has only been incorporated in the developed countries.

Also, computer science has been used in the making of automated wheelchairs. These wheelchairs are specially designed such that the motion may be caused by touch (ITL Education Solutions Limited, 2011).

They are made more so for disabled children and those suffering from chronic diseases as they are weak most of the time and are unable to push wheelchairs. Computer science has been used in the making of bionic legs and arms. They are specially programmed to work as if they were normal arms and legs.

8.4.3. Used in Treatment

Not everyone who has a disability, is also born with it. For some of them, it was due to accidents that had occurred such as car crashes that led them to be disabled. For those who are fortunate, they are given a diagnosis that the disability may not be permanent.

Not only them but also for those born with the disability. Computer science has been used to make the form of treatment in terms of therapy whereby the machines that are used are specially programmed to suit the type of treatment.

For instance, the machines used to help children walk it usually programmed so that once the child makes a step, the machine has a holder where the child supports his or her self on automatically moves forward to encourage continuous motion. The holder is equipped with sensors that are able to detect the child's progress and also the behavioral changes such as the heart and pulse rate.

This is important in that if the sensors detect straining by the child, it shuts down or slows down to enable the child rest. This technology is not only used in children but also among adults.

Computer science has been used in the designing of machines that are used during the scans to check the damage rate of the body and give specifications on the places that need therapy, how much therapy is required and for what duration should the therapy occur.

8.5. BENEFITS OF COMPUTER SCIENCE IN SPACE INNOVATION

8.5.1. Making of Robots

In the recent years, the populations of the earth have been rapidly increasing. This has led to depletion of resources making it hard for a majority of the population to survive. This has prompted researchers to look into the probability of other planets being possible homes for mankind. This has prompted them to carry out investigation of factors that are possibly required for man to survive such as air among others. For them to carry out such experiments they require test subject and since they do not have much will to use man as test subjects, they were required to look for other means.

This is where computer science comes in. Researchers have combined with computer scientists to create robots. These robots are programmed by computer scientists in that once they reach space, they are able to collect data that the scientists need to assist in the research. For instance, the possibility of such planets having air. The robots are programmed and created in a manner in that they are able to scan the planet's atmosphere for presence of oxygen. Not only oxygen, elements such as water are looked into (ITL Education Solutions Limited, 2011).

Even the ability of the soil being able to produce, in other words its fertility. The computer scientists have been able to program the robots in a way that even though they are as far as being in space, the researchers on earth can give it instructions for it to carry out.

8.5.2. Making of Satellites

In the current age, the world has been globalized in a manner that there is easy access to information worldwide. This is because currently, people's information is in the internet which is made possible by people having to sign into research sites such as Google. With such information, it is easy for a person to track down people by use of tracking devices that rely on the satellites. The use of satellites is evidently seen in that, it is used for transition of information and also for entertainment among others.

During the making of such satellites, knowledge on computer science was applied. The researchers partnered up with computer scientist in the creation on the satellites. These satellites are programmed to pick up signals from other planets and give back information to earth. The computer scientists with the help of researchers are able to decode the meaning of the signals. This is majorly used in weather forecasts among others. They also are used for transition of signals in terms of entertainment.

It works in that the satellites are programmed to pick up signals form the various TV media houses. They then turn and reflect the signals received to the various households enabling then to view the broadcasted information. Computer science has been helpful in the making of the satellites and computer scientists are carrying out more experiments to improve the working of such satellites not only in space but also in the various stations on earth (ITL Education Solutions Limited, 2011).

8.6. BENEFITS OF COMPUTER SCIENCE IN LOCOMOTION

8.6.1. Automation of Cars

With the current world that we are living in, everything is being digitalized in the various sectors including travel. Initially, people relayed on manual car where the driver was in control of the vehicle in the entire travelling process and though this has been useful for quite some time, it has had its down fall whereby in the instance of transferring cargo, the drivers for the vehicles would not have had enough sleep but would still drive increasing the chances of accidents occurring.

This has led to automotive engineers working with computer scientists in the making of automatic cars. These cars are designed in a manner that they have computers placed inside them. The computers are not as big but they work efficiently. Computer science has been applied in the programming of such computers. The computers are given the ability to control the car's fuel system, brake and the accelerator among others. The programmers connect the computers to the internet. The computers are programmed like a robot in that it has knowledge on driving skills. It is able to control the accelerator (Smith, 2013).

The cars are also placed with motion sensors in that they are able to sense objects before them and relay the information to the computer which then controls the car's brakes stopping the vehicle. This has been advantageous for the drivers in that they can carry out several trips to transport the cargo to different places that may be far away.

8.6.2. Air Travel

Computer science has played a key role in this type of travel. Air travel has become more and more common and like the cars, this type of locomotion is also being automated. Air travel is more complex and tends to relay more on technology and where there is technology, there is use of computers. This field relays more on computer science. For instance, they have satellites programmed to pick up signals to be able to know where the airplane is and how fast it is moving.

Also in the control towers, there are several computers that assist the smooth running of the air travel. These computers are able to pick up the signals and interpret them for the workers in the control towers. The computers are also fitted in the airplanes to give the pilots information on the altitude and climatic conditions depending on the type of information received from the control tower (Smith, 2013).

Some of the airplanes are also automated meaning that the computers fitted inside them are equipped to fly plane to various destinations designated to them. They rely on signals given to them by the satellites to identify the destination. Though they are automated, the pilots have to be physically present incase anything should go wrong. In airports, there are machines that are programmed to carryout routine maintenance of the airplanes that helps save on time and also lengthens the duration use of the airplanes making computer science a benefit to the air travel industry.

8.6.3. Used in Traffic Signals

Human labor is said most at times to be limited which is true. Earlier, to manage the flow of traffic in the roads, traffic police were employed to regulate it but it has not been that efficient in many countries. This is because at times the police may focus more in certain regions leaving others behind. This was greatly resolved by introduction of traffic lights in various roads. The use of traffic lights greatly relayed on knowledge on computer science.

The traffic lights are programmed and fitted with timers in them such that for some period of time the traffic light will light green allowing the cars in a certain region to move and after the allocated time runs out, the color of the traffic light changes making the vehicles stop and others to move. This has also been created for pedestrians where there are traffic lights that have been created to allow the movement of pedestrians reducing the number of car accidents (Smith, 2013).

Not only have the traffic signals, the traffic lights in the roads also employed some principals of computer science. The traffic light are connected to computers at a central location and are synced together such that when on is put on the rest is also put on. The computer is programmed in that when it reaches a certain time like say five pm the lights are put on and when its morning they are put off.

8.6.4. Trains

Computer science has been applied in the railway travel be it electric trains or the traditional trains. It has been advantageous in that is has save on time and also the number of manpower used. For the traditional trains, the use of computer science has been used in the making of rail gauge. This is whereby there are computers programmed to change the railway gauges move depending on the route that the train is to take.

The computer has trackers such that the motion of the train on the railway gauge is used to determine the movement of the gauge. It has also been helpful to reduce the chances of the trains colliding that's why there are few cases of train accidents. Even for the railway the gauges when the trains are moving, there are traffic lights that there to stop the cars from moving. The traffic lights are programmed such that when the train is moving the traffic light lights light to red and it raises a barrier so that no car crosses the railway as the train moves.

For the electric trains, the computers are programmed to sequence the start of the motion of the trains and also the stop of the trains once it reaches its destination. With the knowledge of networking, the trains are fitted with computers that are wirelessly connected to those in the railway station. This enables the devices to share information such as the location so that they can identify the position of the train.

8.6.5. Making of Elevators and Escalators

The world today as said is keener on comfort and various things are being invented and modified to escalators. They have been embraced by various institutions as they are efficient and also the fact that they save on time. Computer science has been incorporated to facilitate this in the principal of programming.

For the elevators, they have motion sensors at the doors. So they are programmed to open the doors once they sense someone's presence at the doors. It is also programmed to open the doors as it progresses upward or downwards at each floor until it reaches the final destination as per the instruction given by the user. This is different from the escalators. The escalators are stairs that continuously move upwards or downwards towards the specified floor. For the escalators, there are computers that are in place to control its motion (Smith, 2013).

For instance, the computers are programmed so that the escalators move at a specified speed, not faster or slower than the specified. It is also programmed to control the direction of the stairs whether it goes upwards or downwards and as programmed, the motion of the stairs continues to be as they were set to be leading to the reason for the fixed continuous motion. Computer science has had its principles being applied into various aspects on movement apart from it being used in elevators and escalators. This goes to show the positive impact that computer science has brought to the locomotion sector.

8.6.6. Space Travel

This is the recent fascination of mankind. To be able to carry out space explorations to various areas in the galaxy. This has been pushed by the need to look for a planet for mankind in order to ease the population pressure. This has led to the invention of space shuttles to enable space travel to occur. This kind of travel relays on computer science among others. Computer science has been applied in the making of rockets that have been used by scientists in space. The rockets are diverse and complex and that employed teamwork where several computer scientists as well as researchers came together to bring the idea into reality (Tedre, 2014).

For one the rockets are programmed such that when they leave a certain part of the atmosphere, they are able to dismember themselves. Dismembering is where a certain part of the rocket comes off to allow the rest of the rocket parts to move efficiently. The rocket is also programmed and fitted with computers that are able to transmit signals to the satellites that later on transmit the same signal to earth so that the scientists can know the position of the rocket while in space.

The computers in the rocket are also programmed to manage the system of the rocket such as the fuel supply. The fact that the rockets are also automated shows the use of computers science in the making of rockets. The computers are able to cut off the fuel supply one reaching a certain level in the atmosphere (Tedre, 2014).

8.7. BENEFITS OF COMPUTERS TO THE HOUSEHOLD

Computer science has also been advantageous to the household in the aspect of the appliances that are used in the household. The current digital age has made advances such that the houses are more modernized. The appliances in the house are specialized in that they work they fit the required work specified for it. This has been made to make life more efficient and more emphasis on comfort. For instance, computer science has been used in the making of machines such as washing machines.

In regards to washing machines, they are first designed and the programmed to carry put the washing services to be carried out such as the circular motion used in the washing machines even the washing, adding of soap and the rinsing of the clothes. The same principles are applied in other appliances such as the dishwashers and the microwaves. Not only in the making of appliances, some homes are automated in a way that everything is controlled by a computer.

The computers are made in a way that their functioning is synced up with the various equipment in the house. Knowledge in programming is applied in that the computer is given instructions such as at six am all the curtain in the house should be drawn and the computer does so without fail every morning. For others, the house command system is voice activated and the instruction to the computer is given by the voice input.

8.7.1. Interior Design

Computer science does not only major in programming alone. It involves other aspects such as graphics design. This involves coming up with ideas such as drawings or art and bringing them into realization. This has been incorporated into people's living space whereby people nowadays love to incorporate in their living space to make it more lively, fun and exciting.

Graphics design has for a period of time has been majorly used in the creation of websites and high levels of creativity have majorly been valued. The websites have been used in the marketing of businesses and product but graphics design is no limited to just website design, people have expanded their creativity such that they can use their knowledge on graphics design to remodel and refurbish homes to look more stylish (Tucker, 2004).

They first think of ideas that will suit various homes and then they use computers to make the various designs that they have. They later on bring the idea to life by printing the designs on fabrics or any other materials that they use. It has been used to produce curtains and even carpets with unique and stylish designs. Most recently, the graphics design has been printed on wall carpets to give the home a well- defined and welcoming looking and so far this trend is being embraced by several homeowners in various parts of the world. It is considered to be cheaper in terms of maintenance depending on quality of material used.

8.8. BENEFITS OF COMPUTER SCIENCE IN SECURITY

8.8.1. Military Combat

In the current day, there are several wars that have been waged more so to people from terrorist groups that are well known to attack innocent civilians. Computer science has been helpful in reducing cases of insecurity and also theft among others. It has been used in the military for their training if they were to face various circumstances during the line of work. For instance, in the navy, computer science has been useful in the making of simulators. Simulators are part of equipment designed to create an environment of something that is occurring. For the navy the simulators are used to create an atmosphere of the ocean and an accident has occurred.

This trains then on the necessary response that is expected of them. For some, the simulators are used to help them to face their fears. For others, computer science has been used in the making of machinery used in making weapons. For the production of bullets and the guns themselves, using human labor would take longer hours therefore machines have been created to make the guns and bullets. It is helpful when some of the materials used in making explosive are hazardous to human health.

Some military gear has also been automated. It is programmed to fire gunshots and bombs once it receives instructions. In most cases, this happens with a remote button, which when pressed, is expected to launch the missile or bomb.

8.8.2. Making of Security Devices

Security is the major topic on people's mind; more so with the rising cases of insecurity. Computer science has been used to counteract the rising case of insecurity. One of the principals of computer science is graphics. Graphics involves making things visual and can be in video mode depending on the preference of the user. It also involves networking which is majorly communication between devices.

The two principals have been combined in the creation of CCTV cameras. These cameras work in that they record motion of thing in the environment then after a time lapse the recorded video is saved and backed up to a certain device. This has greatly impacted the improvement of security in various institutions whereby the CCTV have been used in identification of various thugs and in case a crime was committed the CCTV footage are used to reveal the perpetrators.

Also, it has been used in the making of trackers. This is mostly made for things such as cars. Knowledge on networking is used to create a connection between the tracking device and the satellites in space. This majorly depends on the use of the GPS signals and coordinates. A network is created between the tracking device and the owner's phone or laptop. The phone is able to request information on the car's location and the tracker gives back the feedback. This has been helpful in cases where cars have been stolen and the owners have been able to retrieve them (Tucker, 2004).

8.9. BENEFITS OF COMPUTER SCIENCE IN EDUCATION

8.9.1. Furthering Education

Education has played a key role in empowering people and increasing their chances of living a financially stable life. It enables people to acquire jobs in various fields of work. This is beneficial for many individuals. In the current trend, people are acquiring more education to increase their chances of being employed in the various fields of work. As some of them cannot easily access education from universities that are in far destinations, computer science has been helpful in bringing the universities to the individuals in the various countries.

This has been made possible through E-Learning which has become a common phenomenon in the world today. E-learning has been developed by employing principles of computer science that include computer software and networking. Networking is referenced in the aspect of being able to use the internet during the learning process. This works in that the computer software is linked to the internet enabling the student to stream the classes as they proceed hence the term online class. The student learns with the rest but is not physically present. This is advantageous for students who carry out long distance learning.

Apart from attending classes, research plays a big role when it comes to education. Computer science has made it possible for students to access research materials through accessing the internet. It has also made it possible for them to upload their research work to their lectures for evaluation and grading. This has greatly benefited students who had financial barriers for education

8.9.2. Digital Learning

Digital trends are being adopted in various areas of human life and this includes education. The education process is being digitalized to improve the quality of education being offered to the students. Digital learning involves use of technology and it involves aspects such as virtual learning. Virtual learning is taken in the instance where a school lacks sufficient laboratories, there are software applications made to create a laboratory simulation of the practical or experiment being carried out.

Digital learning also involves the use of classroom technologies such as the use of smart boards to increase classroom interactions of students. The smart boards have a software that enables the students to interact with the screens and also visualizes concepts being taught by the teachers. It also involves the use of computers, laptops and phones during the learning process of the students (Dasgupta, 2016).

Computer scientists have been able to come up with educational programs that are in-line with the students learning systems. Programs such as counting and word learning sequences have been advantageous for the students. As this type of learning process is visual, it enables the students to easily remember all that they were taught and greatly improves the student's performance rates. It has also employed the use of strategies such as adaptive learning, e-textbooks, learning objects, virtual reality, augmented reality, personalized learning, badging and gamification among others. Digital learning points out clear benefits of computers science for students in the education sector.

8.9.3. Improving the Curriculum

Computer science involves the use of computers and it is greatly involved. It also applies the use of mathematics in solving problems. It is helpful as computers use numbers. To enter instructions into the computers, there are numbers that are used to key in the instructions known as binary numbers. As mathematics revolves around our day today lives, it also revolves around computers. Computers have had an impact on students in high school.

Computer science compels students to be creative and innovative. This is because they are encouraged to create problems and also solving the problems that they have created. This engages them to work more especially when solving mathematical problems as they relate to each other. It challenges them to get better understanding of the various application. This facilitates critical thinking as they think of ways to solve and create possible solution to the problems

A large number of dropouts has been recorded in various high schools. This has prompted the education boards to incorporate computer science into their education curriculums. This is because computer science involves practical skills. The students are able to acquire these skills to handle various problems. These skills they are able to apply in the various subject they learn. This changes their outlook on education deeming it not difficult thereby reducing the number of students who drop out from school. It has led to several students choosing to further in computer science as their career of choice (Dasgupta, 2016).

8.10. BENEFITS OF COMPUTER SCIENCE IN HEALTH CARE

8.10.1. Equipment

In the health sector, there are recent advancements being made so that the quality of health care being offered is the best and of good quality. This majorly revolves around the type of machine equipment being used to cater for the patients. There are several equipments being used in the health industry that are made based on the knowledge of computer science. For instance, the life support machines. They are like computers but their major work is to monitor the patients. For some, they are programmed to make beeping noises once the health of the patient starts degrading.

Even in the process of coming up with the technology to be used, the internet is used in the process of designing the machines to be used and the level of technology to be used. For instance, when designing the cancer screening equipment. Once the equipment was produced, the manufacturers upload the blueprints of the machinery in the internet. This enables other manufacturers to use the blueprints to come up with different types of the machines and the major advantage is that they are able to make some changes in order to improve the working quality of the equipment (Barry, 2015).Computer science contains graphic design as its principles. The use of graphic designs is used to create new models of software to be used in the new models of the equipment and various test runs made so that it can be rendered qualified for human use.

8.10.2. Research

There is research being conducted in order to treat the various upcoming illnesses and diseases. The most recent being ways of treating cancer and HIV/ AIDS. There is extensive use of the internet to conduct the research to develop new medicines for the treatment of such medicines. The research that was initially conducted and the results placed in the internet is used by the upcoming researchers who conduct further research and bases on the findings they develop the medicines.Genomics also utilizes the use of computer science in the form of its artificial intelligence in computers. It deals with genes and their replication in the human cells. This theory is applied in molecular farming where various technologies are used to bring about different genetic mutations in the cell chromosomes. This knowledge is applied and used in the production of bio medicines which will benefit a large percentage of the population.This is because it will enable production of large amounts of medicines thereby reducing the cost of medicines as it is a cheaper way of producing medicines that are effective and that will be in use for longer periods of time. Computers are also used in the production. The genome sequencing machines are used to identify patterns with high volume of genetic data sets. The patterns are then translated into computer models and further used to predict the probability of an individual to contract certain diseases and illnesses. It also predicts the type of therapy to be used to counteract the disease.

8.11. BENEFITS OF COMPUTER SCIENCE IN COMMUNICATION

8.11.1. Expanding Communication

Computer science plays a key role in communication. As a matter of fact, computer science is the mother of communication. The principles in computer science involve networking. This involves communication between devices enabling sharing and receiving of information from one device to another. This has led to communication between people by creating platforms for communication.

Various individuals have made use of the knowledge on computer science to create the social platforms. This social site has grown in the current age and are used by several users in the world today. They include platforms such as Instagram, Facebook, Twitter, messenger and we chat among others. This are majorly text-oriented chatting apps. They allow the users to share documents and photos all over the world. Most recently, the computer scientists have come up with updates for the software enabling the devices to facilitate video calls and phone calls (Barry, 2015).

This has been advantageous for businessmen who have partnerships with companies from different places. With this kind of tool, they just have to carry out e- conferences where they attend the meetings virtually. This has greatly revolutionized the workforce by facilitating e-commerce and also digital marketing. It also has facilitated communication between people who may be in different faces of the earth. This has led to the world being referred to a global village as people are able to easily interact removing distance as a barrier to communication.

8.12. BENEFITS OF COMPUTER SCIENCE CATASTROPHE MANAGEMENT

8.12.1. Prediction and Avoiding Catastrophes

Apart from computer science being used to predict human behavior with the aid of artificial intelligence, it is also able to predict climates, seasons and ocean currents. It is mostly used by the meteorological department extensively. It involves the use of computers in increasing the capacity of handling data and also carrying out mathematical experiments simulating the experiments with the atmosphere making it efficient to work as the data on weather tends to be voluminous.

The department used various technologies to link the satellites with the computers in the department. The satellites are able to pick up signals of the atmosphere and transmit the signals to the computers. The information received is then processed by the computers and translated and used to give predictions on expected weather conditions. These predictions are then given to the citizens so that in case there is a prediction of upcoming heavy rains, the government as well as the citizens are able to carry out planning to make good use of the rains (Barry, 2015).

If there are strong storms coming, the government is able to decide so that the storms experience do not cause much damages to the citizens. Computer science is also used in that meteorological programmers are growing with the current trends of the latest computer languages. The use these languages, Python, C++, Objective C, or PHP, in programming and also making the climatic prediction economical. This points out the benefits of computer science to meteorology (Barry, 2015).

8.13. BENEFITS OF COMPUTER SCIENCE IN INDUSTRIES

8.13.1. Reducing Cost on Labor

Computer science has been greatly used to revolutionize the industrial sector with several processes being automated and bringing about industrial technology. The industrial technology involves using engineering and manufacturing technology to improve the production process making it faster, simpler and efficient for the manufacturers. Computer science has also been used to identify and solve some of the problems experienced in industrial engineering.

Computer science is applied in the machine learning process and the use of artificial intelligence in the production process. This involves the integration of machines such that they are able to carry out the manufacturing process on their own. At a set time, it is programmed to start the production process and end at the set time. It is also programmed to send messages to the company's computers indication a problem during the manufacturing process hence it is easier to solve the problems encountered. (Tucker, 2004).

Computer scientists work hand in hand with industrial engineers to come up with new software and technology to make the manufacturing process more easily and cheaper in the long run. Machine learning is used in the process as it enables the creation of various algorithms in solving technical problems experienced in production. This information is useful to the computer scientists and industrial engineers when they are coming up with new technologies so that the newly established technology is free from the challenges that were previously experienced in the previously experienced technology.

8.14. BENEFITS OF COMPUTER SCIENCE TO THE SOCIETY

8.14.1. Directly Meeting Needs

Computer science has had outright direct impact on the society. The impacts being mostly positive and advantageous to the society. This is because the computer scientists are able to easily access applications that address the various societal issues that affect the society such as unemployment, poverty, global warming among others.

For instance, the association between the computer scientists and the meteorological departments enable the prediction of the future weather patterns therefore people know the type of climate to expect predicting the type of clothes to wear and preparations to make in terms of farming and food production (Tucker, 2004).

By being able to access the applications, they make it possible to produce possible solutions to the identified problems. Such as in the case of weather forecast. If there is a prediction of upcoming catastrophic conditions, the government is able to come up with solutions to avoid very serious damages.

The solutions are then used nationally benefitting all the citizens of the country. By using this approach, computer scientists and other technology professionals to be able to identify and meet the needs that arise in the various communities.

There are also social sites that can be used as resources for all the computer scientists that want to put their knowledge and skills in solving global problems.

They facilitate the computer scientists with the necessary funds and support to enable them come up with projects and actualize them in order to change the lives of several people (Tucker, 2004).

8.14.2. Empowering People

Computer science has majorly impacted the society by enabling the creation of software that can be used by people from all walks of life. This means that it is freely distributed to all and they are able to use it as a key resource tool for positively impacting their lives. For instance, computer science has created job opportunities for people who have been undermined enabling them to financially support themselves and also create job opportunities for others (Tucker, 2004).

The internet provides them with resources that enables them acquire knowledge and skills to create, run and manage their businesses. This has been a major advantage to the youth in developing countries as they are known to face challenges of unemployment hence entrepreneurship is more likely to work for them. It has given several businessmen and women platforms to market their businesses. In the current age, people use the various social media platforms to market their goods and services hence they have a larger audience and are able to get more clients without using much of their finances on advertising. It also has enabled the employers to find and sort out the most suitable candidates to hire as their employees.

The use of platforms such as "LinkedIN" enables the employers to get more information on the candidates and create dates for interviews with the candidates. This increases the chances of several candidates getting jobs thereby empowering them. This points out the role computer science has played in empowering citizens.

8.14.3. Paving the Way for Equality

Computer science has been used to level barriers in the playing field. There are various barriers experienced in the playing field. They include gender, racial and ethnical barriers among others. The most frequent being gender discrimination. Computer science has been used to overcome this barrier by creating a platform for women empowerment. This is done by enabling platforms sort to encourage women to venture into various fields.

For many years, fields such as computer engineering and software engineering have been seen and deemed to be male-dominated. The fact that women are taking up such courses as careers are changing the perception of women. This has led to women being offered more chances of employment in the male-dominated fields of work. This is paving way for women to obtain equality in gaining employment opportunities. The same case applies for the ethnical and racial difference whereby people are hired based on their qualifications and are not undermined by other factors.Equality has also been created by the use of the internet where people are able to access various information. This includes information concerning their rights and freedoms as citizens of a certain country. This enables them to identify scenarios where their rights and freedoms have been violated and they are able to clap back and seek for justice. They use the internet to knowledge on the appropriate route to take when seeking justice in the different places of law. This shows the contribution computer science has brought into improving equality.

8.14.4. Impacting Every Area in Society

Computer science has made major impacts to the society economically and socially for the better. Socially, it has greatly impacted interactions among people by enabling them to send and receive information from people in different areas of the world. This has been done through sending of emails, messages, video conferencing, e-commerce and cloud computing among others (Tucker, 2004).

This is experienced globally through the easy access to information on the internet, use of peer to peer networks, use of proxy servers and production of copyrights certificates. From an economic perspective, it has been beneficial to individuals as it has created ways to be able to get employed or be self-employed by helping them the required skills required for the job. It has also created a variety of employment opportunities that would cater for the large numbers of people who are unemployed (Tucker, 2004).

It has also been greatly used by businessmen to market their products and also advertise their companies by use of social media platforms and also carrying out digital marketing that has seen many businesses getting more clients hence increasing the business profits. It has also brought about security for individuals by creating programs and applications such as ant viruses that protect the user from damage. The user's privacy is also protected by creating barriers for other parties so that they have limited access to information reducing cases of violations such as cybercrimes. These among others are the positive impacts of computer science on the various areas in society.

Chapter 9

Barriers to Studying Computer Science

CONTENTS

9.1. INTRODUCTION

When looking at students in general we have to admit that computer science (CS) has never been popular among students. Out of all students beginning post-high school studies only 7.6 % decide to major in computer science. With a dropout rate of 38%, computer science has decrease in enrolments of all computer science students between 2000 and 2018. As software engineering training grows at the more significant level, we should be mindful so as to guarantee that CS neither fuels existing value holes in instruction nor upsets endeavors to differentiate the field of CS. In this chapter, we talk about auxiliary and social hindrances that impact African Americans, Latinos, and female students.

9.2. ABSENCE OF TEACHERS

Universities are not graduating huge quantities of CS students. To compound this problem, even if a student decides to major in CS, they choose an employment in the industry instead of pursuing graduate studies. The reason for these employment choices is a salary inequality: an industry job can pay twice as much as a job in academia or education. This is causing a serious conundrum: a deficiency of software engineering instructors is making it harder for some students to get exposure to subjects they would like to pursue before they graduate.

The interest in CS education has been enormous and the quantity of instructors who are prepared to educate ICT can't fulfil the current needs. There are more understudies ready to be shown registering aptitudes than there are instructs to move the skills. The issue additionally exists at private establishments, since industry pays so much better, yet additionally on the grounds that there is a deficiency of CS Ph.D. applicants, and a doctorate is a prerequisite for residency track positions.

The utilization of ICT in the homeroom is significant for giving chances to understudies to figure out how to work in a data age. Examining the hindrances to the utilization of ICT in training may help instructors to beat these boundaries and become effective innovation adopters later on.

Studies show that instructors had a powerful urge for to coordinate ICT into training; however, that, they experienced numerous hindrances. The significant obstructions were absence of certainty, absence of skill, and absence of access to assets. Since certainty, capability and openness have been seen as the basic segments of innovation joining in schools, ICT assets including programming and equipment, viable expert improvement, adequate time, and specialized help should be given to educators.

No segment in itself is adequate to give great educating. Be that as it may, the nearness of all segments builds the probability of brilliant joining of ICT in learning and instructing openings. By and large, this paper gives data and suggestion to those liable for the coordination of new advancements into science training. Having doctoral understudies help with the instructing is lightening the issue of understudies getting shut out of software engineering classes, he says. Kumar, a CS graduate, mentions that his area of expertise has a few people who work in industry showing low maintenance, "however, the number is little. A similar time, enlisting both residency track and non-residency track software engineering staff stays a test, for workforce, both showing personnel just as residency track staff."

The base of the two issues is the equivalent: a critical deficiency of instructors qualified to show software engineering. This is valid at both the secondary school and school levels. Just 75 instructors moved on from colleges prepared to show the subject in 2016. Contrast that with the quantity of graduating instructors arranged in arithmetic (12,528) and technical studies (11,917 across general science, science, material science, and earth science). For some current basic, center, and secondary school employees who need to know software engineering, getting guaranteed isn't a probability. While each state gives clear pathways to affirmation in arithmetic and science, just hardly any states have comparable approaches for software engineering teachers. At the school level, by far most of advanced education organizations additionally experience the ill effects of a software engineering personnel deficiency. Purposes behind this incorporate an absence of residency track software engineering positions, and a moderately low number of Ph.D. applicants in software engineering.

Indeed, only 2 percent of all degrees presented in software engineering are doctorates an investigation on PC graduate by college association. The basic instructing foundation to help software engineering training is rising, however, surely not hearty. Thus, there are low quantities of understudies moving on from secondary school intrigued by software engineering and much less from school just in light of the fact that there is no one to acquaint them with the subject, give motivation, and help them to imagine themselves as PC researchers. All over the world there is lack and to solve this is only by developing new attitude towards computer science, accepting to enroll and government support.

9.3. GENDER DISPARITY

Innovation industry expressed the determinations of an as of late distributed examination: this century won't see ladies distributing the identical measure of software engineering research as men, in view of the most idealistic investigation of past patterns. With a clear increment in the portrayal of female researchers and coding associations that guide underrepresented gatherings, it was dampening to hear that there is still a very long time before equality is anticipated to be accomplished. It shows up as though this pattern has been happening for a considerable length of time – ladies keep on confronting boundaries to section in innovation fields, even with the coming of new items and openings for work, however, any expectation for a reasonable arrangement is covered in long stretches of generalizations and profoundly established snags in industry and the scholarly world the same. With both a sexual orientation hole and pay hole in STEM fields, in what manner can approaching PC researchers counter a framework that is by all accounts worked against them?

On a social scale, apparently young ladies presented to software engineering may avoid the field dependent on the generalizations around it. An investigation led through Microsoft found that 91% of young ladies and 80% of young ladies would portray themselves as inventive, which clashes with the conventional depiction of programming as a simply coherent occupation. Putting the entirety of the various parts of STEM under a particular name represses individuals from making associations with different pieces of the field that may not all fall in that class. Numerous understudies may not investigate STEM fields on account of the customary portrayals of tech, and without having starting courses or direct encounters with the field; they may always be unable to touch off their enthusiasm for STEM. As indicated by BBC, a report from the Council for the Curriculum, Examinations, and Assessment found that young ladies were frequently awkward with contemplating PC related trains and felt a strain to perform better in the event that they ended up seeking after registering (Anderson, Ferro, & Hilton, 2010).

The fundamental issues that add to the sex hole in software engineering likewise incorporate generalizations and access to assets. As indicated by the Harvard Business Review, ladies are regularly restrained from seeking after vocations in building similarly as men are repressed from seeking after professions in female-commanded fields like nursing. While we would expect that a flood of new advancements would prompt an expansion in openings for work no matter how you look at it, 60% of these open doors in most states are opened in male-ruled fields. Countering the disgrace behind seeking after a vocation in specialized work is certainly an issue that should be tended to, however, making answers for increment chances to work in more current advancements is additionally a bigger issue that must be considered. The United Nations expresses that experts in the field of man-made reasoning are just 22% female comprehensively, as indicated by the World Economic Forum's Global Gender Gap Report. Even if these generalizations are oblivious, the innovation business could seriously confine its potential achievement later on if its establishment acknowledges a similar kind of disgrace that past enterprises have neglected to address. The Guardian refers to a connection among organizations in the top 25% for sexual orientation decent variety and ethnic assorted variety and acquiring preferable outcomes over their rivals. Recognizing the advantages of assorted variety is a vital initial step yet actualizing these systems in rising and imaginative businesses is basic to predictable development pushing ahead (Henderson, 2009).

So how would we fix a framework that has been broken for a considerable length of time? It's vital to gain from an earlier time and perceive how progressions can step by step be made. The BBC refers to an examination that found that having solid good examples could urge young ladies to ponder figuring. All things considered, having the option to see somebody's voyage is moving to any individual who needs to pursue a comparable course. From a meeting with two ladies who had contrasting encounters in seeking after a vocation in tech, Forbes found that encouraging groups of people were a key part of why one of the interviewees had the option to proceed with her investigations in software engineering. An interviewee likewise referenced that "a more extensive social move" was required. Furthermore, to locate a long-haul answer for the divergence between the sexual orientations in software engineering, the facts confirm that such retribution is vital.

Regardless of whether a blend of the previously mentioned arrangements or an accentuation on one idea is important to upset the divergence in sex portrayal in software engineering, it must be recognized that changes do should be made. Tech is pushing the world ahead – we consider it to be our day by day lives as much as we see it in the motion picture (Henderson, 2009) s. Our consistent utilization of more current bits of innovation just alludes to the world we may live in ten, a long time from now. Along these lines, pushing for change in the tech business must be an objective that we progress in the direction of together to help the two ladies and men. Instead of referencing innovation as another industry that neglected to keep away from the mix-ups of past ventures, we should focus on it to be a brilliant illustration of fruitful social change. That starts with urging young ladies to consider vocations that they might not have been presented to and to separate the generalizations that restrain male and female understudies the same from seeking after their inclinations.

9.4. CULTURAL BARRIERS

"Grating isn't only a wellspring of contention – it's a wellspring of learning," said Ian Arawjo, doctoral understudy in the field of data science and first creator of "Registering Education for Intercultural Learning: Lessons from the Nairobi Play Project," which won a decent notice for best paper at the forthcoming Association for Computing Machinery Conference on Computer-Supported Cooperative Work and Social Computing, Nov. 9-13 in Austin, Texas. The paper was co-written by AriamMogos of the Nairobi Play Project; Steven Jackson, partner teacher, and seat of the Department of Information Science; Tapan Parikh, partner educator at Cornell Tech; and Kentaro Toyama of the University of Michigan.

In 30 after-school sessions drove by educators who are themselves outcasts, understudies learn essential figuring ideas and create computer games with network-based subjects. Applying socially significant instructional method is critical. The apparent significance of processing, the oddity of the gadgets, the need to share hardware, new methods of reasoning and open door for giggling are among the elements that add to intercultural participation, Arawjo said. Numerous understudies – whose normal classes in exile camps have understudy educator proportions of around 100 to 1 – said they likely wouldn't have been permitted to take part in some other sort of class.

"My mom approves [the class] on the grounds that I am the principal individual in the family utilizing a PC," a Somali young lady told questioners. For the examination, specialists watched classes, talked with instructors and understudies and directed reviews both when the program. They found that in spite of obstruction – or now and again, as a result of it – the structure of the computational class empowered far-fetched fellowships between understudies from altogether different foundations.

For instance, a Somali young lady at first communicated protection from working with a South Sudanese kid, yet said he "was my computer mate and become my closest companion" after the two shared a workstation for a month. A Congolese kid and a Sudanese kid fortified over language troubles. Two Dinka understudies quit going to the class in the wake of taking in their instructor was from the Nuer clan, on the grounds that their two clans were in dynamic clash. The educator visited the young men to urge them to return and complete the program, which they did.

The predetermined number of gadgets implied the understudies needed to sit together and participate. When asked how he made companions from various foundations, a kid stated, "Our educator disclosed to us that you should sit together – for instance, you're Congolese, you're Sudanese. They blend us. ... We need to impart. Since there is just a single PC. You can't make something without the PC."

Programming expects understudies to think about an issue from the PC's viewpoint – like seeing from others' perspectives, Arawjo said. Instructors based on these associations. New instruments and troubleshooting programs additionally would in general move humor, the specialists wrote. An instructor exhibits computational apparatuses to understudies in the Nairobi Play Project.

None of these associations happened naturally. The analysts found that, as in the United States, social power orders could be repeated if educators didn't perceive and turn away them. Instructors should have been skilled and experienced enough to make the most of chances for intercultural learning. Also, the gadgets could divert the understudies, particularly if the web was accessible.

Educators likewise confronted the test of contentions emitting in class. One culturally diverse group of young men made a computer game in which vagrants recover their properties by slaughtering every single male individual from another clan; worried about fortifying xenophobia, the educators urged them to discover another arrangement. "Struggle is available," Arawjo said. "In any case, it additionally can be settled, and the goal of contention offers amazing open doors for learning." Arawjo said future research will investigate adjusting bits of knowledge from the Nairobi Play Project concentrate to differing software engineering study halls in the United States.

The investigation was somewhat bolstered by UNICEF Kenya and Cornell's Mario Einaudi Center for International Studies and Judith Reppy Institute for Peace and Conflict Studies. To decidedly affect understudy accomplishment and vocation decision, especially as it identifies with the STEM field of registering sciences. Social hindrances, for example, early presentation to innovation, understudies' impression of their own potential in the field, and the absence of socially pertinent social help, regularly hinder African understudies from seeking after vocations in STEM fields, especially registering sciences. In spite of the fact that there is a shortage in the writing with respect to how to grow the pipeline to figuring sciences utilizing socially explicit practices, this investigation delivered results that recommend socially responsive practices as a viable technique for expanding interest in processing.

9.5. LACK OF MOTIVATION

Inspiration and enthusiasm are transitory and untrustworthy. Order, structure, and placing in exertion consistently are what will cause you to turn into an incredible PC researcher as well as programming engineer. Countless understudies drop out in the primary year of their Bachelor's examinations in Computer Science (CS). It is an issue in numerous nations around the world. An investigation was finished with a mean to build up a scale for estimating the inspiration and recognition factors that impact understudies' choice to begin considering Computer Science (CS), and to discover the contrasts between these variables. A survey was directed dependent on anticipation esteem hypothesis to quantify understudies' inspiration and recognition. Information were gathered from 140 understudies who began their Bachelor thinks about in CS at a college in Estonia. The scale, named FICSS (Factors Influencing Computer Science Studies), was led and approved utilizing exploratory and corroborative factor examinations. Two models were recognized: a four-factor model portraying understudies' inspiration ("Intrinsic worth," "Utility worth," "Social impacts" and "Time for family") and a five-factor model ("Satisfaction with decision of to acclaim," "Social debilitation," "Mentioning work," "Remuneration and expert strength" and "Cultural position") that portrays understudies' perception. "Characteristic worth" and "Utility worth" were the most elevated evaluated inspirational variables. The most reduced evaluated factor was "Social impacts." Among the observation factors, the elements with the most elevated methods were "Fulfilment with decision of claim to fame" and "Pay and employer stability" while "Social deterrence" was appraised least.

An examination investigating ladies' choices, influencers and early encounters of figuring to all the more likely see how ladies' inspirations and related knowledge influence their choice to consider software engineering (CS). The rise of a sexual orientation balance target and government goals for Scottish college courses has tested software engineering as a control over the 14 colleges in which software engineering is as of now educated. The subsidizing body target is that there ought to be an increasingly equivalent sexual orientation balance, with no course having less than 25% of one sex, prompting an expansion of sex activity designs over the college segment. Obviously, the marvel of under-portrayal stretches out crosswise over created and creating nations on the planet. At present, the level of ladies considering figuring in the UK is 17%. The absence of female candidates to courses recommends that subject choices have been made through past encounters preceding choosing a course and college.

Reviewing current software engineering understudies (n=185) an investigation on ladies' and men's purposes behind contemplating software engineering, their influencers and their initial encounters of processing. The point of the investigation was to look at the inspirations and impacts that drove them to a positive decision of software engineering so as to discover proof on which to construct a sexual orientation activity plan. We found that ladies were acquainted with processing at various stages (counting home, early tutoring and optional tutoring), though men were bound to have been acquainted with PCs at home. Ladies likewise referred to somewhat all the more changing explanations behind choosing CS, while men were bound to choose is dependent on close to home intrigue. The two people were affected by loved ones. Be that as it may, men were somewhat more probable than ladies to settle on the choice to ponder registering independent from anyone else, not referring to some other impact. Another factor being negative impact. Software engineering has been viewed as one of the hardest course to take by most understudies. This clarifies an avoid the course the same number of will in general abstain from burning through their time just to drop off later. College around the world haven't kept a lot of intercession towards inspiration on taking the course. High evaluation to join the course being another explanation. This is as per study from understudies applying for college courses referring to absence of college classes in software engineering. Enthusiasm for hypothetical Computer Science, programming, and configuration, isn't really equivalent to enthusiasm for PCs themselves, as devices. The greater part of the men we talked with who were keen on CS got intrigued at an opportune time since they were entranced by the PCs themselves.

They would in general have more experience working with PCs before coming to school, and at home in a "programmer" culture. Ladies, conversely, frequently incidentally found an enthusiasm for Computer Science later in their scholarly vocations than their male partners. From one viewpoint it could be conceivably distancing to enter a field wherein numerous individuals, the greater part of them men, have substantially more experience than yourself. Then again, it has been proposed that some social desires may really work to a lady's preferred position, making her increasingly capable or bound to openly seek after CS out of premium and love of the theme, as opposed to being pushed into it for profiting. As Computer Science turns out to be progressively noticeable as a field, increasingly male and female understudies are probably going to give contemplating it a shot of interest. A well-structured basic course could be an important selecting instrument for potential majors as a rule and ladies specifically.

9.6. BIASES IN CLASSROOM

Discrimination has been on the rise for many areas of computer science faculty. Ranging from fewer funds to the faculty and gender disparity. Students tend to avoid computer science faculty as it is believed to be a male area.

An absence of software engineering essentials can averse to understudies specifically and the nation when all is said in done. Equity in digital learning remains an issue and despite widespread connectivity, a majority of schools and libraries lack the bandwidth to drive digital learning, says Jonathan Zarf, executive director of the Center for Promise, the research institute of Americas Promise Alliance, an organization that focuses on raising graduation rates and increasing classroom access to technology (Tedre, 2014).

In total, Unconscious Bias is a nontrivial issue in instruction, particularly in CS and STEM training, and it isn't effectively tended to by means of conventional instructive arrangements and intercessions. In any case, intercessions that distinguish and change the as often as possible oblivious mental procedures that mischief people's results are at present being created and guided. Educator confronting intercessions, which can be regulated to both pre-and in-administration instructors, are especially encouraging. To some extent, this is on the grounds that by tending among educators, we can help shape the whole study hall setting in steady manners. Moreover, instructor confronting mediations are conceivably practical and adaptable, in light of the fact that framework for educator preparing is as of now set up.

Zaff tells Good Call, while digital learning is supposed to be a tool for helping to bridge the economic divide, the fact remains that several communities and homes, especially in provincial and distraught neighborhoods around the nation, do not have the capacity to either manage the cost of the computerized gadgets or assets to appropriately utilize them. When schools don't have the right classes, instructors and physical resources, Zaff warns students may lose valuable time developing a computer science skillset, which in turn, may undermine their chances for success in college and beyond. Less than half (40%) of the U.S.

We tend to hold innate inclinations about individuals that impact our conduct and associations in manners we don't understand. At the point when educators' concealed frames of mind and convictions about understudies depend on race, ethnicity, as well as sexual orientation, they may accidentally impart negative messages to their dark, brown, and female understudies about their capacities to handle STEM (science, innovation, building, and math) subjects. Unpreventable banality pictures of analysts and other STEM specialists (figure Albert Einstein) may furthermore invigorate to these understudies that STEM employments are critical, yet are not for them the dark astrophysicist Neil Tyson tended to how it feels to be forced to bear this kind of predisposition when he was approached to deliver a discourse at his grade school. He reacted, "I am the place I am not a result of what occurred in school, however, regardless of it, and that is likely not what you need me to state. Get back to me, and I will address your educators and give them some appropriately harsh criticism." Computer science in most secondary school and universities have been dismissed because of their low no of understudies. This has led to inclination in framework improvement in the field with the greater part of this homerooms displaying old age materials. This is rather than the 21śt century rapid hardware. This leads to trouble in examining and generation of understudies benefit graduate. The systematization of negative portrayals of ladies in CS exhibits a seriously lopsided male influence in the field. Since CS has since quite a while ago confronted a deficiency of ladies, it is obvious that the materials reflect freedom.

Initially male-focused points of view. These outcomes in continuous ages of understudies gaining from materials that are established in imbalance. In this manner, they will proceed to utilize and propel the field utilizing the one-sided institutionalized materials, framing an endless loop.

9.7. TECHNICAL BARRIERS

Software engineering education is essential to the present current, advanced society. Understudies, guardians, educators and directors keep on valuating CS learning in Year 2. More than Nine of every 10 guardians feel that chances to learn CS are a decent utilization of school assets. While support for CS learning keeps on being solid, all understudies don't yet approach CS learning openings in school classes. Be that as it may, many get presentation to CS through school Supported clubs or exercises and when CS is joined into different classes at school.

The utilization of ICT in the homeroom is significant for giving chances to understudies to figure out how to work in a data age. Examining the hindrances to the utilization of ICT in training may help instructors to beat these boundaries and become effective innovation adopters later on. This paper gives a meta-examination of the pertinent writing that means to display the apparent obstructions to innovation joining in science training. The discoveries show that instructors had a powerful urge for to coordinate ICT into training; however, that, they experienced numerous hindrances. The significant obstructions were absence of certainty, absence of skill, and absence of access to assets. Since certainty, capability and openness have been seen as the basic segments of innovation joining in schools, ICT assets including programming and equipment, viable expert improvement, adequate time, and specialized help should be given to educators. Nobody segment in itself is adequate to give great educating. Be that as it may, the nearness of all segments builds the probability of brilliant joining of ICT in learning and instructing openings. By and large, this paper gives data and suggestion to those liable for the coordination of new advancements into science training.

While CS learning openings are not all around available, they are expanding. In particular, schools keep on detailing that they have such a large number of different classes that help required testing for understudies, which may immobilize a few schools from including CS contributions, particularly in lower grade levels. The Computer Science Field is one of the quickest developing and most lucrative profession ways on the planet. Nonetheless, there is a lessening supply of instructors and understudies intrigued by Computer Science. This is to a great extent dependent on how presented understudies are to innovation and assets just as whether the understudies are being urged to investigate the universe of software engineering.

Teaching understudies in software engineering is likewise gainful to those not inspired by the software engineering field. Given the speed of developments in this computerized age, there is a need to create intelligent reasoning and critical thinking, which touches every piece of the software engineering educational program. Understudies, paying little mind to intrigued field, must be energetic in utilizing PCs whether it be to make a record, compose a report, or inquiring about a specific subject. Additionally, the employment opportunities with information on software engineering are developing in each industry and each state; employment opportunity are anticipated to develop double the pace of any activity. It's imperative to uncover understudies, anyway the fundamental concentration with software engineering has been on white understudies. There has been an absence of spotlight on young ladies, blacks, and Latinos understudies. Indeed, students of color are bound to not have classes committed to software engineering than white students.

This absence of assets and educators training software engineering makes an instructive hole between white guys and hued/female students. Although greater part of guardians, instructors, and principals the same feel that Computer Science would be significant and a decent utilization of school assets, not all K-12 schools has actualized classes to educate it. Be that as it may, many have made access to Computer Science by outside school-supported clubs and exercises. A principle issue for bringing Computer Science into schools is the absence of educators that can teach it. Secondary school principals who run schools without CS programs express this is the fundamental motivation behind why they don't offer CS classes.

The time factor is a significant obstruction in the use of PC. Educators don't prefer to utilize PC innovation since it can abbreviate learning time for students. The genuine time spent for instructing and learning isn't sufficient for educators and this may stop them utilizing the PC innovation (Roszell, 1995). 29 conditions were distinguished by Roszell (1995) that affected the utilization of PC in educating. The outcomes demonstrated that one of the most significant conditions affecting educators' status to remember innovation for their training is the need of time for creating exercises that utilization PC innovation. Absence of time is a boundary that stops instructors utilizing PC innovation (Mumtaz, 2000). This boundary shows up in two strategies: (a) Release time and (b) booked time. An examination was finished by the U.S. Division of Education and National Center for Education Statistics (2000). Discoveries acquired from this investigation demonstrated that 82% of the members accepted that inadequacy of discharge time halted them rehearsing PC innovation in their classes. Instructors said that with their planned classes, they needed adequate chances to work on applying PC innovation in their classes. About 80% of the educators expressed that there was insufficient time booked for their understudies to use PCs. It tends to be expressed that the absence of time expected to utilize PC into the prospectus is a significant subject.

9.8. STEREOTYPE THREAT

To identify generalization risk on harder points in basic Computer Science. Understudies in the benchmark group were approached to distinguish their statistic data before stepping through the examination though understudies in the test bunch were approached to do as such in the wake of finishing the test. Along these lines, the benchmark group was by implication helped to remember generalizations before stepping through the exam, when it could influence execution on the test, while the exploratory gathering was reminded after the test when it couldn't influence test execution. Tests on two distinct circles were utilized, alongside an incomplete traverse plan: an arbitrary gathering of understudies filled in as the benchmark group on one test, and the exploratory gathering on the other and the other way around. Blended factor ANOVA examination of the information indicated that every one of the understudies scored essentially higher when not helped to remember generalizations before the test paying little heed to sex or race.

Moreover, normal/beneath normal understudies scored fundamentally higher when not helped to remember generalizations before the test, once more, paying little respect to sex or race. In this way, on harder themes in Computer Science, generalization risk influences every one of the understudies, and specifically, the less-readied understudies. At the point when sex and race are related with positive or negative generalizations in a control, helping understudies to remember the generalization. An examination was led before to check whether generalization risk could be identified with regards to testing in Computer Science (Rex & Ruben, 2019).

In the examination, generalization risk was considered among initial Computer Science understudies utilizing on the web tests on coherent and task articulations. Since generalization danger was seen on task articulation test, yet not sensible articulation test, and understudies saw task articulations as harder, the investigation presumed that generalization risk might be all the more promptly clear on harder subjects in Computer Science (Barry, 2015).

This outcome agreed with discoveries revealed in writing for learning Math (Rex & Ruben, 2019).

Another finding of the previous investigation was that generalization risk was critical on task articulations just when understudies who had scored 100% on the test had been dispensed with from thought. As it were, generalization danger was increasingly apparent among understudies who had not effectively aced the material. In the investigation, generalization danger was inspired certainly by requesting that understudies distinguish their statistic data, i.e., sex, race, scholastic status and major. In writing, different components have been recorded for inspiring generalization danger, e.g., scientists evacuated objects cliché of Computer Science, for example, Star Trek blurbs and computer games from a homeroom and supplanted them with non-cliché items, for example, nature notices to build the enthusiasm of female college understudies to the degree of their male friends, through a procedure called "encompassing having a place (Krohn, Layton, & Weingart, 2012)."

In another investigation, specialists utilized the sex of the experimenter as an inconspicuous generalization risk sign (Krohn, Layton, & Weingart, 2012, and proposed a double procedure for how obtrusive and unpretentious generalization danger signals can affect execution.

There are different manners by which generalization risk can be evoked, and in this way, it should be kept away from any isolations: A class isolated by sex either during guidance or testing (as may be done in certain societies). Students are situated for a test not haphazardly yet by some statistic basis, (for example, major) to demoralize undesirable coordinated effort during the test.

Two distinct tests are passed out, or understudies are approached to answer odd or even-numbered inquiries on a test put together not with respect to arbitrary request, however, on some statistic paradigm (for example, scholastic status). An additional field is remembered for the test book for the understudy to enter "original surname" or credits earned so far towards a degree (Tucker, 2004).

The wording of the test questions isn't sexually impartial. The teacher may coincidentally inspire generalization danger, which can thusly prompt less fortunate execution on the test. Given that generalization danger can be inspired in any number of ways both unmistakable and inconspicuous, it contrarily influences the test execution of both decidedly and adversely stereotyped understudies on harder subjects in Computer Science, and it particularly influences less-readied understudies, Computer Science educators ought to be conscious of the potential for generalization risk and play it safe to keep away from it when directing tests. Such precautionary measures are critical to guarantee that social elements don't influence understudy execution on the tests, and tests survey just specialized information. This is even more significant given the declined enlistment and proceeding with steady loss issue in Computer Science and the anticipated increment in the interest for Computer Science graduates throughout the following decade all around the globe.

9.9. ELECTRONIC WASTE/E-SQUANDER

E-waste is one of the quickest developing waste streams the world over. In 2004, there were 183 million PCs sold all inclusive; by 2010, it's assessed there will be 716 million new PCs being used. With a normal life expectancy of only two years, that will be a great deal of PCs set out toward landfills sooner rather than later. Electronic waste, in some cases alluded to as e-waste or waste electrical and electronic gear (WEEE), is a profoundly changed stream of risky waste. This waste stream is included any electronic things that a shopper or business expects to discard, or is never again valuable for its unique reason. E-squander has produced a lot of open and political enthusiasm because of a conversion of elements, including: the exponential ascent in the age of e-squander, the potential benefit of reusing the loss so as to recuperate valuable metals and different components, and the ecological and human wellbeing dangers related with inappropriately putting away, discarding, and reusing e-waste. A portion of the significant reactions to the rising age of e-waste (and developing interest for auxiliary crude materials that it contains) have incorporated the improvement of maker "reclaim" enactment, mechanical advancements in reusing forms, and the arrangement of organizations to encourage the exchange of e-waste between the casual and formal reusing divisions (Tucker, 2004).

Consistently, 20 to 50 million tons (18 to 45 million metric huge amounts of) of e-squander is produced [source: Greenpeace]. In spite of the fact that you might be enticed to toss your wrecked VCR in with your ordinary trash, e-squander shouldn't be hurled into the normal garbage in light of the fact that a significant number of electronic items contain poisonous or possibly hazardous substances is being presented as another subject in the school educational program in numerous nations, and as a significant piece of casual learning openings in others. This carries with it both fervor and difficulties, concerning any new subject. For educators confronting educational program change, how to encourage it is exceptionally appropriate. Presenting new substance doesn't only imply that educators need to outfit themselves with new subject information, which obviously by and large they do Teachers likewise need to learn suitable instructional methods for conveying another subject, especially in those parts of software engineering that identify with calculations, programming and the improvement of computational reasoning aptitudes.

E-squander is an extraordinarily perplexing waste stream, as it incorporates a wide scope of things and the precise structure of numerous electronic segments are viewed as prized formulas, which means they are the classified data of the producer. Generally speaking, "current equipment can contain up to 60 novel segments The affiliation in like manner progresses the reusing of used PCs and parts to help diminish e-waste. So with PCs turning into a basic piece of the present learning techniques, and private organizations and charitable associations attempting to guarantee that understudies have a school PC, state-funded schools are driving our children on an innovative wave that sets them up for the employments of things to come (Krohn, Layton, & Weingart, 2012).

Simultaneously, our schools are probably going to produce a far higher level of e-squander than singular homes or even a few organizations in the territory, as PCs become basic parts of how the study halls operate. Computers for Kids is attempting to make it similarly as normal to include "hardware" to that rundown. The non-benefit has an after-school program that is driving the manner in which with regards to electronic or e-squander reusing. While they frequently acknowledge gave PCs that can be reused, they perceive that a ton of gave PCs just never again work and can't be restored. Their objective, at that point, is to work with schools to guarantee those PCs are reused, so the parts inside them can be effectively used to make new items.

What's more, there are natural exercises here too for our schools, our educators and our understudies. As per the Environmental Protection Agency, in excess of 4 million tons of e-squander winds up in our country's landfills consistently. This is a developing ecological risk since a ton of that e-squander contains harmful and hazardous synthetics and substances, including lead and mercury. On the off chance that those poisons leak out into the dirt and water, this postures wellbeing dangers to the individuals living close by, and to our untamed life. As Computers for Kids has noted, giving understudies a PC is an extraordinary idea, on the grounds that those children would then be able to return home and show their relatives the abilities they've learned. What's more, schools can likewise show those children to become incredible promoters for our condition by presenting exercises about reusing.

Chapter 10

Leveraging Current Momentum in Computer Science and Technology

CONTENTS

10.1. INTRODUCTION

Ensuring that every student gets an equal chance to learn computer-science is vital to the growth of the sector. It helps scholars to build the abilities they'll require for the future, such as coding, creativity, problem solving and collaboration. Going into the future, around 65% of youngsters will work in occupations that don't currently exist—such as developing new technology, promoting artificial intelligence, and providing better methods of analyzing data.

To flourish in careers across different sectors, students require a solid basis in computer science knowledge and expertise with using modern day technology. Still, research has shown certain inequities in the access to computing education.

Stakeholders are meanwhile working hard to fill up these gaps, in order to give the students—right from elementary to graduate school—the resources, skills, and inspiration they need to feel self-assured working with technology.

Additionally, some tech companies like Microsoft have partnered internationally with nonprofits, states, educators, and companies to ensure that all youth get access to virtual skills training plus inclusive computer science training.

Based on study results from Google, educators from rural and small township schools suggest that the greatest obstacles to improving accessibility to K-12 computing classes are lack of instructors with adequate skills and funding for preparation or hiring of teachers.

Apart from teaching masses of youngsters digital skills and computing, organizations like Microsoft further guarantee that well over 200,000 teachers with relevant skills will get the opportunity for teaching this subject all across the world.

They also ensure that boys and girls alike get equal opportunity for studying computer science.

10.2. TEACHING COMPUTER SCIENCE IN ALL HIGH SCHOOLS

Figure 10.1. *High school students enjoying a computer science lesson with their teacher.*

Source: https://today.uic.edu/helping-students-prep-for-computer-science-careers.

Teaching computer science is an honorable profession that combines creativity, with problem-solving and coding skills. There are various pre-made curricula which are available for IT and computer science courses, plus a considerable amount are absolutely free. You might use the curriculum draft of a pre-made lesson to help in designing the scope, as well as sequencing your particular class and selecting the specific activities that you like. If you have several preps, then choosing your favorite training module for computer science becomes easier.

10.2.1. Effective Teaching Practices for Computer Science

No matter what curriculum is being used, as an IT or computers instructor always ensure you fully understand what your pupils will experience. Accomplishing the exercises as well as labs shall help you to better help students and possibly anticipate mistakes.

You might also need to learn new coding languages or computing programs. Even for instructors with degree qualification in Computer Science, it's still advisable to update their knowledge with modern innovations like App Inventor and p5.js. It's advisable to acquaint yourself with up-and-coming technologies as much as possible, in order to better answer students' questions.

Similarly, try to develop a classroom culture where inquiries are encouraged among computer science students, so that they can have an opportunity to grow and increase in knowledge. Creating software isn't just about getting the answers, but also promoting the ability to unravel things out through using the available resources like the web, as well as leveraging on skilled teachers.

Similarly, it's advisable to establish coherent expectations for the use of computers. In class you don't want learners playing games, when instead they ought to be operating programming exercises. For your classroom management agenda, include clear guidelines for computer use, such as the fact computers should only be utilized for relevant class activities (Amuno, 2019).

Furthermore, based on the students' average age group, consider setting up schedules for computer use also. Students generally have trouble listening to instructors when their class computers are open, engrossing their attention. To avoid this, let them set their computers at an angle of 45 degrees or wholly closed in case you require their utmost attention.

10.2.2. Establishing Principles for Academic Honesty in Computer Science

With so much coding available on the Web, ranging from Scratch courses to AP Java systems, it's important to establish ground rules for your students so that they don't simply copy the existing programs and take them to be their own.

Even though professional programmers utilize the web as a data resource, students are still operate within an academic setting whereby they're required to script their own code plus apply their own effort so as to learn and grow. Currently, many schools use Harvard's CS50 course which has a collection of academic honesty polices which can be utilized in the high school setting. Some of the honesty guidelines you must consider when teaching computer science in your syllabus include:

- Be rational: don't copy solutions directly from the internet. Instead, encourage learners to discuss the topics with their peers.
- When requesting for help, learners might show some peers their code, use and quote online resources, plus ask the instructor for help.
- When providing help, students may not reveal to other peers their code. Instructors may also critique a learner's code and request for guiding questions to assist a peer to find the solution.

Preferably, discuss the guidelines with your students from day one, plus even provide the students with some hypothetical cases that they can consider as misuses of academic integrity or not!

10.2.3. Applying Pair Programming

Pair programming is different from an uncomfortable silent classroom, where apart from the sounds of typing, students silently tussle to solve complex equations.

Here, the class buzzes with on-topic discussions and debates among the students.

While computers can indeed isolate students, they don't necessarily have to when using pair programming method since the students can do most works and solve problems in pairs.

By joining efforts, students can help solidify one another's programming knowledge while also keeping their peers on task. This way computer science students can enjoy the class better and become less frightened by the subject.

Pair programming can become a great transitional step between grasping a new concept, and trying to solve the issue personally.

As an instructor, always make it a routine for your class to participate in pair programming, and provide students with an opportunity to showcase skill on their own.

Generally, to develop and become a remarkable computer science instructor, experience and professional growth are required (Tucker, 2004). When you gain experience in teaching computer science as a subject, you become better in it over time.

10.3. ALLOWING COMPUTER SCIENCE TO COUNT

Figure 10.2. *In some schools, computer science is ranked within the same group as mathematics and sciences.*

Source: https://theconversation.com/computer-science-now-counts-as-math-credit-in-most-states-is-this-a-good-idea-123424.

Schools are encouraged to place more emphasis on training students for jobs in the modern century. It looks like a common thing that students should enjoy credit for STEM subjects, but in almost half of states around the U.S. and many other countries, computer science subjects still don't count in arithmetic or science graduation prerequisites.

However, organizations like Microsoft are currently advocating for more governments to pass policies which allow computer science subjects to be included toward high school mathematics and science graduation prerequisites. In a year, the average number of American states which have achieved this feat has nearly doubled, which shows that progress is being made in making computer science count in schools. However, there's still some work to be done, since lots of schools worldwide don't provide computer science courses, whether due to economic or logistical problems, or an absence of resources for instructors (Tucker, 2004).

One thing most computer science experts agree on is the requirement for more classes and tutors in this field. According to Microsoft's VP, the fact is that if you're looking forward to having a job going into the future, you should have some understanding of computer science.

Data from Code.org reveals that at current pace, developed countries like the U.S. will generate around 1 million new job opportunities in computer science, compared to students who will be graduating in this field by the year 2020. On average, computer science jobs are increasing in popularity at twice the countrywide average. For a few states like New York, Delaware and Connecticut, the average rate of computing jobs is expanding at around four times the country's average. However, 90% of schools nationally don't provide computer science classes.

Normally, students can register for computer science programs as electives, though they won't count as the main course prerequisite for graduation, mentioned Cameron Wilson, who is the operations officer for Code.org. The organization entered into an agreement with Microsoft in 2013, advocating for statewide policy changes to ensure computer science satisfies a graduation prerequisite.

While it doesn't mean that schools must have to offer it in class, students are encouraged to have some motivation in learning it as a main course rather than an elective. There's still more to be done, especially in local jurisdictions where this requirement should filter down up to the most basic levels of society (Barry, 2015).

10.3.1. Efforts to Promote Computer Science an Important Subject

Some school districts have taken it upon their shoulders to make computer-science subjects available. Just recently, Indiana's Purdue University also announced that it will start offering introductory computer science classes and programming course freely to Indiana high schoolers. Even though the course shall be ungraded and won't count for any credit, it still prepares students to sample freshman programming courses available at Purdue as well as other universities.

Some public schools are furthermore striving to roll out K12 computer science courses, which will benefit students with basic computing skills. Throughout the next coming years, a number of learning institutions are expected to provide some foundation for students who want to pursue this science field. They will be at a better position and understand more computer science concepts that shall be useful later on in their careers (Barry, 2015).

Moreover, the number of students who are interested in computer science fields is steadily rising. A recent finding by the Cyber Security Alliance group established that around a quarter of youngsters aged between 18 to 26yrs old showed interest in a cyber-security career, though around 64% mentioned that their institution didn't provide sufficient exposure for computer science and cyber security courses.

However, improving access to the computer science programs in high school may be tasking, since teachers usually feel like they don't get access to the necessary resources and training for mentoring their students. Unlike other ordinary subjects such as English or Math, computer science is still a developing field and therefore there aren't many colleges offering it.

A 2013 survey on computer science instructors found that around 40% of teachers believed the single most challenging factor in teaching this subject, is the lack of proper support from school staff. While another 35% said that lack of learner interest and enrolment were the top challenges. Similarly, rapidly shifting technology and inaccessibility of learning resources were mentioned as other possible challenges by roughly 25.5 to 30.5 percent of computer science teachers (Tucker, 2004).In some occasions, schools are dejected from preparing computer science courses due to economic and logistical reasons. Since most computer lessons are designed to cater for small sized class – with roughly 20 pupils per class rather than 35 – schools may prefer to save resources by not providing the courses at all.

10.4. REMOVING BARRIERS TO STUDENTS CHOOSING WHETHER TO TAKE COMPUTER SCIENCE COURSES

Figure 10.3. *Schools should allow computer science to count as credit for math and science graduations.*

Source: https://www.kenoshanews.com/news/local/education/university/wall-street-journal-columnist-to-speak-at-uw-madison-winter/article_ba8a0871-be87-54e0-9dac-8096cede9d61.html.

At various institutions today, scholars that aren't computer science majors experience severe enrolment restraints and diluted or limited courses.

In the modern times, college students require a computer science subject, while some need at least two or more. Educators are starting to distinguish this truth, however, are still a long journey from fulfilling the need.

In 2013, several stakeholders in the tech world merged together to start a non-profit called Code.org. Its purpose was ensuring as many students as possible enrol for computer science courses into schools. So far in their mission, they have managed to influence graduation policies in around 42 states. These regions now allow computer science courses to count instead of math classes such as Algebra 2. Before the organization's contribution, just a handful of states accepted computer science to be counted for math credit before graduation, but that has since changed (Krohn, Layton, & Weingart, 2012).Furthermore, another 29 states passed laws allowing computer science courses to pass for graduation requirements instead of science subjects. When computer science starts to count in place of math or science, then it's logical to ask whether these changes are assisting America's students or just limiting them.

10.4.1. The Concern

Some computational professionals and education researchers that teach in college have concerns that, permitting computer science courses to count as a requirement for math or science can make students significantly less primed for college. Also, there's concern that lack of sufficient math and science training in high school may artificially limit the variety of options for pupils who may otherwise have bright STEM careers (Tedre, 2014).

Definitely, computer science is vital to teach in schools. Experienced instructors can lead efforts towards training other high school science and math teachers coding skills, while working with them to incorporate more science and math courses into their curriculum.When considering computer science courses in schools, some of the factors to take note of are: What type of computer science is it, rigorousness of the content, plus what subjects ends up excluded to create room for this? Even though there are certain exceptions, the majority of school computer science courses have impacted greatly on mathematics and science learning. There's worry that students might take computer science simply to avoid the tougher math and science subjects they require for university. Computer science may be a method for pupils to bypass graduation requirements while grownups look the other side (Tedre, 2014).

10.4.2. Career Preparation

Computer science might be taken as a practical course which helps pupils prepare for actual middle-class jobs. In fact, you can't live in the modern society without handling technology or computers in day to day life. There are some significant studies behind this sentiment.

Notwithstanding a rise in the number of students registering for computer science courses in college, there's still considerable demand for computing studies and software engineering experts than there's supply. Possibly due to this demand, incomes for computer science occupations are expected to be as high as 40 percent more, compared to careers in other fields (Tedre, 2014).

Despite these opinions, there are still considerable motives to query computer science replacement policies. Being a present-day electrician, for instance, needs some basic comprehension of algebra as well as trigonometry. Learning these subjects in college can prepare one for a career in fields like electrician later on in life. Even for individuals who plan to learn computer science as a professional course, taking Algebra 2 or other higher algebra subjects are also crucial for engineering.

Some studies approximate that roughly 40 percent of university freshmen in America require remedial mathematical courses. That ration may move up if fewer pupils are taking a conventional math subject in high school.

Registering for remedial mathematics courses such as Algebra II in college needs students to spend larger amounts of time and resources than they might if they only registered and passed 4yrs of mathematics in high school. Based on one study, roughly half of all pupils that take remedial math courses actually don't complete it. Therefore, skipping Algebra II in high school may end up preventing many scholars from graduating college after all (ITL Education Solutions Limited, 2011).

10.4.3. Implication

Many colleges and universities provide the opportunity for students to take multiple courses they want in math, science and just about any other field, provided by faculty members within that particular discipline. Similarly, students should be provided with the same opportunity for computer science. Though at quite many institutions today – comprising those in prestigious countries around the world – pupils who haven't registered as computer science majors often face enrollment caps, including subsidized computer science subjects for non-majors subjects. But students who take computer science courses definitely deserve better than this.

10.5. INCREASING THE NUMBER OF QUALIFIED COMPUTER SCIENCE TEACHERS

Figure 10.4. *There's need for more computer science teachers in schools to promote digital literacy.*

Source: https://www.microsoft.com/en-us/corporate-responsibility/skills-employability/computer-science.

The overall amount of computing jobs is growing fast and capturing the notice of educators as well as the industry at large, towards the pressing need for holistic K-12 computer science training. Computer science knowledge is clearly in huge demand, though low supply. Tech giants like Microsoft, including data Analytics Company You Gov presented survey information on computer science lessons in K-12 classrooms. Based on Microsoft, its studies provide intuitions into the root of the workforce gap—by promoting K-12 computer science training.

As the computing industry continues growing at breakneck speeds, teachers are feeling pressurized to expound computer science education plus ultimately produce more specialists to enter the marketplace. Based on data from Labor Statistics Bureau, there would be nearly 1.4 million accessible computer science careers by 2020 plus less than 1/3 of those available jobs shall have skilled graduates to occupy them. There's a rising demand, not only for high-tech professions, but for every job that requires some form of computer science skill (ITL Education Solutions Limited, 2011).

Experts believe that preliminary introduction to computing can help meet that workforce shortage. In a survey involving 500 K-12 instructors across the nation, Microsoft discovered that 88% of instructors believe computing is necessary to the impending career success of students.

Beyond mere coding, computer science might teach pupils other important skills. Learners begin to develop some understanding concerning the types of skills and expertise and methods of thinking which ultimately will position them to consider a computer science course. Based on the survey, teachers mentioned that problem solving as well as reasoning are crucial skills that computer science might help develop. Furthermore, 83% of teachers surveyed are of the belief that coding certainly builds students' creativity.In spite of the growing need for computer workers and the advantages that computer science provides students, Microsoft discovered that schools are not supporting and implementing computer science courses. Based on survey data, roughly 2 out of 10 educators mentioned their pupils don't learn anything on computer science totally. Microsoft discovered the main reasons why teachers often fail to incorporate computer science training in their classes are because of poor supporting curriculum, and lack of resources (Henderson, 2009).Even though educators readily recognize the significance of computer science knowledge in their students, roughly 30% mentioned they feel not well qualified to prepare learners for a bright "digital future," whereas 20% mentioned that they feel overwhelmed.

With inadequate computer science teachers and program resourcing, the American education system isn't providing extensive access to this crucial subject, the research found. Statistics from Microsoft show that teachers believe improved government and industry participation can help avoid some of these impediments. Close to 80% of instructors believe that large tech companies such as Microsoft, Google and Apple must incorporate computer science in schools, whereas 75% of teachers are worried the government isn't performing enough to develop computer science education.

Many technology giants have willfully answered this call, providing computer science courses for K-12, such as Verizon's Innovative Learning or Amazon's AWS Educate, plus committing several millions of dollars into bringing computer science subjects to more learners (Henderson, 2009).

The state has further taken active measures towards supporting computer science teaching. For instance, recently in September 2019, the U.S President pledged around $200 million per year towards expanding access to "great quality" STEM training, with an emphasis on computer science. Moreover, industry and educational stakeholders have started to respond to calls for improved computer science training, equipping pupils with 21st-century abilities which can equip them for all aspects of career and education. This early preparation will connect students with an inner desire to be inventive and creative, while socially solving problems which are crucial to them.

10.5.1. Inadequate Instruction

Typically, students who look forward to studying computer science as their major aren't fully prepared for taking up the role—thus they lack the computational thinking or mathematical background needed to excel in college-level projects. There's also not enough effort being put to widen interests in computing: and the ratio of female computing majors still remains to be low, at just 14.1 percent, whereas several racial minorities furthermore are considerably underrepresented. Based on statistics from Code.org, a nonprofit organization focused on promoting access to computing training in K-12 schools, around 26 states allow computing courses to be credited toward school graduation, as compared to just 9 states in 2010. No U.S. states, however, really need a computer science course for graduation. Therefore, the greater majority of pupils in the country don't take even one computer science program throughout their K-12 training, while only 25 percent of principals mention that their school provides a computing course that covers programming (Arnaldi& Bianchi, 2016).

10.6. DOUBLING THE NUMBER OF STEM CHARTER SCHOOLS

Figure 10.5. *STEM subjects should be taught often in schools to prepare students for computer science courses.*

Source: https://hechingerreport.org/new-orleans-loses-teachers-at-double-the-rate-of-other-cities-like-it/.

The society's interest with science, technical subjects, engineering, and mathematics is vast. Ranging from an obsession on applications and effects of robotics and artificial intelligence, over to a persistent interest in startup ventures and innovation entrepreneurship.

Despite these findings, evidence from global standardized exam performance and career vacancy data indicates America has a mathematics and science competency shortage. The ratio of STEM bachelor's qualifications has actually decreased over the past several decades, falling from 24 percent in 1985 to only 18 percent in 2009. Therefore, despite the finding that the highest paying careers are mostly in STEM subjects, the incapacity to staff these particular positions is becoming a major bottleneck for companies (Dasgupta, 2016).

Developing a STEM-capable staff creates more qualified public policymakers. It also prepares students for a future of technology. With an uncertain working-class whose jobs are increasingly being lost to automation, science and math provides a reliable and profitable opportunity for secure work opportunities. How policymakers and instructors develop that workforce is still an evolving matter with many solutions, though will comprise innovative training, following school programs, STEM-specific high schools, and improved teacher training.

10.6.1. Understanding the STEM Solution

It's a clear concern that both relatively and absolutely, the education system of many countries is failing to fully educate pupils in STEM subjects. For instance, Americans' performance on global exams such as Program for International Scholar Assessment (PISA) is ordinary in reading and science but below average in mathematics;

Similarly, America ranks 29th out of 109 nations in the ratio of 24yr olds having a math or science degree. Even though arguments on "global competitiveness" raise significant queries on topics as broad as migration policy and countrywide security, the outcomes of this skills deficiency are far more direct. Whereas the 8.6 million science-based careers in America by 2015 represented around 6.2 percent of the overall American employment. With STEM jobs as of May 2015 representing around 6.2 percent of U.S. employment, it's expected to grow by around twice the same pace as other jobs in the market (Dasgupta, 2016).

Come 2020, it's expected that demand for specialized technologists shall exceed the overall number of applicants by a figure of 1 million. Education, especially STEM education, is vital for filling up these jobs. The Labor Statistics Bureau found that well over 99 percent of STEM careers normally require some kind of postsecondary education, whereas only 36 percent of other careers require that amount of education.

Data further shows that 73 percent of necessary degrees in STEM careers that require postsecondary training are bachelor's degrees, in comparison to 21 percent of typical jobs. Studies further show that students aren't leaving K-12 systems with the tools that they require to thrive in postsecondary education, plus in their careers.

As for educators, this isn't news, though a holistic and bilateral teaching methodology at K-12 level plus at college and university can help educators to better answer the trials of STEM education.

Basically, policymakers must help educators to better prepare the students, to promote the economic growth machine that's STEM and allow students to realize higher financial success (Dasgupta, 2016).

10.6.2. Ways that STEM Develops Incomes

A STEM degree provides a great boost to the student's earning potential, since STEM jobs generally pay well beyond the national average. Data shows that 93 out of the best 100 STEM jobs pay well above average salaries, while the average STEM profession salary is roughly $87,570, nearly double the non-STEM average in the U.S. Furthermore, the Education Department found that university STEM degree holders earn around $15,500 more yearly, compared to their colleagues post-graduation plus are more probable to be employed full-time, rather than temporary like their peers from other professions.

With careers in STEM developing at a rate of 50 percent more than the countrywide growth average, it provides more opportunities for experts joining the field. For computer-based professions alone, an area expected to develop by 12.5 percent year after year from 2014 up to 2024, workers will provide half a million fresh jobs this decade only.

The dependability and accessibility of STEM occupations makes them particularly enticing options for students coming from low-income households. Policymakers concerned on both income disparity and lack of financial mobility should recognize the opportunities that STEM education provides; steady, in-demand job with great pay across a wide range of growing industries (Dasgupta, 2016).

10.6.3. Possible Challenges to STEM Learning

Setbacks in STEM education can be summarized in two key ways, which are usually interrelated problems. First, students usually start but seldom finish their STEM degrees, plus less still of those qualified are women or individuals of color. Hispanics, Native Americans, and African Americans constitute around 27 percent of the workforce, though only 11 percent of STEM workers.

10.7. CREATING INCENTIVES FOR MORE TERTIARY COMPUTER SCIENCE

Figure 10.6. *Colleges must create better opportunities for students who want to major in computer science.*

Source: https://www.sciencespo.fr/learning-lab/en/what-is-the-impact-of-students-use-of-computers-in-class/.

Within the past 50 years, there's been an uprising in computing and associated communications technologies. Contributions made by industry as well as university researchers towards this uprising are evident; less widely acknowledged is the significant role that the federal government puts in promoting the computing revolution plus sustaining its momentum. In the U.S., the federal government has provided substantial contributions towards research for computing technology. This support has covered a substantial portion of the overall financing for computing research within America and the greater majority of college research funds within the sector. This funding has sustained both the advancement of new technologies, as well as student training (Reilly, 2003).

The federal government has further funded public research infrastructure, giving majority of the financing for research apparatus in college divisions of computer science as well as electrical engineering, plus has sponsored courses to increase access to and provide infrastructure for high-grade computing and networking. These contributions didn't single-handedly propel successive development of the country's computing industry; instead, they formed a portion of the greater innovation system which united the efforts of states, universities, and industry. Still, they played a vital role in the sector's development (Reilly, 2003).

10.7.1. Promoting University Research Capabilities

Federal funding has similarly maintained university research contributions in computing. Universities rely mostly on federal backing for research courses in computing and electrical engineering, which are the two school disciplines most significantly aligned with computing and communications. As of 1973, federal organizations have provided approximately 70 percent of the entire funding for college research in computing.

As for electrical engineering, national funding has dropped from its highest of 75% of overall university research funding during the early 1970s, though still represented roughly 65% of such backing in 1995. Extra support has also been received in form of research apparatus. Colleges need access to modern equipment so as to perform research and coach students. Even though industry contributes certain equipment, still funding for college research apparatus has come mostly from federal contribution since the 1960s (O'Regan, 2012).

Such investments have managed to ensure that scholars have access to contemporary computing facilities, plus have allowed them to further increase their abilities of computing and networking systems. Colleges play a vital role in the invention process, they typically focus on research with a broad application across businesses and product lines plus sharing new information openly.

Since they aren't normally subject to business pressures, college researchers often have more ability compared to their industrial counterparts in exploring ideas with indefinite long-term payoffs. Even though it can be difficult to decide how much college research contributes openly to industrial innovation, it's revealing that each of these case studies including other significant examples observed by researchers—interactive databases, the web, hypothetical computer science, robotics and virtual reality—incorporated the participation of college researchers. Learning institutions play a significant role in distributing new knowledge through supporting open publication of study results.

Furthermore, they have served as training grounds for scholars who have carried fresh ideas with them onto existing businesses or began their own companies. Transmission of knowledge on relational databases, to give an example, was enhanced by scientists from Berkeley's University of California, who established the source code to be used for their Ingres program and made it accessible free of charge. Many of the top researchers for this project set up companies to help commercialize the innovation, or conveyed it back to preexisting companies where they supported its use (Shelly, Freund, &Vermaat, 2010).

10.7.2. Advantages of Federal Research Funding

State research funding has been influential on the growth of the computing sector in U.S. Federal research funding has delivered a solid basis for testing fresh concepts, designs, and structures in computing, besides it has helped fast-track the commercialization of innovation developed in company laboratories.

This effect has revealed itself in various ways, including the development of new products, solutions, businesses, and billion-dollar sectors which are dependent on federally backed research. Including in the development of university research abilities in computing and electrical engineering, formation of human resources which have propelled the computing revolution; plus, capacity of federal bodies to better achieve their public missions.

Nevertheless, quantifying all the advantages of state research support may be hard, for various reasons. To start, the research output is usually intangible. Majority of the benefits available take the shape of fresh knowledge which subsequently might be fulfilled in fresh hardware, software, and systems, though is in itself challenging to measure. In other occasions, the benefits may take form of schooled individuals who bring fresh ideas or perspectives into an organization. Secondly, the delays that happen between the period a research program is done and the moment the products covering the research results have been sold, could make measurement a little bit more challenging.

References

1. Amuno, A., (2019). 20 Common Uses of Computers. Retrieved from hubpages: https://hubpages.com/technology/20-Common-Uses-of-Computers (accessed on 4 February 2020).
2. Barry, P., (2015). Overview of Computer Science (pp. 1–238). Department of Computer Science and Engineering University of Minnesota-Twin Cities.
3. Dasgupta, S., (2016). Computer Science: A Very Short Introduction (p. 147.). London: Oxford University Press.
4. Gary, B. S., Steven, M. F., & Misty, E. V., (2010). Introduction to Computers (p. 40). Boston: Cengage Learning.
5. Greg, A., David, F., & Robert, H., (2010). Connecting with Computer Science (pp. 2–42). Boston: Cengage Learning.
6. Henderson, H., (2009). Encyclopedia of Computer Science and Technology (p. 580). New York: Infobase Publishing.
7. ITL Education Solutions Limited, (2011). Introduction to Computer Science, 2/e (pp. 27–77). New delhi: Pearson Education India.
8. James E. McClellan III, & Harold, D., (2006). Science and Technology in World History: An Introduction (pp. 5–99). Maryland: JHU Press.
9. Krohn, W., Layton Jr. E.T., & Weingart, P., (2012). The Dynamics of Science and Technology: Social Values, Technical Norms and

Scientific Criteria in the Development of Knowledge (pp. 29–59). Berlin: Springer Science & Business Media.

10. LaMarco, N., (2019). Uses for Computers in Business. Retrieved from smallbusiness.chron: https://smallbusiness.chron.com/uses-computers-business-56844.html (accessed on 4 February 2020).
11. Moreira, T., (2016). Science, Technology and the Ageing Society (pp. 14–71). London: Taylor & Francis.
12. O'Regan, G., (2012). A Brief History of Computing (p. 262). Berlin: Springer Science & Business Media.
13. O'Regan, G., (2016). Introduction to the History of Computing: A Computing History Primer (pp. 1–101). Berlin: Springer.
14. Reilly, E. D., (2003). Milestones in Computer Science and Information Technology (p. 380). Westport: Greenwood Publishing Group.
15. Rex, P., & Ruben, G., (2019). Essential Logic for Computer Science (p. 304). Cambridge: MIT Press.
16. Schäfer, G. E., (2013). History of Computer Science (pp. 7–117). Berlin: BoD.
17. Simone, A., & Luca, B., (2016). Responsibility in Science and Technology: Elements of a Social Theory, (1–70). Berlin: Springer.
18. Smith, P. J., (2013). Science and Technology for Development (p. 160). London: Zed Books Ltd.
19. Sofia, S., Rupinder, K., & Mandeep, K., (2016). The Analysis of Computer Applications in Various Fields . International Journal of Advanced Research in Computer Science and Software Engineering, 439–445.
20. Tedre, M., (2014). The Science of Computing: Shaping a Discipline (p. 292). Florida: CRC Press.
21. Tucker, A. B., (2004). Computer Science Handbook. London: Taylor & Francis Group, LLC.

INDEX

D

E